Almost Anastasia

the Life of

Franziska Schanzkowsky

Vera Green and *Victoria Hughes*

Whistling Swan Press

EVERGLADES

Almost Anastasia /Vera Green and Victoria Hughes. —1st ed.

Contents

Chapter One

I

The Fall

The death of a family: eleven people—a mother, a father, four sisters, a younger brother, a doctor, a maid, a cook, a valet—all shot, bayoneted, or beaten to death in the borrowed house of a mining engineer. The surviving pictures of the house show a Siberian mansion furnished in a sinister art nouveau, lots of mahogany and bronze tendrils, the walls done up in a figured paper. A hallway reveals the shadow of a wood and wicker wheelchair, also paneled doors opening on to other dark recesses. Here is the girls' room. They are all dead now; we know this because their plain enamel chamberpot sits in the middle of the floor for all to see. Above is a hideous metal and glass chandelier—an inverted bouquet of red, maw-like lilies and huge heart-shaped leaves.

There were eleven executioners too, local political functionaries and soldiers, each with a mandated victim, an opposite number. Anastasia, a seventeen-year-old girl who liked to act in plays and climb trees, was one of the last to die. A rigid corset stuffed with diamonds which had made her life a trial in the hot weeks of her last summer prolonged her final moments.

Four nights earlier an uncle and his secretary had been shot outside Perm, not very far away. The following night an aunt and a clutch of

1

male relatives would be done to death outside the nearby town of Alapaevsk.

All wound up interred in the birch and pine forests of Siberia, most concealed in disused mine shafts or in hurried excavations, roofed with railroad ties tamped down by the heavy truck which carried them there. The smell of gasoline and pine sap seems to hang over the memories of these sites, as well as the screams of a woman, perhaps singing, the raised voices of men, the whine of mosquitoes and an overheating engine, then silence. On the surface so little was left: a finger, a belt buckle, corset stays, a ruined pearl earring, a pocketful of coins, and bits of wire and scrap metal.

It was the end.

II

Before the Fall

Any story so complex and tragic can be started at an almost infinite number of points. Here is one: the nursery wing of an imperial palace, bright with floral prints and lemonwood furniture on a winter morning in the last days of peace. A cousin would longingly recall the toys there, in particular a French doll with her own silver toilet articles—every kind you could imagine, and all in the best belle epoche style; another would remember the fine dresses by Lamanova of Moscow and whole trays of ruby and diamond brooches. The girlies, the empress calls her daughters. OTMA, they call themselves: Olga, Tatiana, Marie, and Anastasia.

Even as young women they dress alike and share bedrooms. As they grew, they earned the right to put their hair up, to wear longer skirts and bigger necklaces, yet remained oddly the same. Nobles, churchmen, and revolutionaries alike would wonder at their naivete, purity, or immaturity. The words varied, but the quality they described did not.

In the memoirs of their era the imperial daughters often get a single paragraph which seeks to capture them in a series of masks: Olga, the dreamy one; Tatiana, the disciplinarian; Maria, the soft-hearted one; Anastasia, the tomboy.

Its occupants think of the Alexander Palace as an unpretentious family home, but it is an imposing neoclassical edifice of over one hundred rooms rooted in a landscape of ornamental lakes and parkland about fifteen miles south of St. Petersburg. It is only one of the palaces of Tsarskoe Selo—the "Tsar's Village." The windows of the nursery look out on gardens and guardhouses, and faintly, through the grille of a high iron gate, an ordinary street corner.

The Mauve Boudoir is Empress Alexandra's favorite retreat, a drawing room decorated in a particular pinkish opalescent shade. The lamps are lit and the heavy drapes drawn against the cold. The walls seem to groan with painted portraits of her immediate family and literally hundreds of icons.

In the Victorian manner, objets d'art cover almost every available surface: brilliantly enameled picture frames, gold clocks with rock crystal faces, miniature cossacks and bears, a diamond and moonstone encrusted bell push to summon servants. The fabled Faberge Easter eggs occupy a special cabinet, secrets at rest beneath their jeweled surfaces. Here Alexandra lies on her chaise lounge until well into the day, surrounded by banks of yellow roses from the Crimea, embroidering cushion covers, knitting for charities, writing notes and diary entries. In the spring an imperial train will convey them to their summer palace, where they will celebrate the festival of an Orthodox Easter. The eggs make their appearance here, beginning with the Coronation of 1896 (the year of the Revolving Miniatures). They are virtual state secrets until their presentation fresh from the Faberge workshops. Their themes—hopeful, nostalgic, proud, fantastic—ring throughout the year.

Alexandra was a granddaughter of Queen Victoria and a princess of Hesse-Darmstadt in her own right. Her mother died when Alexandra was very young, and a brother died of hemophilia before he came of age. Alexandra took it hard, becoming a doleful looking woman despite her beauty. Bad luck was catchy, some felt, and Alexandra's closed, unhappy face seemed to radiate it. When she left home to marry her tsarevich, at least a few Hessians were happy to see her go. They had nicknamed her *Pechvogel* ("bird of ill-fortune") and shouted *Geh und nimm Pech mit dir* ("Go, and take your bad luck with you") as she departed. None of this seems to have mattered to Nicholas; they were a true love match, even if the death of her father-in-law soon after her arrival would be remembered as a bad omen by many Russians.

Alexandra, so German in temperament and appearance, thought of herself as an Englishwoman, an identity that seems to have existed simultaneously with a passionately Russian persona. This contradiction was a common one in her family, resulting in Germanic princes wearing highland evening dress or the caftan and sword of Cossack cavalrymen. The casual adoption of these national identities often reflected a rather superficial understanding of the countries themselves (comfortable England, mysterious Russia).

Although Alexander III's demise was unexpected, he had left his empire with sound finances. Huge gold reserves backed an overwhelmingly agricultural economy only beginning to develop an industrial capacity. Apart from this, Alexander had made an alliance with France, avoided war at all costs, and maintained an iron control over domestic politics.

Alexandra, a shy but proud woman, was tormented by her public duties yet defended her prerogatives fiercely. Caught up in the awesome rites of her new faith, she saw herself as the *Matushka*, the Little Mother of her adopted country, and resented the foreign, cynical tone she detected in the court that revolved around the Winter Palace in St. Petersburg. *Petersburg is a rotten town, not one atom Russian*, she wrote. For their part, the aristocracy saw their empress as a prude and were embarrassed by her religious enthusiasms. Those below found her cold and distant, when they could be bothered to think of her at all.

When you see someone sad, try to cheer them up and show them a bright sunny smile … Now that you are a big girl, you must always be more careful and not show those feelings. One must not let others see what one feels inside—

Alexandra, who had such trouble controlling her own effect on others, demanded exquisite control on the part of her daughters. Their wing was a virtual household of its own with bedrooms, bathrooms, sitting rooms, and a dining room. There were English governesses and Russian nurses, at least one of whom wore an authentic peasant costume, and tutors of various nationalities. Photographs show tables with crisp cloths, straight-backed chairs, sometimes a free-standing blackboard. There was lots of dictation, and some recitation. They had abundant religious instruction, literature, and Russian history, though little of that went beyond the medieval period. Also music, needlework, and sketching. Basic arithmetic; nothing of science past mushroom and flower identification. The main intellectual achievement of their extended family—the ability to write letters and make pleasant conversation in at least three languages—came slowly to them.

Olga had the most subtle mind of the group, refined and cautious, watchful. She was mature enough to have her own money, and to be considered as a future crown princess of Romania, but was still too attached to her family to leave home. Tatiana, born in the year of the Coronation Egg, was Alexandra's favorite. She was a canny girl with great willpower; the only one, people said, who could be fairly described as haughty. In her writings to her mother she seems the most beseeching, the most passionately self-denying. This may have been sincere, but it may also be that she had learned this was what suited Mama best.

The younger pair seem more spontaneous, somewhat less repressed. They were true granddaughters of Alexander III, a vigorous and simple man. Marie, born in 1899—the year of the Madonna Lily Egg—was perhaps the most natural of the lot. A sweet girl, empathetic and strong; she could see herself marrying a soldier and making a life in a backwater town, and likely would have made a success of it, given a chance. Anastasia, who arrived in 1901—the year of the Trans-Siberian Egg—would be the one people would wonder about most later.

Perhaps she stuck in people's minds because she was the youngest of the girls, the least formed, the most mysterious. Potential was there—her French teacher would note that she easily had the best accent of the group—but also a peculiar waywardness; either a lack of will, or a superabundance of it applied in unpredictable ways. She was physically strong, but not gentle. Like many younger siblings, she cared a lot about games and could be spiteful when she lost. Her notes are filled with a barrage of details and thoughts sometimes meant to startle. While the others write about their daily walks, Anastasia writes about toenails, worms, roughhousing. At the same time she was a pious girl, and endlessly patient with the sick.

Beyond Tsarskoe Selo the cities and countryside began to simmer, little noticed at first. Pogroms had traditionally been tolerated as an outlet for peasant anxieties and hostilities, but now the pogroms only seemed to ignite larger fires. The people on the estates, always somewhat inscrutable to their noble landlords, seemed sullen, even menacing. The cities were full of people who had managed to educate themselves in state supported universities but now found they had little hope of tangibly improving their lives. These people, often Jewish, joined the many illegal political parties forming all over the country, courting arrest and exile or worse at the hands of the Okhrana, Nicholas' secret police.

The Russo-Japanese War—that "short, victorious war" suggested by Nicholas' advisers as a panacea to the disaffection spreading throughout the empire—nearly upended everything. The Japanese, thought to be "little yellow monkeys" who would flee at the sight of a Russian soldier, were brave, clever opponents. Their sudden naval attack on Port Arthur in 1904 (the year of the Colonnade Egg), was closely followed by the Bloody Sunday slaughter of women and children on the steps of the Winter Palace; disaster abroad, disaster at home. A wave of assassinations, strikes, and mutiny paralyzed the cities by mid-October. In the countryside the burning of estates began.

The long-awaited heir, Alexei, had appeared in August 1904, but there were no unmixed blessings in that thoroughly unlucky year. Alexandra had inherited the hemophilia gene and Alexei would soon show signs of the disease, hemorrhaging horribly from ordinary childhood accidents. He was a bright child, good-hearted, but a little spoiled—his illness was so painful, so debilitating, that his parents and tutors were loath to discipline him when he actually felt well enough to misbehave.

In the end, only the issuing of an Imperial Manifesto granting freedom of speech, and an elective Duma would slow the slide towards anarchy. The Manifesto was a sham; the Okhrana continued to suppress dissent, and Nicholas reserved the right to appoint and dismiss ministers, and to close the Duma at will. Any real movement towards a constitutional monarchy—an option which might have been better suited to the political realities and personalities involved—was adamantly rejected by the tsar and tsarina alike. The moment passed.

The rhythm of life within the Imperial Household appeared to proceed much as it always had. 1906 was the year of the Swan Egg, a lavender enamel and diamond shell that concealed a mechanical platinum swan which seemed to glide across a polished oval of blue-green aquamarine.

The snapshots the Imperial Family mounts into its massive albums reveal a jolly clockwork universe, one full of genial instructors who always gave top marks, picnics, games of tennis, and dances held on the deck of the imperial yacht, the *Standart*, as it cruised the Gulf of Finland for two weeks every June.

The picnics can be held on the grounds of any number of palaces, hunting lodges and private beaches, but the effect is so much the same that a span of several years can seem like a single golden afternoon. The women wear white dresses, straw boaters, and carry parasols and malacca walking sticks. Wicker picnic gear is set up by sailor servants among the wild flowers. The scene is remarkably informal—we see the empress barefoot with her skirts hiked up to reveal pale, slender ankles.

The photos also disclose a new member of their intimate circle. Anna Taneyva Vyrubova, a heavy-set young woman of dog-like devotion begins turning up in about 1907 (the year of the Rose Trellis Egg). She quickly became "our big baby," living in a small house near the Alexander Palace and taking dinner with the family most nights, staying on as they read uplifting books, stuck pictures in the photo albums, and did fancy stitching. After she left they retired to their rooms and wrote to each other, memorializing walks, recording weather statistics, correcting false impressions. The minutiae of their lives was fossilized in shoals of notes like shells deposited by a shallow, tepid sea:

Today it is the 49th day that I am ill, tomorrow begins the 8th week ...

Even before the stress of Alexei's illness prematurely aged her, Alexandra had been prone to psychosomatic complaints. Heart, back, legs, head—they were all the locus of affliction at one time or another. Distinguished specialists failed to find anything physically wrong; this was left to the obliging Dr. Botkin, her court physician. Prayers were welcome, but were not expected to relieve her distress:

When God thinks the time comes to make me better, He will, and not before ... loving your poor old Mama who is always ill does not make life bright for you poor children ... He has sent His cross which must be borne. I know it's dull having an invalid mother, but it teaches you all to be loving and gentle. Only try to be more obedient, then you make it easier for me ...

Her daughters plead with her to feel better:

I am so sorry your heart is still No. 2 ... You don't know how sorry I am that you feel bad. It is awful to see how you suffer. You are so patient that I cannot understand... Mama, sweet, I am so awfully sad. I see so little of you ... I hope you will sleep well my darling angel and I will see you not in bed with a bad heart, but feeling well and in your sitting room ...

Inevitably their efforts fall short and there are choruses of contrition too:

Perhaps I have lots of folts but please forgive me ... really, really my sweet one I WILL try and be as good as I can and never tire you ... Write to me please a word only that you forgive me and then I can go and sleep with a clear conscience ... Please, darling angel, forgive me ... Say, darling, that you are not angry ...

The notorious Grigori Rasputin was also becoming an intimate member of the royal circle. Anna Vyrubova was a devotee and served as an intermediary between the empress and the Siberian "Man of God."

Alexei suffered, and she in turn suffered, as minor incidents turned into potentially lethal emergencies. Rasputin alone seemed able to calm Alexei and slow the bleeding. This might not have been a scandal if he had not led a lurid second life drinking, seducing women, and making compromising statements about his closeness to the empress ("the old lady"). Alexandra, engrossed in mystic ideas about holy fools, not only refused to believe these tales, she marked their bearers as personal enemies and worked to limit their influence on her husband. A governess who tried to restrict Rasputin's access to the girls as they prepared for bed was silenced. As Tatiana wrote: *I hope our nurse will be nice to our friend now.*

A downward spiral was beginning but this was somewhat concealed by the glittering events of 1913, the 300th anniversary of Romanov rule. The imperial family embarked on a round of public appearances, generating a warm response at every stop. The effort gave Alexandra and her suite an exaggerated sense of security: "Now you can see for yourself what cowards those State Ministers are," she told a lady-in-waiting. "They are constantly frightening the emperor with threats of revolution and here—you see it yourself—we need merely to show ourselves and at once their hearts are ours."

Reassured, everyone went back to what they were doing, little realizing that it would take more than waving at crowds to retain the loyalty of those unknown, unknowable masses. Brass bands, the chance to see something grand, and time off work created happy crowds, people who cheered and waved back before going home to hash over the latest rumors about the imperial family.

Rumormongers had a lot to work with. The talk about Alexandra and Rasputin circulated in ever wider circles. Anna Vyrubova and the daughters were said to be involved too; Tsarskoe Selo was the scene of religious mania and wild orgies. The rest of the family had too many problems of its own to act as a counterweight. The dowager empress spent much of her time abroad, a casualty of her quarrels with Alexandra. The grand dukes and duchesses, leading lives of great privilege and little responsibility, made bad marriages and bickered and conspired amongst themselves.

I am simply stifling in this atmosphere of gossip and malice, Nicholas himself would write in 1913.

The coming of war, and of unimaginably vast and hideous means of warfare, came as a surprise in Russia, as it did elsewhere. The assassination at Sarajevo and the subsequent Austrian and German threats to Serbian autonomy brought Russia, long a player in Balkan affairs, into the fray in the summer of 1914 (the year of the Mosaic Egg). The war inspired a patriotic fervor that led to enlistments in every social class, men who went off by train and by foot, singing of their longing to defend Holy Russia.

At first Alexandra and her elder daughters threw themselves into the war effort, becoming Red Cross nurses and spending long hours with patients in the hospital they had established at the Catherine Palace. An adjacent chapel was converted into a second, smaller hospital in the names of Maria and Anastasia, as yet too young to take the nursing course. The early and devastating loss at Tannenburg darkened the public mood. It had become apparent that a great struggle had only just begun, and that victory would take longer, and cost more than any had suspected.

In 1915 (the year of the Red Cross Egg) intense anti-German feelings began to be vented against the Imperial Family, and against Alexandra in particular. While she continued to see herself as the *Matushka*, to many Russians she was simply "that German woman." Unruly crowds in Red Square called her a spy and demanded that she be shut up in a convent; even her daughters found the situation confusing. Anti-German statements were made and then explained by a note from Tatiana:

Please forgive me, my Mama Sweet, if I ever hurt you involuntarily by saying something about your former home, but if I really do say something, it is always without thinking that I can hurt you, or something like that, because really, when I think of you I only think that you are our angel, Mama dear— a Russian, and always forget that it was not always so.

Alexandra only directly involved herself in politics after Rasputin became a figure of national disrepute. "Our Friend" needed to be protected from his enemies and supported by friendly ministers in the government. The need for protection and secrecy had become so great that when the Commander-in-Chief, the Grand Duke Alexander Nicholaevich wished to meet privately with the empress to relay some unpleasant truths, he was forced to make an appointment through Olga, now acting as the gatekeeper of the Mauve Boudoir.

Alexandra's primary target was the the Grand Duke Nicholas Nicholaevich, an intimidating presence who managed to keep his devastated armies in the field and was a veteran opponent of Rasputin. All along she had been urging her husband to assert himself by taking direct command. In the summer Poland fell and an opportunity presented itself. After much prayer, the emperor, against all official advice, asked for Nicholas Nicholaevich's resignation, took personal control of his armies, and left Alexandra to rule in his name.

The end came quickly once this fatal moment was reached. 1916 (the year of the Steel Military Egg) was the final year of the Russian war effort, and the last full year of the dynasty. Members of the Imperial Family were involved in the assassination of Rasputin; it was the wrong thing to do, and too late, also. Military collapse and civilian bread riots in St. Petersburg followed.

Sick with the measles, Olga, Tatiana, and Anastasia were sequestered in a darkened room in a palace which now lacked a reliable household guard. The tsar, stranded between home and headquarters, abdicated. The final nights of Alexandra's consortship would be spent praying with her handful of defenders, writing notes to her husband— *we shall see you again on your throne, restored by your people and troops to the glory of your reign*—all the while awaiting the advance of a mutinous army in the ominous silence.

The girls emerged from their quarantine into new, trackless days. Did any of them see it coming? A.A. Mordvinov, an aide-de-camp of their Uncle Michael's thought so. He had sat with them the long night they learned of Rasputin's murder. It was cold and they huddled together on a sofa in one of their bedrooms, visibly upset but never actually uttering his name in front of their visitor. Mordvinov thought they were not only mourning their spiritual adviser but sensing doom: *The stormy sea of political passions, calumnies, posturing and the most decisive threats, had now in reality come to this flowering, monastic little haven.*

1917 will be the year of the Twilight Egg—it seems that Faberge did make an austere, dark blue egg for the empress and even tried to deliver it but was turned away by the Provisional Government headed by Alexander Kerensky. House arrest at Tsarkoe Selo was followed by exile at Tobolsk, the Bolshevik revolution, imprisonment at Ekaterinburg, a plunge into an unmarked grave (naked, faces obliterated by rifle butts), and seventy years in the earth (everyone truly Russian at last).

All this is in the future. On this winter morning, the lamps are still bright as the empress, feeling better, selects a pen and begins to write.

Alexandra

Anastasia, Nicholas, Olga, Alexei, Tatiana, Alexandra, Marie, c. 1914

Anastasia

Olga, Nicholas, Anastasia, Marie, Tobolsk 1917

Ipatiev House, Ekaterinburg, c. 1918

Chapter Two

I

August 16, 1916.

As the Grand Duchess Anastasia, fifteen, wakes up in the Alexander Palace at Tsarskoe Selo, a thousand miles away Franziska Schanzkowsky, twenty, clatters down the steps of Neue Hochstrasse 17 in Wedding, a working-class suburb of Berlin. Red Wedding, they call it, because of the communist sympathizers and old-time socialists who live in the grey apartment buildings set around rear courtyards where women string laundry and gossip, and where you might still find outhouses.

Over a quarter of a million people live in Wedding's six square miles, some of them in rundown tenements like the the squalid Meyer's Hof on Ackerstrasse where two thousand souls are crammed into 230 tiny flats. Franziska is an unskilled laborer, conscripted for work at the Allgemeine Elektricitats Gesellschaft [AEG] on Brunnenstrasse. AEG has been converted to a munitions plant for the duration of the war. With men fighting and dying on the front, women have taken over factory jobs. The war that started so gloriously with the kaiser leading the soldiers through the Brandenburg Gate for the glory of the Fatherland has caused many casualties.

Franziska's fiance is among the dead. She thinks of him all the time, and as she dashes along the street on this warm August morning, she touches his medallion through the thin blue cotton of her work dress.

She could be attractive, a little woman with full lips, a tilted nose and high cheekbones. Her eyes are a startling blue and her wavy light brown hair is caught back in a bun. There's a Slavic touch about her, a roundness and lushness offset by the ironic, sometimes sad look in her eyes.

But no one notices as she hurries over the cobblestones. She's just another working woman, a girl from the provinces who's come to the big city to work. Tired looking; she works ten hours a day. Hungry; everyone is hungry these days. Her lunch consists of ersatz bread smeared with ersatz fat—*Streichfett.* Maybe a boiled potato, but not an egg. Eggs are rationed, one every fortnight.

Franziska doesn't know that on this day she will drop a hand grenade on the assembly line, an accident that will kill the foreman and send her to a mental hospital.

As unlikely as it might seem, she will also become a famous, even legendary personage. As Anna Anderson, she will live in castles, in luxurious spas, and in a Fifth Avenue apartment. Books will be written, movies made, and years of court proceedings embarked upon, all in hopes of demonstrating that she was in fact the Grand Duchess Anastasia of Russia.

How, her supporters reasoned, could an impostor have so closely resembled Anastasia? How else could she have known so many telling details about the Russian Imperial Family? And would an impostor have acted as "Anastasia" did? Until her death in 1984 she behaved in an autocratic, often selfish way, not caring if she alienated princes, dukes, and other supporters.

There had been other claimants over the years, but they had been quickly exposed and ridiculed. Anna Anderson was in a class of her own.

By 1994 DNA tests performed on a sample of her intestine, preserved after an operation, proved that she was indeed Franziska Schanzkowsky. Even so, many supporters have remained loyal. There must have been a conspiracy; "Anastasia" herself had said that she would never be recognized. Such is the magic of royalty and the mystery of Anastasia's death. The words "princess" and "murder" resonate. Some supporters who have grudgingly accepted the Schanzkowsky identity feel Franziska herself had come to believe in her own legend, as if by some force of will or karmic transference, the woman they knew did possess the magic of a lost and haunted princess.

But Franziska Schanzkowsky, the "Polish factory worker" had fooled them all.

The phone rings. It is Waltraud von Czenskovsky, returning my call. I had tried to reach her at the telephone number in Hamburg given to me by a British contact, but a relative informed me that Frau von Czenskovsky was on holiday in Spain. Finally we can talk.

I am calling about Franziska Schanzkowsky, I explain after introductions.

"Yes, Franziska, my aunt," Mrs. v. Czenskovsky says in a friendly, matter-of-fact, and youthful voice. I had been led to believe she was elderly, probably ill, perhaps even dead: I'd better hurry and call her.

"My father's sister."

So simple this is. A voice thousands of miles away connects to the real Franziska, the young woman who had stumbled onto the Anastasia identity and lived under variants of that name for more than sixty years. Can it be so simple? I think, as Mrs. v. Czenskovsky tells me that Franziska saw her brother Felix at Wasserburg and asked him to say she was not his sister.

I know the reference to Wasserburg. This was in 1927, when Harriet von Rathlef, who later wrote a book about "Anastasia," brought Felix Schanzkowsky to an inn to refute what she referred to as the "Schanzkowsky legend." At first Felix said Franziska was his sister, but changed his mind after he and Franziska talked privately.

"And my father did this," Waltraud goes on, "because he did not want to see Franziska return to poverty. Franziska told him that she didn't want to do farm work anymore, or work as a maid again."

Had Waltraud ever met her aunt?

"No, I didn't know her. We never met."

Had her father had contact with his sister?

"The only opportunity they had to talk was at Wasserburg." I could hear her sigh. "It was hard for him, a great sorrow. She was his favorite sister."

But the German words say it better. Not seeing his sister was a *Belastung* for Felix, a burden. And Franziska was his *Lieblingsschwester*, his darling sister, the sister you think about in your heart, the sister you remember always. And then the *Belastung* comes, that great sorrowing sadness that spreads and grows throughout the years, recalling childhood memories. And beginnings.

The beginning. Franziska Schanzkowsky was born on December 16, 1896, in Borowy Las, also known as Borek, a village twenty-three miles to the west of Karthaus, now Kartuzy, in Pomerania, to Anton and Marie Schanzkowsky. The Schanzkowsky family had once been minor nobility. Waltraud uses the spelling Czenskovsky, as well as the noble "von," which her father had discovered was the proper and legal form. "A prince ennobled a great-grandfather for service," Waltraud explained, "but that was long ago. My grandfather, Anton, was a drinker."

King Jan Sobileski ennobled an entire regiment of Kashubian soldiers for fighting against the Turks, a gesture cheaper than pensioning them off.

According to Dr. Zygmunt Klimek, of the Instytut Jezyka Polskiego PAN, the original spelling of Schanzkowsky/Czenskovsky was Czestkowski, meaning "somebody who was the owner of, or who came from a locality called Czestkowo." Klimek did not find a record of the Schanzkowsky family nobility, but *Polish Genealogy and Heraldry* lists a crest for a family named Czenstkowski.

Historically, Poland was filled with nobility, which in some areas comprised ten percent of the population, a larger ratio than any other European country. The suffix "-ski" often signified a noble background.

There were five children: Valerian (also known as Walter), Gertrud, Juliana Marie ("Mariechen"), Franziska, and Felix, born February 17, 1903, in Stolp, a small city along the Baltic coast.

The family moved from town to town. Waltraud does not know what her grandfather did, but he died when Felix was five or six. By the time Franziska went to school, the family lived in Hygendorf (also spelled Hugendorf), a hamlet a few kilometers from Butow, where the Schanzkowskys belonged to the Roman Catholic church. They were poor, honest, straightforward.

Hygendorf was in Pomerania, near the Polish-German border. Today it is part of Poland and the village belongs to Butow (now Bytow), which lies about twenty-five miles southwest of Danzig (now Gdansk). It is a lovely area, with forests, sparkling lakes, and fertile fields. Picking mushrooms is a common pastime. Potatoes have long been a major crop. There is a Kashubian museum at Wdzydze and a castle with four great towers built by the Teutonic Knights at the turn of the fifteenth century at Butow.

The ordinary folk had few opportunities. Elementary school was compulsory, but not many could afford further education or training. Men toiled in the fields or practised carpentry or smithing. Girls worked as daily help for the local gentry, carrying bath water, cleaning floors, peeling vegetables in the kitchen.

Village women did the laundry once a month, hauling it by wagon to the mill for rinsing. The washerwomen sang, a countess noted nostalgically, but she herself was educated away from the village. Everyone helped with the harvest, an occasion enlivened by wagons bearing coffee urns to the field workers.

"I could have been anything, a doctor," Mr. D. of Toronto says. "But there was no opportunity, no money for studying. It was *Guten Tag, Herr Graf*, and off with the cap when the count rode by."

"We were German, not Polish," Waltraud stresses. "There was some Polish on our maternal grandmother's side, but we always considered ourselves German, of Kashubian background. There were Poles in the village, of course, and so Franziska learned a little Polish."

Franziska was the brightest of all of them, Felix told investigators. She did well in school, he said, completing her compulsory schooling in six and a half years; four and half for the lower school, another two for the upper school, which she left in November 1911, at age fifteen. His sister spoke good High German, good *Platt* (low German) and a little Polish.

Franziska's teacher, Otto Meyer, told a detective that he considered her rather limited intellectually. Waltraud disagreed. Franziska loved to read, she told me, and always borrowed books from the Butow library. Franziska made herself elegant for these trips to Butow, in dresses she sewed herself, hat, gloves, and high heeled shoes.

"People laughed at her, especially at the high heels," Waltraud said. "High heels in those days! In a village! Everyone shook their heads!"

Already Franziska was different. She hid in a wagon, reading, while the others brought in the hay. She already seemed to be distancing herself from them, wrapped up in an increasingly absorbing inner life. There is a famous photograph of Franziska which once belonged to her mother. It shows her standing in a garden, wearing a dress and patterned apron, like the "print-gowned housemaids" who swept the streets after a royal procession.

When you look closely at the picture, you see the maid's cap strings dangling over the collar of Franziska's dress. The cap itself is invisible, as if Franziska had pushed it to the back of her head where it would not be seen. Her long, tapering fingers, which Prince Felix Youssoupov said reminded him of the hands of the Empress Alexandra, are held in the same manner in pictures of "Anastasia," with fingers extended and draped.

The face is serious, unsmiling, with a high forehead and enigmatic eyes. She would later be described as coarse, "big-boned," but the general impression is of an attractive, dignified young woman. A secretive woman. She has read books, she is only a maid in disguise, her look says. She comes from good stock. Perhaps she has seen the kaiser and his family when they visited their estate near Danzig.

Franziska Schanzkowsky, c. 1914

II

In 1914 Franziska and her elder sister Gertrud traveled to Berlin, looking for work. Twelve hours on the train, eating their *Brot und Wurst* in their lap, watching the Prussian countryside. They would have arrived at the main railway station, where "Anastasia's" supporters would argue that Franziska had been picked up by the serial murderer Karl Grossmann, who rendered gullible country girls into the sausages and potted meats he sold to butchers.

Two girls fresh from the east, in long dresses and carrying cheap suitcases. Franziska perhaps in a nicer dress, one she had made herself. Jostling, gossiping, kidding. Arguing. Franziska had a temper even then, as did her brother Walter. In Hygendorf people talked about Walter and his temper. Dreaming … maybe she is dreaming about England. Franziska always wanted to go to England, home of Queen Victoria; she has read about Queen Victoria and Anne Boleyn and Camelot. Green lawns and tennis and ladies in white hats. Putting on airs, Gertrud would say. But Franziska could see herself coming down the wide steps at the front of the house, greeting visitors as they came for tea …

Not much chance of getting to England in 1914, but for the meanwhile Berlin would do just fine. With its population of over two and a half million, the city was a marvel: parks and lakes, wide boulevards and big stone buildings, palaces, the famous Kurfurstendamm and the Friedrichstrasse with its cabarets and restaurants. You could go to the theatre, the cinema. Franziska would come to love the cinema and wept at sentimental films. Maybe she could become an actress …

And perhaps you could see the kaiser riding in the Tiergarten, or walk by the Charlottenburg Palace. Franziska had always wanted to see that. They had talked of Berlin food shortages in Hygendorf, and the horrors of war, but Berlin also meant *Kaiserzeit*, the Kaiser Time, the old values and traditions, mirrored in the palaces and wide streets. "All of Berlin is stately and substantial," Mark Twain wrote, "and it is not merely in parts but uniformly beautiful."

Franziska got a job as a maid. In 1916 she was conscripted for work at AEG on the assembly line, putting together hand grenades. Originally she had rented a room from the Backers, but in 1915 she moved to the flat of Frau Wingender at Neue Hochstrasse 17. Mrs. Wingender ran a knife-sharpening shop in the basement and had a young daughter, Doris. Franziska often visited the Wingenders for chats and had asked if she could move in; Mrs. Wingender agreed.

Although Berlin wasn't what she had dreamed it would be, life there was not devoid of comfort. The Wingenders gave Franziska her own room. Franziska borrowed history books from the local library and went to the cinema. The Wingender flat was filled with old furniture, but was clean and tidy.

The younger Doris was an admirer, sharing confidences and scrubbing Franziska's back. Franziska window-shopped, but this was not always a pleasant occupation. In later, more prosperous days she would speak of looking and not being able to buy, even of being laughed at for not being able to buy. It leaves a sharp tang, the memories of a woman who keenly resented her limitations.

The war was on, she told herself. Wait.

At some point Franziska argued with Gertrud and broke off relations. Gertrud returned to Hygendorf. "Our Franziska was more excited about the fight with Gertrud than was necessary," Mrs. Wingender remarked.

She also acquired a fiance. Franziska wrote home about her engagement, but her family never met the young man, who was soon killed on the Western Front. He must have been poor; Franziska had no money for a dowry. He would be her secret life. Later investigators would probe the memory of "Anastasia," seeking details of royal nurseries and Finnish cruises, but the secret life of Franziska, her real memories, were of no concern to anyone. The mystery beneath the mystery.

An estranged sister, a dead fiance. These things troubled and preoccupied her. She dropped a grenade at work, and was wounded in the arm. The shrapnel killed her foreman.

Franziska's injuries were minor but she had a nervous breakdown and was hospitalized at an asylum in Berlin-Schonberg in August. Only a month later the doctors there declared her "not dangerous, but incurably insane," and released her.

What did they mean by "incurably insane"? It's difficult now to catch the precise nuances of these brief, cryptic comments. Perhaps the shock of the accident had tipped the balance between her waking dreams and the sudden—explosive, violent—horror of her real life. Perhaps a new balance was eventually reached; she was steadier but retained distorted ideas about the world and her place in it.

And then what? Back at the Wingenders', where she stayed in bed and turned her face to the wall, or stared out the window? AEG paid for her hospitalization and it is likely that she remained in Berlin and received disability benefits. The following year she was in another asylum, this time Neuruppin, in the Brandenburg countryside. Franziska did not give her name or any details about herself. She refused to provide a handwriting specimen and said nothing. It seems unlikely from this that she was a voluntary patient, or that she had been committed by people she knew. Had there been an incident of some sort?

The diagnosis of her mental illness remains a mystery. She would be moody and temperamental all her life, and would be "certified" again in the Thirties, when she was living in New York. Other doctors insisted that she did not suffer from a mental illness of any kind.

Her history suggests otherwise. Later, after she disappeared for good, Felix would say he had thought she was either dead or "locked up" somewhere. This is the voice of someone who had long since resigned himself to his sister's illness. The whisper of "psychopathic" symptoms arises, but again, it is difficult to know what this meant. At the very least it suggests a deep, deceptive sort of disorder, something which may not have always been apparent at the surface but ran to the very core of her personality.

It did come to the surface sometimes. She would become depressed, brooding, solitary. There were other, more alarming occasions when she lost control and the fierce, unreasonable suspicions she held about the people around her roared out, transforming her into a madwoman.

After the Neuruppin doctors discovered her identity, they released her into the care of her mother in Hygendorf. The hospital records have disappeared, but the discharge ledger remains and states that Franziska Schanzkowsky was "better" but not cured. Imagine the trip back, by train. This time there was no bustling city to look forward to, only home.

In 1918 Franziska found work in Butow, in a brewery. Mr. Vorbau, keeper of the motor cars, remembered her washing bottles. In March 1919 she was in the Berlin area, at the Friederikenhof estate in Marienfeld, a village that had been incorporated into Berlin. She worked as a cutter in the fields. Chief of Police Schupenhaver remembered her as "secretive, retiring." A woman with thick feet, "a heavy walk." Other girls from Butow worked there; had her mother encouraged Franziska to go with them? She arrived towards the end of March 1919 and stayed until November 17, 1919.

Soon she was taking the streetcar to her old friends the Wingenders, who were glad to see her again. Why not return to Wedding? She could have her old room back; there was no farm work in the winter anyway.

How good our Franziska was, bringing food from the country. Mrs. Wingender fried potatoes. They sat over the table, talking about the recently concluded war, the communists and the Social Democrats. About the revolutionaries Rosa Luxembourg and Karl Liebknecht, who had been murdered and thrown into the Landwehr Canal, where so many people committed suicide that there was even a song about it: *Don't grab the bodies, they'll come apart in your hands!*

Two days after Franziska left Friederikenhof she signed the required notification of the move at the police station. Among other things she attested to her status as a boarder and said that she was

"Undecided" as to whether she would stay there longer than three months.

Berlin in the winter of 1919 was cold, gray, wet. The Wingender apartment was gloomy and damp. They roasted potatoes on the stove, drank ersatz coffee. The political upheavals continued, but they were used to that. The feeling is one of boredom rather than excitement or fear. Franziska's birthday came and went. She spent more and more time in her room. Her head ached. She read or stared out the window at the wet courtyard.

"Franziska was very bizarre in the last time with us, having no doubt a lover and absenting herself often before disappearing February 15, 1920 ... Our Franziska read a lot but when she was in a bad mood she spent entire days in bed, her head turned to the wall and wouldn't speak to anyone," Doris Wingender would say later.

Sometimes Franziska roused herself, dashing into the streets at noon. "She did so very mysteriously," Doris said. "She always made some sort of excuse. She didn't say where she was going. We thought she was meeting a friend or something like that and was making a lot of fuss about it."

"If I told you about it, you would only laugh at me," Franziska said when asked about her absences.

That was Franziska, spinning mysteries. Did she really have a lover? The *Berliner Nachtausgabe* later reported that Franziska had met a man on the estate at Friederikenhof who used to visit her in Berlin, but this was never mentioned again. Doris also agreed when Felix said that Franziska was devoted to the memory of her fiance, and continued to wear his medallion.

Or—who knew? All kinds of things went on in the streets. Prostitutes stood on street corners, drug addicts were everywhere. There were speeches, marches, and brawls in the streets between the communists and the right-wing.

Maybe there was no mystery, except the one Franziska wanted to create. She might have only gone for a walk. The apartment was dreary, but the winter streets were even worse. Perhaps she thought of going to the cinema, seeing *Madame du Barry*. It was the kind of film she liked, but the effort of going was too great. She had little money, only a small disability pension. Few clothes, only one undershirt which she washed out one night a week. That was reality, that and the prospect of returning to Friederikenhof in the spring. The three months were almost up; she'd have to sign another notification in March.

What then? She plainly didn't know. She didn't even have a winter coat, but had to borrow Mrs. Wingender's heavy shawl. She wore the shawl when she left the Wingender apartment one Sunday. It was February 15, 1920.

No one ever found out what Franziska did for the next few days. She did not return to the Wingenders, who assumed she had found a boyfriend. They did not report her missing—Franziska had left before and returned—until March 15. Anyway, the police hadn't been too concerned. Franziska was just another girl who'd run away with a fellow, they said.

Chapter Three

I

Much later, Franziska would say she had walked to the gates of the palace of Princess Irene, sister of the Empress Alexandra. She was in despair ... but that was the story of "Anastasia" and in February 1920, Franziska hadn't become Anastasia yet.

In another version, she stayed in a pensionne on the Friedrichstrasse, that lively street of cabarets, bistros, and prostitutes. "Near the railway station," Franziska remembered.

The only thing known is that she roused herself from her depression and bought a sentimental birthday card for her brother Felix. In the greeting she lies, says she's been working. She doesn't want him to know how she's really been living. She would never write to her family again.

February 17, Felix' birthday, was a Tuesday. At nine o'clock in the evening Franziska jumped off the Bendler Bridge into the Landwehr Canal. Policeman Hallman heard the splash, dove in and rescued her.

They gave her a blanket and tea at the police station and questioned her. Wasn't she aware that attempting suicide was a crime? Didn't she care about her family? Why had she tried to kill herself? Who was she? What was her name? Where did she come from?

"I have asked for nothing," she said, muffling her voice to alter it. If they identified her as Franziska Schanzkowsky, with her record of mental instability, the authorities could have committed her for life. She realized this as soon as Hallmann hauled her onto the banks of the canal. Luckily she had left her papers behind at the Wingenders. And her fiance's medallion? Had she disposed of it before leaping into the canal? It was not found at the Wingenders'.

The police took her to the Elizabeth Hospital on Lutzowstrasse, where the nurses gave her a bed on a ward. They noted her dress: a linen blouse, black skirt, stockings, the shawl, and boots that laced up. No identifying marks on any of it. This was less surprising in an era when women often made their own clothes or re-worked old ones. It might also be that the lack of identifying marks was deliberate; that she meant to spare her intensely Catholic family the shame of a suicide. This might explain the fate of the medallion as well—perhaps it had been engraved with initials, a date or endearment that would have tied Franziska to her past.

The doctors and police questioned her for six weeks. She didn't answer their questions, but admitted she was a working woman. She had no relatives, she said, adding that her mother had recently died. She was terrified, defiant. Terrified because they might find out who she was if the Wingenders reported her missing. Defiant, because she was determined that the doctors and police would not break her as they had at Neuruppin.

Berlin was in turmoil. There was a general strike in March—on the day the Wingenders reported Franziska missing the power was off throughout the city. The right-wing Kapp Putsch, led by authoritarian elements of the old army determined to overthrow the Social Democratic government, raged. People were fleeing, hiding … Franziska kept her mouth shut. She pulled the covers over her head and turned to the wall. At the end of the month they sent Franziska to the asylum at Dalldorf. Everyone in Germany knew about Dalldorf. The nuthouse. Say "Dalldorf" and people knew what you meant. Even the kaiser: "Anyone in Germany who does not believe that Franco-Russia is not working at high pressure for an early war against us deserves to be sent straight to the Dalldorf lunatic asylum," Wilhelm had said at the beginning of the war.

Franziska at Dalldorf, 1920

"Miss Unknown"—Fraulein Unbekannt. That was what Franziska was called at Dalldorf. The picture taken after her arrival there shows her in a hospital gown of thick cotton. Her face looks puffy, heavy-lidded. She was twenty-four at the time, but looks older, and heavier than her recorded weight of 110 pounds.

Would she not tell them who she was? No. She squirmed for the police photos, front and side. They examined her; she was not a virgin. What about her boyfriend? She must have one. She protested in good

German and took to her bed in House 4, Ward B, which she shared with fourteen other "quiet" patients. Visitors to the ward sent her scurrying beneath the bedclothes and she seemed to dread the garden.

Dalldorf was only a few kilometers from the AEG plant and Neue Hochstrasse. No wonder she hated visitors and being outside. They would later say that "Anastasia" had been afraid of being discovered and murdered by the Bolsheviks, but Franziska herself feared an ex-neighbor or co-worker might recognize her.

"Very reserved," it was reported. "Refuses to give her name, family, age or occupation. Sits in a stubborn posture. Will make no statement, says she has her reasons for this and that if she wanted to speak, she would have done so already ... The doctor may believe what he likes, she will tell him nothing. To the question whether she hears voices or hallucinates, she is said to have replied, 'You are not very well informed, Doctor'. She admits to having tried to kill herself but declines to give any reason or explanation."

Maybe she was coming to enjoy the mystery. And the power of mystery. She hinted at fears of persecution. They sent people to look at her. Maria Andrecewsky's brother came from Posen and shook his head. Unlike later confrontations with witnesses, Franziska laughed, making no attempt to conceal her face or voice her indignation at being forced to meet a stranger.

Time passed and no one connected her with the missing Franziska. The Wingenders had come forward but gave the wrong date for her disappearance, placing it on January 15. Her picture was posted in police stations, but without result. She must have known that the Wingenders wouldn't make too much of an effort; they weren't keen on the police and wouldn't want to make trouble for her anyway.

But what about her family? They would inquire, but would be careful too, remembering Neuruppin.

"She used to write regularly," Franziska's mother said. "We gave notice of her disappearance to the police magistrate at Hasse, but had no success."

Fraulein Unbekannt was the suffering type, the nurses said. Psychopathic symptoms, the doctors noted, but they disagreed. She was really so nice, so polite. Not like the other patients. She wasn't insane, it was only that she would not give her name. It was obvious that she didn't come from a rough background. What tragedy made her refuse to say who she was? What was she so afraid of? It was such a mystery.

At some point during her stay, a young man, unremarkable in appearance, visited Franziska. They spoke for an hour in a foreign language, it was said. A boyfriend? Felix? Someone must have known that Franziska was at Dalldorf, but the visit didn't distress her, and she never made much of an effort to explain it. Perhaps someone she trusted had seen her picture in the police station and had come quietly to Dalldorf to check on her. Later she would hoist her visitor up the social ladder, claiming that he had carried a silver-headed walking stick.

When she felt well, Fraulein Unbekannt borrowed books from the Dalldorf library. She liked to read about the kaiser, about royalty and ancient warfare. Was she German? She spoke good High German, but sometimes, in her sleep, other words escaped her. Polish? Russian? Low German?

Some nights it was hard to sleep and the mystery woman crept to the nurses' station for some decent conversation. Miss Unknown discussed the books she read and German royalty, once speaking of the Prussian crown prince "as if she were personally acquainted with him." She might buy an estate one day, after her release, and ride horses, she said.

To the nurses she was becoming the person she wanted to be: a mysterious lady of high station who felt safe with them. Sometimes she was haughty, "even a little overbearing. In general, however, lovable, though rather reserved." They excused her from the chores other patients were expected to perform.

"During her residence at Dalldorf, [Franziska] behaved not as a working woman, but as a lady of the highest circles of society," said nurse Anna Chemnitz later.

Did Miss Unknown really know the kaiser, as she hinted? These were turbulent times; was she somehow connected to high places? Is that why she feared for her life? Was that why she said she could not leave Dalldorf until "times were different"? The kaiser had abdicated and would never return to Germany. Things had been better in his time, the *Kaiserzeit*, before the war.

"The Germans were living as though they were at the railway station, no one knowing what would happen the next day," wrote Ilya Ehrenburg, a Russian intellectual who had come to Berlin in 1921. "Shopkeepers changed their price-tickets every day: the mark was falling. In the poorer quarters several bakeries were looted. It seemed as though everything was bound to collapse, but factory chimneys went on smoking, bank clerks neatly wrote out astronomical figures, prostitutes made up their faces ... the end of the world was postponed from one day to the next."

It's no wonder that the nurses found Fraulein Unbekannt's gentle hints and mysteriously refined manners a calming diversion. In October 1921 they noticed Franziska looking at a newspaper picture of the murdered Romanov family.

II

An article had been published in the *Berliner Illustrierte* stating that a Mademoiselle Berditch had turned up in Paris, claiming to be the Grand Duchess Anastasia. She was said to have been saved by one of the guards at Ekaterinburg. This imposture was immediately debunked, but the curiosity that prompted the article remained.

Ekaterinburg had fallen to the White Russians soon after the killings, but subsequent investigation had failed to unearth the bodies. The secrecy surrounding the fate of the imperial family and the chaos in Russia meant that official versions of the murders did not appear until the mid-Twenties. In the meanwhile the aura of splendor and tragedy evoked by their disappearance suffused the stories published in the popular press.

The magazine found its way to Dalldorf and Franziska read it, as she read so many things. But how did it happen that they came to think she could be Anastasia, or at least one of the daughters? Nurse Bertha Wiemuth said she often saw an article about the massacre of the Romanovs in Franziska's hands. And then, a subtle hint, a suggestion? There was a look about Fraulein Unbekannt, around the eyes … Franziska turned "pale" when they showed her a photo of the tsar shoveling snow in Tobolsk. Nurses Buchholz and Walz agreed: Miss Unknown looked like the Grand Duchess Anastasia.

A nurse later said that she spoke Russian at Dalldorf, a language Franziska never learned. But a Polish phrase, muttered in her sleep— could that not sound like Russian?

The nurses were easily impressed. Franziska didn't know much about the Romanovs, only what she had read in newspapers, but she didn't have to say a lot. People were eager to believe, to fill in the blanks, to help tell the story.

She asked Nurse Chemnitz to run away with her to Africa to join the Foreign Legion because the doctors at Dalldorf were working for the Bolsheviks. The Jewish doctors—everywhere. Unlike her nurses, Franziska's doctors rarely appear in the drama unfolding in Ward B. The destruction of her records there means little is known of what they thought of her, apart from the ominous mention of "psychopathic symptoms." Their absence among her early supporters is conspicuous in light of her later successes. She must have gotten better at handling doctors as she went along, because she seems to have made little headway here, and saw them as hostile, even dangerous.

Franziska would later complain about Dalldorf, saying "I wondered why people did not feel any pity for me. Does somebody who despairs of life not deserve pity? Of course they could not know all I had been through, but was that a reason for regarding me with cold aloofness, even with disapproval? I could not eat. Every day had the same diet— potato soup, greasy gravy, a cup of coffee, and a roll. This eventually became so repugnant that they had to resort to artificial feeding ... I was so weak that I could not hold a spoon in my hand, and spilled everything I tried to put in my mouth."

Actually, life wasn't bad at Dalldorf. Franziska was not dull or unworldly; she had always managed to ride things out, to avoid the worst of the strife around her. The food wasn't good but people were starving in Berlin. There was an adequate library and people who took her to be a fine lady, perhaps even a daughter of a tsar. Franziska didn't have to do chores or think about working in the fields or in a factory. Two years had passed; she no longer worried as much about being identified as Franziska Schanzkowsky.

Perhaps she would have been released one day, to return to her family or to show up again at the Wingenders, but suddenly her peaceful existence was threatened.

Franziska learned that she, along with the rest of her ward, would be transferred to an asylum in the Brandenburg countryside—Neuruppin, where she had been before, where she had also refused to identify herself, only to be found out. A return to a life as a former fieldhand and incurable madwoman was suddenly certain. She told the nurses she worried about her safety in rural Brandenburg, where Bolshevik agents would surely kill her.

They sought to reassure her, but it was no good now. The oncoming disaster sent her back to bed where she laid sleepless, suffocating blankets pulled over her head. The nurses were kind, but useless in an official matter like this one. The doctors were worse than useless, and she knew better than to go to them with her stories of Bolshevik peril.

By this time Clara Peuthert had been admitted to Franziska's ward. Clara was a strong-willed, talkative Berliner of about fifty. She said she had worked in St. Petersburg and Tsarskoe Selo as a seamstress sewing dresses for "court ladies." Sometimes she claimed to have been a governess there; others claimed that she had been a laundress or an agent for the Germans. She had ended up at Dalldorf because of her bad temper, it was said. She was not mad, she stressed, "only pathological."

Clara came at just the right time. She seemed good-natured, a motherly, strapping, take-charge person who knew how to manage. Clara and Franziska used the familiar *Du* with each other, implying an easy, immediate intimacy.

She soon learned of Franziska's impending transfer. Later Clara would say that Franziska had asked her to contact the Russian monarchists now living in Berlin; maybe they could do something to keep her from being sent away to Brandenburg.

"I know you! You're the Grand Duchess Tatiana!" Clara cried out to Franziska as the rest of the ward looked on.

Franziska put her finger to her lips. It is easy to imagine the story, through hints and suppositions, further developing between them. The nurses thought Franziska looked like one of the tsar's daughters. Why shouldn't Clara see the resemblance too? She claimed to have seen the grand duchesses in Russia, and could describe their coats, their hats, the crowds as they drove by. Clara was interested in royalty, and she knew a lot.

But which daughter was Miss Unknown? Franziska wouldn't say. Clara studied the photos of the tsar's family and came to the conclusion, as so many would later, that Franziska most resembled the Grand Duchess Tatiana.

Yes, it might be so. This strange young woman did look like Tatiana. Clara knew what to do; she would write letters to important people. Clara would take charge of the whole matter and see it through. Maybe these people could prevent the transfer, Franziska suggested.

Clara was released on January 20, 1922, but she visited Franziska regularly, bringing treats and magazines. She also brought a copy of the *Almanach de Gotha*, the tome outlining the intricate bloodlines of the German aristocracy, so Franziska—"Tatiana"—could learn more about her "relatives."

Miss Unknown didn't speak Russian? She *wouldn't* speak Russian. Why should she, after what those brutes had done to her family? And if Franziska's mouth was a bit large, well, hadn't it been deformed by injuries in Ekaterinburg?

In the meantime, Clara wrote to the Grand Duke of Hesse on February 22 about his "niece" at Dalldorf. She also wrote to Princess Irene, the tsarina's sister, and to Irene's husband, Prince Henry, brother of the exiled kaiser. She went to the Danish embassy because the dowager empress of Russia was a former Danish princess who had returned to her native country after the Revolution.

There was no reply to the letters and Clara got nowhere at the embassy. Time was running out. Franziska's transfer was set for the second or third week of March.

III

Clara decided to approach someone influential in the White Russian community. Berlin was filled with Russians. The Whites were there because they had fled the Soviets, the Reds because they thought a German revolution was in the offing. Up until April 1922, Serge Botkin of the Russian Delegation was authorized to issue passports to Russians, enabling Russian exiles to travel to and from Germany.

Russians of all varieties mingled in the cafes and restaurants. "At every step you could hear Russian spoken," wrote Ehrenburg. "Dozens of Russian restaurants were opened ... There was a little theatre that put on sketches. Three daily newspapers and five weeklies appeared in Russian. In one year seventeen publishing firms were started."

Konstantin Stanislavski brought his theatre company, Wassily Kandinsky his paintings. Vladimir Mayakovsky gave poetry readings. The Soviets had a table at the Allaverdi, where former grand dukes served the customers.

The White Russians had been involved in the Kapp Putsch; they brought the anti-Semitic *Protocols of the Elders of Zion* to Germany and fought among themselves. In 1921, over one hundred White Russians met at Bad Reichenhall in Bavaria in an attempt to achieve political cohesion. They were secretly backed by the arch-conservative General

Erich Ludendorff and openly organized by Max von Scheubner-Richter, an important adviser to the up-and-coming Adolf Hitler.

The monarchists among them expected to see a monarchy reestablished in Russia. The big question was which of the two pretenders to support: the Grand Duke Kyril, a controversial cousin of Nicholas II's; or the Grand Duke Nicholas, the commander-in-chief of the army who had stepped aside for the tsar. A second Russian Monarchist Congress was slated for March 22, at the Rotes Haus restaurant in Berlin.

On March 6, with only a week to go before Franziska's transfer, Clara went to the Russian church on Unter den Linden, where Captain Nicholas Adolfovich von Schwabe was selling monarchist pamphlets and photographs. A handsome young ex-officer, he had once been a member of the dowager empress' personal guard. Now he edited *The Double Eagle*, the newsletter of the Supreme Monarchist Council. A Russian grand duchess at Dalldorf? He was immediately interested. Clara identified Tatiana in a photo of the tsar's family. Schwabe remembered the case of Miss Berditch, the supposed Anastasia of Paris. No one had taken this pretender seriously, and there had been other impostors as well, but the Dalldorf patient sounded intriguing: fearful of giving her name, reserved, occasionally haughty.

But the important thing, Clara emphasized, was that "Tatiana" was petrified of being sent to an asylum in rural Brandenburg, where Bolshevik agents might assassinate her.

Could Schwabe help?

Schwabe promised that he would visit the "grand duchess" as soon as he could and contacted Nicholas Markov, known as Markov II, head of the Supreme Monarchist Council. Before the revolution, Markov had owned an estate in Kursk and had spoken violently against socialism in the Duma. In Berlin he wrote about ritual slaughter and international Masonic conspiracies.

The idea of discovering a living daughter of Nicholas II must have been riveting, just two weeks before the Congress met. He contacted Madame Zinaida Tolstoi, a friend of the tsarina's, and asked her to visit

Dalldorf the next day. Early the following morning he sent an agent to the Elizabeth Hospital to learn more about Fraulein Unbekannt and dispatched others to form a guard at Dalldorf.

Clara, not privy to these plans, worried. What if Schwabe hadn't believed her? What if she hadn't presented a strong enough case? She appeared at his door to argue Franziska's cause again.

The grand duchess, she explained, didn't like to speak Russian after what had happened to her family, but read English, French, and Russian; she was refined and had impressed the nurses with her aristocratic manner. She was religious and feared Bolsheviks and Jews. Schwabe hastened to reassure his visitor.

Clara must stay at home, he stressed. Let the monarchists handle things for now, he said, hustling her away.

Later that morning Madame Tolstoi, accompanied by her daughter and Captain Stefan Andreievsky, arrived at Dalldorf. They brought Dr. Winicke, who had looked after Franziska at the Elizabeth Hospital, in the hope that he could persuade the Dalldorf staff not to transfer "Tatiana"—they hoped she was Tatiana—to Brandenburg. Schwabe hovered in the background.

Franziska refused to meet them in the downstairs visiting room. She had spent another sleepless night after not hearing from Clara.

The monarchists trooped upstairs.

Franziska had no idea who these visitors were. Crazy people, yelling in a strange language, pacing, whispering, and worst of all, trying to pull the covers away from her face. Finally Dr. Winicke sat down and spoke softly in German.

He got the covers down a few inches. She recognized him at once as someone who had interrogated her at the Elizabeth Hospital and yanked the blanket right back up. Did this have something to do with Neuruppin?

In those few seconds, Madame Tolstoi and her daughter recognized Tatiana's eyes. Miss Unknown was shorter than Tatiana, they thought, but the eyes—yes, the eyes were the same. The unknown, mysterious patient had to be Tatiana. Yes, yes, yes: Tatiana. One wonders when

Franziska realized she had passed muster as a Romanov. It must have all seemed so improbable, so far beyond the sly hints at the nurses' station.

Markov sent next for Baroness Sophie von Buxhoeveden, a former lady-in-waiting to the tsarina. She had accompanied the imperial family to Tobolsk until forcibly separated from them by the Bolshevik regime. At the time of Markov's call she was staying at Hemmelmark, the country home of Princess Irene.

Schwabe worried. There was something not quite right about the meeting with Madame Tolstoi. The patient had been so frightened and she clearly didn't understand Russian. He decided to visit her again, privately.

On Wednesday Schwabe returned with Fritz Jannicke, a German friend and Nazi party organizer. Jannicke went armed in case there was trouble. They brought chocolates, a copy of *The Double Eagle* and a photo of the dowager empress.

Once they arrived, the same old thing: Franziska in bed with her face covered. She was unresponsive when Schwabe began questioning her but when he handed her the picture of the dowager empress, she actually looked at it.

The photo reminded her of one Clara had shown her. Could this visit possibly be Clara's work? Was something going to come of all that crazy talk about monarchists?

She asked Schwabe who had sent him. Clara Peuthert, he said. Franziska immediately asked him if he could prevent her transfer. That was what this was all about, after all.

He would do his best, he said. Dr. Winicke had promised to intercede, but Schwabe kept this information to himself. Markov and the Council were waiting to see what Baroness Buxhoeveden had to say when she arrived in Berlin on Friday.

Franziska accepted the chocolates and the newspaper. She told Schwabe that she read Russian. Franziska's smile and nod when they left impressed Schwabe and Jannicke as aristocratic.

It was a close run thing. If Clara hadn't gone to the Russian church that Sunday, it is probable that Franziska would have been sent back to Neuruppin, where the staff would have recognized her at once.

Franziska's meeting with Baroness Buxhoeveden took place on March 11 or 12; accounts differ as to the date. The baroness arrived with her father, Zinaida Tolstoi, Captain Andreievsky, and Schwabe. Franziska refused to come downstairs.

The entourage entered the ward, where they found Franziska—where else?—in bed, chatting excitedly with Clara, who had been sent ahead to prepare "Tatiana" for the meeting. When Franziska spied the visitors she dove under the covers.

In the baroness' own words: "The nurse and Madame Tolstoi told me she always acted this way when visitors wanted to see her, but that she liked to gossip with an old woman, Mademoiselle Peuthert, a former patient at the hospital in whom she had confidence and who was present when I arrived ... She was speaking German with Mlle. Peuthert. Although she was allowed to get up, she liked to stay in bed as long as possible ...

"She wore a white nightshirt and bed jacket, the front open, the hair tied in the back in a very simple style ... I tried to catch the attention of the young woman and I caressed her hair, while addressing her in English, using tender phrases which I used to speak to the Grand Duchesses ... She didn't respond at all and I saw that she didn't understand a word I said, because she let the cover slip a bit and I saw nothing in her eyes that showed she knew me ...

"The eyes and the forehead had a certain resemblance to the Grand Duchess Tatiana, but it was a resemblance which disappeared when her face wasn't covered. I removed the cover by force and I saw that neither the nose, the mouth, [nor] the chin were like those of the Grand Duchesses. The hair was lighter, the teeth—several were missing—were formed completely differently from the Grand Duchesses' teeth, which were lightly inclined. The teeth of this young woman were totally straight. Her hands were also different ... We couldn't tell her height exactly as she was lying in bed, but I realized that she was in any case smaller than me, while the Grand Duchess Tatiana was ten centimeters taller than me. I was able to verify her height from measurements made at the asylum.

"I tried to revive the memory of the young woman by every way possible. I showed her an icon with the dates of the [1913] Jubilee ... then a ring given me by the Empress in the presence of the Grand Duchess Tatiana. But none of these things seemed to evoke in her the least remembrance. She remained completely indifferent, content to whisper several incomprehensible words into Mlle. Peuthert's ear ... When Mlle. Peuthert saw that the Unknown remained mute and showed she didn't recognize me, she tried to get her attention and whispered several words in German into her ear as she showed her photos, saying, 'Tell me, isn't this the Empress'?"

Markov dropped the case after Franziska's meeting with her. Baroness Buxhoeveden said that she wasn't Tatiana and that was enough for him. Miss Unknown was an impostor.

Franziska's supporters would later claim that the baroness failed to recognize her because she came looking for Tatiana when the claimant was in fact Anastasia, but the witness remained firm: "I learned later that one thought she was the Grand Duchess Anastasia, but she didn't have the least resemblance to her either. She didn't have the least particular trait which would have allowed anyone who knew the Grand Duchess Anastasia well to identify her."

Baroness Buxhoeveden's opinion would carry much weight with European royalty over the years, including the British Royal Family, according to one of Franziska's opponents.

Clara, Schwabe, and Madame Tolstoi had all tried their best, but Franziska had not tried at all, remaining hidden and saying nothing, not speaking Russian and not answering questions, and in that manner she found the result she sought.

The transfer to Brandenburg was canceled. Within two months Franziska moved in with a Baltic baron and said she was the Grand Duchess Anastasia, miraculously saved from the massacre of her family.

Chapter Four

I

Russians continued to visit Franziska even after Baroness Buxhoeveden's negative verdict. But which of the grand duchesses was
she? She had never actually said she was Tatiana, she informed
Schwabe. He chose not to dwell on the fact that she had allowed him to
believe it. Who then? Schwabe produced a list of the grand duchesses
and asked Franziska to cross out the names that didn't belong to her.

She left "Anastasia." It was her only choice; at 5'2" she was simply
too short to be any of the others. The lack of facial resemblance was
something she would have to live with.

The visitors seem to have taken the change of identity in stride.
They crowded her bedside, sharing photos and memories: Here was
"Mama;" here was "Papa" rowing the boat. Did she remember Spala,
the hunting lodge? Everyone looked forward to Spala in the fall. And
who was this ... wasn't it ... didn't she recognize this?

Franziska pulled the covers over her head and turned away. Sometimes she cried. She was feeling sick these days, coughing and losing
weight.

Poor "Anastasia"! Remembering was so dreadful, after all she had
been through. The rifle blows at Ekaterinburg had caused amnesia as
well as loose teeth. Maybe they explained why questions had to be put
into German before she could answer them.

Franziska listened and said little. It was what she would do most of
her life. Other impostors trumpeted their claims loud and clear, but
not Franziska. Talking to the nurses had taught her the power of making oblique statements, of letting her audience do most of the work in
creating the story.

And then Baron Arthur Gustovich von Kleist, his wife Maria, and their daughters Gerda and Irina came to see her, bearing chocolates and flowers. Baron von Kleist had been a regional police officer in Russia. He and his family lived in a large, comfortable apartment on Nettelbeckplatz. The baroness believed immediately. The nurses said that Fraulein Unbekannt came from "higher circles." She had the graceful, flawless hands of an aristocrat, the "Empress' shoulderline," and spoke German with a foreign accent.

Captain Paul Bulygin, who had followed the Romanovs into Siberia hoping to discover what had become of them, disagreed. He and his companion, Baron Osten-Sacken asserted that she "spoke German quite fluently." Actually, Franziska was proud of her good High German. Would the nurses have seen her as refined if she had spoken badly? One wonders when she learned that the real Anastasia had only known a little German. Not yet, probably.

She could only be herself with Clara, who continued to visit, offering encouragement, advice, and relief from the Russians. A lady must have manicured hands, Clara instructed, drawing on the old belief that after generations of hard labor, the hands of peasants were innately rough and short-fingered. An aristocrat had fine hands with long fingers, and always took the time to push the cuticles back. Peasant or not, Franziska hadn't worked in years and had the soft, cultivated hands to prove it. From the beginning she worked this prejudice to her advantage, gracefully extending a properly "aristocratic" hand to visitors. For some, this gesture would be enough to convince them of her authenticity.

Things suddenly got serious when the Kleists offered to take Franziska into their apartment. Her first reaction seems to have been to decline. Nettelbeckplatz was too close to the Landwehr Canal, Franziska protested. What memories that location would bring back! What she didn't say was that it was also dangerously close to Wedding. She might be recognized by a former neighbor right on the street. And what if the baron saw through her? Could she keep on pretending? Especially as she was feeling more ill every day?

Clara thought that Franziska should go to the Kleists. They would buy her new dresses and there would be a maid to wait on her. Franziska wouldn't have to worry about earning money, either. She could always leave and come to Clara's apartment on Schumannstrasse if it didn't work out. Didn't she want to be with her own kind? With nobility?

On May 30, 1922, Franziska left Dalldorf with the Kleists.

II

Franziska climbed into the taxi that would take her to her new life. It was a miserable beginning; Franziska sick, terrified behind a heavy black veil. The veil was a protection against old neighbors ("Bolsheviks," she said). She was now almost toothless. Although Franziska entered Dalldorf with a full set of teeth, sixteen were missing by the time she left. She told supporters that rifle blows at Ekaterinburg had loosened her teeth, causing constant pain, but she admitted to a Dalldorf guard that she had had healthy teeth removed to change her appearance. She also plucked hair from her hairline in an attempt to change its shape. Did these attempts to alter her features happen before she was taken for a daughter of the tsar, or after? The changes could have had as much to do with Neuruppin; she may have also hoped that the losses would make it more difficult to recognize her as Franziska Schanzkowsky.

Franziska's broad mouth was her least Romanov feature, and she seems to have known this, hiding it whenever possible. The effect is odd; at some points she seems to have adopted the Anastasia persona quite passively, even playfully, but the pulling of teeth was an indication of the steely purpose behind the games. The extractions disfigured her. For the rest of her life she clutched collars, paper napkins, fans, and scarves over her crumpled lower face. The false teeth which might have restored her normal appearance were rejected.

The baroness was surprised at the additional missing teeth. Franziska said that she was afraid of being recognized as Anastasia.

The Kleists were jubilant to have won the confidence of "Anastasia." Germany and the Soviet Union had just signed the Treaty of Rapallo, and were resuming formal relations. This recognition of the Soviet state had led to even closer ties between the monarchists and their sympathizers on the German right. The much-anticipated congress at the Rotes Haus had ended in violence and police action when Vladimir Nabokov, the father of the novelist, was murdered by monarchist extremists. Everyone agreed that a strong leader was needed to unify the cause and give it legitimacy. A grand duchess, a daughter of the fallen tsar, would certainly be a rallying point.

No one recognized Franziska as she stepped from the taxi at Nettelbeckplatz 9. The baron politely allowed her to walk ahead up the four flights of stairs. The apartment was filled with Russian icons and pictures, books, a samovar. From a worker's room to a baron's home—what a change in two years. All she really cared about was the fact that she had her own room there, where she could take off the veil and hide. She must stay in her room, she told the Kleists. No one must know who she was.

A doctor was sent for. Dr. Schiller first visited on June 1. Franziska was anaemic, pale and suffering from pleurisy. Her pulse was weak and she had eruptions on her skin. He was with her on the 4th and then back again on the 6th. She complained that her eyes were swimming and that her head ached, especially behind the right ear. He noted a scar on the finger of her left hand, two centimeters long, with associated stiffness. Franziska had cut herself washing dishes but she wasn't going to admit that. She refused to tell him who she was, also.

"I thought they did not know my true identity," Franziska later said of the Kleists, but this was nonsense. She even suggested that they call her "Anny," short for Anastasia, and also a form of Franziska's second name, Anna.

She had to mollify them. Sick as she was, Russians were congregating at the Kleist apartment, Madame Tolstoi, Schwabe, Bulygin, and

Osten-Sacken among them. Sometimes twenty at a time peered at the "grand duchess."

Franziska said little, and listened to their stories. Some had known the Romanovs personally. Zinaida Tolstoi had been close to the tsarina; Schwabe knew someone else. Who? Who were Vladimir, Andrei, Marva? Sergei?

Photos came out, books. Madame Tolstoi played the piano. Did "Anastasia" remember the tune? Franziska nodded, smiled, gave her hand. She tried to memorize the faces in the pictures, the names and facts. To "remember" events. Yes, she had visited a school in Moscow, she conceded. And the students ... the students wore ... uniforms ... they had given her ... couldn't Anny recall? Was it—perhaps—could it be—a doll? Yes, a doll! It was a doll! "Anastasia" remembered!

And so it went, as it would for many years. Hints and nudges, clues. She remembered what they said, and used the information to impress the next questioner. When she didn't know she kept quiet.

Remembering was so hard for her poor head, they agreed. To help her, they made gifts of postcards and photos, books, and magazines. She, who had lost everything, could at least have the solace of these mementoes.

III

Imagine this ... a hot summer day in Kleists' apartment.

First there was tea-drinking, and then *zakuski*, the afternoon round of drinks and appetizers with guests. Franziska can sometimes get out of this, but not today. She avoided the vodka and nibbled on pickled mushrooms and eggplant caviar. Now she is rather reluctantly having an evening meal with the Kleists. The table is well-set—they're doing quite well despite the depression. Franziska wrings her hands under the table as she waits for the soup course to be served.

Baron von Kleist sits at the head of the table. His baroness, sitting at the foot, has just given a signal to the maid who will serve as footman tonight. Across from Franziska sit Irina and Gerda. To her right sits a young White Russian officer, one she believes she was not supposed to have known in Russia. It is possible that the young officer knows more than he is letting on—they seem determined to push him at her, and that must mean something—but there is very little that Franziska can do about it. The baron is a genial host, but also a former policeman … she can literally feel the eyes of the women upon her as she stares into the little bowl of iced bouillon that has been placed in front of her. How can she eat? It wasn't enough to get it right once; every meal must now be carefully navigated. She had tried to simplify this by begging the Kleists not to observe the full courtesies extended to a visiting grand duchess, but much formality remains to catch her up.

Franziska slurps her soup and notices Gerda smirking. What does she know? The tsarina herself would have made noise drinking soup, if she'd been missing so many teeth.

She passes on the kalatsch—hard rolls now impossible to chew—with a tight little frown and a shake of the head (grand duchesses never thank anyone).

The fish course—this was tricky. Spine straight, shoulders back, elbows loose but held close to the body. Breathe! Which fork are they picking up? Tines up or down? All this fuss over a bit of baked codfish!

Conversation begins in German, although side conversations go on in Russian. The baron tries to draw Franziska in, but she largely ignores him and her dinner partner (who can do all this and talk?). She crumples and smooths the linen napkin in her lap as she waits between courses. The entree arrives and she allows herself an almost inaudible cluck of amusement: some sort of meatballs and buttered noodles, dressed up with parsley and a dollop of sour cream, accompanied by a limp green vegetable.

Not much for the table of a baron! They might have had meatballs at home, but there'd be more of them, a whole pot full, with a big pot of potatoes besides. Mushrooms! She would fill up on them, and on the strawberry kissel tart to come later. When the tart comes she allows herself to be served a small glass of dessert wine, her first drink of the day.

Can she get away with asking the young officer to exchange desserts? She worries that the servants hate her for making extra work and doesn't trust them not to tamper with a slice of tart meant for her. He has already tucked into his portion though, and she redirects her attention to the conversation.

What are they saying now? They have reverted to Russian and she keeps an ear open for references to "Anastasia" or "Romanov." The impression that she understands Russian is useful when it keeps them from using it to talk about her right in front of her face. The baron also has more confidence in her when she seems to understand, but this tends to lead to exhortations to speak and remember. She feels too unwell for that tonight.

The cups of demitasse make their rounds. It's almost over now. The best part is when she stands up, places her mangled napkin on the table and walks away, leaving all those dirty dishes behind her.

Tonight she announces her intention to retire early.

IV

If only the Russians would stop asking questions! It was hard to refuse the baron, especially when he began asking them in an organized way and formulating her answers into a series of protocols.

The direct question format was never a good one for Franziska. She doesn't seem to have prepared anything in advance: "I arrived in Berlin in the middle of the month of February 1920. I arrived alone, having come from Russia and passing through Romania ... Once in Berlin, I changed clothes because it seemed to me I was followed. I don't remember now where I changed my clothes. I was at liberty less than a week before I was placed in the Elizabeth Hospital."

Franziska was then "seized with strong emotion."

That evening he presented her with the names of Tatiana and Anastasia written on a piece of paper. Again, she selected "Anastasia." At
least the hedging about that was over.

The questions went on: hadn't she come to Berlin with Clara Peuthert? One wonders why the baron thought this might be true.

She was always there, he sighed. Elbowing her way in. She and Anny conferred, whispering in corners. It was very strange. What could
they have in common? Kleist wanted to ban Clara, but Anny would be
so upset ...

Franziska was getting sicker. She had head and chest x-rays on the
8th. Auscultation showed her left lung had very little function. She was
spitting blood on the 10th. Later the weather was hot and close and
Franziska was aloof. She refused to eat and was "psychically very excited." Then "Patient is sorry for her behavior of yesterday."

When she was feeling well, she went sightseeing with Gerda. The
Charlottenburg Palace reminded her of Tsarskoe Selo, she said, and
she showed terror at the sight of an Orthodox Jew on the street, certain that he was a Bolshevik.

Unfortunately she mistook a doctor friend of the Kleists' for a Romanov cousin. They were still talking about her failure to speak Russian, although she made what she thought were appropriate comments
when the baron read the Russian newspapers to her.

On June 20, as if sensing their suspicions, "the young woman I took
in from the lunatic asylum, invited me into her room, and in the presence of my wife, asked me to protect her and to promote her rights. I
told her I was at her disposition but on the condition that she frankly
answer my questions.   The reply was categorical ... She was the Grand
Duchess Anastasia Nicholaevna, the youngest daughter of the Emperor
Nicholas II ... "

Franziska went on to say that she had been present at the massacre
of her family and that she had saved herself by hiding behind her sister
Tatiana. She felt rifle blows, fainted, and when she came to she found
herself with the soldier who rescued her. She went to Romania with

this soldier and his wife. After he died, she came alone to Berlin to earn her living, selling jewels to pay for the journey.

"All these trials profoundly depressed me so that momentarily I lost all hope of seeing better days. Although I speak Russian, I decline to speak it, because this language evokes in me painful memories: the Russians did us great wrong, me and my parents."

Why Romania? It was an impulsive choice, but not a bad one. While no details confirming Franziska's story ever emerged from investigations there, nothing would directly contradict it, either.

Franziska readily agreed to the baron's suggestion that she consult a lawyer to help with the deposition of witnesses, and to meet a Prince Dolgourov, who had been attached to the dowager empress' service, as soon as he came to Berlin. The interrogations continued. Franziska's lung condition, the onset of tuberculosis, worsened. She kept on fabricating details, affirming her identity as Anastasia yet again.

Most of all, Franziska added, she wanted to see the Grand Duchess Xenia, Nicholas' sister. She loved this aunt very much: "I am sure she would recognize me better than the others, although I don't understand at all why other people who knew me well seem not to recognize me now."

It seems that some of the visitors hadn't thought that she was Anastasia. "She ruined every chance of being recognized," Gerda would later say. Franziska agreed to write a note to Xenia, but she was so nervous the baron had to guide her hand.

And what about her features? Why didn't she look more like Anastasia?, the baron wanted to know.

She said that while in Romania her companion had obtained an iron device which she wore over her face. The mask helped to slightly alter the shape of her nose and mouth.

The face-altering device would never be mentioned again. The baron translated her words into his protocols, making her hesitant responses sound more definite than they probably were. All the same, the business about the iron mask sounds like an imagination stretched to its absolute limit. Is it any wonder that she collapsed at the end of

July? "Choking feeling, pain in left lung, dazed ... hazy statements," noted Dr. Schiller. He administered morphine and "digalen."

V

Franziska had been well-behaved at Dalldorf, but at the Kleists', she had become both needy and imperious, behavior that would become all too familiar in years to come. The days were shaped by the demands of the visitors and by the baron, who continued to create the protocols which attempted to form Fraulein Anny's "memories" into a coherent account of her escape from Ekaterinburg and eventual appearance in Berlin.

The raw material for this quest seems to have been collected at night, when the women of the house drew together in Franziska's room. She was unpredictable, quick to anger. These agitated moods, exacerbated by the intense scrutiny, were frightening enough to convince the Kleists that Franziska might harm herself if left alone. She was even watched in her sleep by one of the Kleist daughters or by Madame Tolstoi.

On the 4th, Franziska had strong pains in her chest and once more had an injection of morphine. That was the day that Madame Tolstoi told the baron that two nights before Franziska had said something about the soldier, Alexandre Tschaikovsky, who had saved her. Tschaikovsky, Schanzkowsky. The names were almost the same. Probably Franziska had uttered the first name that had come to her during a long night's conversation.

Franziska's story went on. She had left Russia with this Alexandre and his family: his mother, Marie; his sister Veronika; and a younger brother, Serge. They had all gone to Bucharest, where she stayed until 1920. They lived near the railway station on Sventi Voevosi Street. In 1920 Alexandre was murdered. She came alone to Berlin, where she took a room on Friedrichstrasse. She couldn't remember the name of the pensionne.

The most startling news was that "Anastasia" had given birth to Tschaikovsky's son on December 5, 1918. He would be almost three now, with his father's hair and her eyes. She had left the child behind with Tschaikovsky's mother, and wanted him brought to her.

December 5 is St. Nicholas Eve, when German children put their shoes in the window so St. Nicholas can fill them with chocolate. Is that why Franziska blurted out this date? It was an unfortunate choice, since a child born then would have been conceived when Anastasia was still in Tobolsk.

What were they to make of this? A son, a possible claimant to the Russian throne? A bastard claimant, the son of a peasant soldier? It was technically true that the boy could not be heir as descent would be through the female line, but in these turbulent times, the tsar's grandson, even a bastard grandson, might be acceptable to some. This was not particularly good news when the monarchist community was already split between the claims of the Grand Dukes Kyril and Nicholas.

There was another problem, as well. Franziska had hinted to Madame Tolstoi that she had been raped, but even so, a grand duchess sleeping with a Siberian prison guard … it was distasteful. Zinaida Tolstoi left, and informed the baron by letter that she wanted nothing more to do with Fraulein Anny.

Undeterred, Kleist pressed for more details. Franziska went on to tell him that she had married Tschaikovsky in a Roman Catholic church in Bucharest so her son wasn't really a bastard. The baby was baptized at the same church. Her name on the marriage license was Anastasia Romanska, she added.

There is a reckless, "so there!" quality to the story. The baron wanted details, he had details. Franziska even used the Polish form of Romanov, although she might have thought it was the same in Russian. His protocol for this date is short, terse, grim.

Franziska told his wife a tale about vast deposits of Romanov money sitting in banks in England. She didn't seem to care what she said or did now. Kleist caught her writing down a number out of the telephone directory. He tried to get at the paper, but she swallowed it.

She'd be gone soon, anyway. She may have thought the game was up when Tolstoi denounced her.

That night the baron finally barred Clara from his home.

VI

Franziska ran back to the Wingenders. What a relief to see her old friends again, to talk naturally around a kitchen table. It was Saturday morning and Frau Wingender came right up from the shop.

Why, look at Franziska! What wonderful clothes—a lilac dress and a real camel hair coat. She had a suitcase of things, and a wallet with money in it. Her hair, her hands—so elegant. A shame about her teeth, though.

But what on earth had happened to her? They had been so worried … but careful, Frau Wingender emphasized. They'd put down that she had disappeared in January, not February.

Oh, she had been with some Russians, idiots who took her for someone else, Franziska said. They'd bought her lots of clothes though, and didn't expect her to lift a finger. Maids, you know. What fools they all were, and so sure they were better than everyone else too.

She was finished with the dirty Russians, she added. It was a big mess. They'd pushed her into a canal, rescued her, and made her say she was someone else. But then she said she'd met this man on the street … Franziska pulled out her photographs of the Romanovs. These idiots believed anything you told them. But oh, if they found her, she'd be in trouble. They'd drag her right back. Awful people, Franziska said. Awful. Did the Wingenders have any idea what these people were capable of?

Five years later, Mrs. Wingender would claim that she had gone with Franziska to the office of the *Red Banner* where Franziska denounced the Kleists, alleging that they had held a meeting in their apartment in which the murder of a prominent communist was planned. She did not hesitate to sign the deposition with her full name, Franziska Schanzkowsky.

An attorney hired by Franziska's supporters found no evidence to support the story. Not so, said Mrs. Wingender. The files had been destroyed during a raid on the office.

Did Franziska really report the Kleists to a communist newspaper? Political murders were relatively common in Berlin at the time. Only weeks before, the German Foreign Minister, Walter Rathenau, had been assassinated by right-wing extremists. Although it seems unlikely that the baron was mixed up in a murder plot, Franziska doubtless knew that there were monarchists who did such things, and may have felt she had plenty of reason to try and make trouble for him.

Mrs. Wingender also said that she bought "gold and silver" which Franziska had stolen from the baron. Franziska later told vicious lies about supporters she had cast off, but never, ever was there talk of her stealing from them. But why would the cagey Mrs. Wingender make up information about knowingly buying stolen goods? Perhaps Franziska had received the jewelry as gifts and then claimed she had stolen them in order to show her contempt for the Kleists.

Franziska wasn't planning to return to the Kleists. She had packed a suitcase and was trying to raise money. You needed to notify the police even if you moved across the street in Germany, but as long as she kept away from Neuruppin—that old bugbear—no one could say for sure that it was Franziska Schanzkowsky who tried to kill herself in 1920. She may even have had some idea of visiting Hygendorf.

Franziska had another reason for returning to the Wingenders. She knew they would have kept her papers, documents she needed if she ever wanted to re-establish herself as Fraulein Schanzkowsky. Franziska left Doris and her mother on Sunday morning, saying she had to see a woman on Schumannstrasse who would give her more money. She didn't return until midnight.

The Kleists had already reported Anny missing to the police. In the meanwhile, the baron and his friends searched Berlin for her. They went to Clara's Schumannstrasse apartment, but Clara said that she hadn't seen Anny. She told the police the same thing when they called.

No one will ever know what Franziska did away from the Wingenders, but it may have gone like this:

Clara was not surprised to see Franziska when she turned up on Sunday morning. Did Clara still believe Franziska was Anastasia? Years later she would denounce her as a fraud, but it is likely that in August 1922 Clara knew Franziska wasn't Anastasia, and that Franziska knew this, but they continued the pretense, heaping scorn on the Kleists, polishing the story, rationalizing and explaining. Clara thought Franziska had acted hastily in leaving the Kleists. The monarchists looked down on "Anastasia" for marrying out of her class? What choice did she have? Maybe she could tell them that the Tschaikovskys were originally from the Polish nobility, Franziska suggested. She needed money, but it was Sunday. The bank was closed. Come back in the morning, Clara said.

Franziska returned to the Wingenders late at night, when no one would be looking for her. In the morning she asked Doris to trade clothes with her so she wouldn't be recognized. Doris gladly exchanged a blue suit and a flowered straw hat for the lilac dress and camel hair coat the baron had bought Franziska at Israel's department store. They also traded underwear while they were at it.

Franziska handed over white panties embroidered with a monogram—"A.R." Not "A.R." for Anastasia Romanov, but for Anna Rheims, old Kleist's married daughter, Franziska laughed. She had snitched the panties too, Mrs. Wingender said.

In the morning, Fritz Jannicke found her. Near the Tiergarten, some said. What had happened to her? Jannicke demanded. Where had she been? Where were her clothes? Where did she get the outfit she was wearing? Franziska wouldn't say.

Jannicke took her to his apartment because she still refused to return to the Kleists, but the baroness couldn't stay away. She found Franziska weeping: "I have been so dirty."

Was Franziska glad Jannicke had found her? Had Clara convinced her that she still had a chance as Anastasia, despite the clumsy, concocted story? Or was she afraid that Jannicke would fetch the police if she tried to get away from him? Maybe Clara knew too much; later it would come out that she had a friend in the Wingenders' building.

Franziska had left all her personal papers—the medical card, police registration form, insurance certificate, and work book—back at the Wingender apartment. Was this playing it safe, or did she intend to return for the papers once she had the money from Clara?

The missing three days. That is how both supporters and detractors referred to Franziska's weekend away. The "famous three days" her lawyer would call them: "The most important item, however, is the stay of the invalid during the famous three days." The debate about them would continue for forty years. They would be Franziska's only serious attempt to escape from being "Anastasia."

Franziska at the Tiergarten during her "escape"

Chapter Five

I

Franziska's next refuge was Funkenmuhle, a country house near Teltow, just to the south of Berlin, that belonged to Dr. Grunberg, a Police Inspector who had interested himself in her case. The landscape was of farmland interrupted by small lakes and stands of forest. Franziska would later say that she had "felt in heaven" there. Mrs. Grunberg went out of her way to make her guest comfortable. Grunberg's duties meant that he could only visit his farm on weekends, leaving Franziska with weekdays free of interrogation and systematic observation.

Anastasia and her sisters had been enthusiastic wild mushroom hunters. Franziska was herself a village girl from a region renowned for its mushrooms. Visitors would tell of her prowess in the field, of her ability to sort the deadly from the delicious at a glance, of her beautiful and precise pronunciations of arcane folknames.

There were long afternoons in the garden too, a block of drawing paper across her knees. The grand duchesses had been watercolorists; a bit of desultory sketching was an untaxing way of fixing her identity in the minds of her hosts. The stormy scenes were not repeated here. She willingly took meals with the family and seems to have made few demands.

The interrogations were carefully managed. Grunberg decided that she was "mentally shattered" and proceeded carefully. The new information came out in fragments as Franziska sat in the garden. She gave a description of the wallpaper in the basement execution chamber of the Ipatiev house. Grunberg, who had never visited the site, announced that she had described it "quite exactly and correctly." The paper had a striped pattern plainly visible in the photographs taken by the invading Whites. Grunberg had seen these photographs but it doesn't seem to have occurred to him that Franziska had seen them too.

Franziska seized the opportunity to rework certain elements of The Story, as it came to be known. Alexandre Tschaikovsky was a Polish exile who owned a house in Ekaterinburg. She moved the date of the child's birth forward and made it vague. The implausible image of "Anastasia," still too confused to know what day it was setting out for Berlin and spiriting herself across the German border was fixed too: she had been accompanied by Alexandre's brother Serge who, strangely uninterested in the rewards of presenting himself as the rescuer of the tsar's daughter, had promptly disappeared. Her goal in coming to Berlin had been to go to her Aunt Irene, but she gave in to shame and despair and wound up jumping in the canal instead.

Franziska was aware of the discrepancies between what she had told Kleist and what she was saying now. Her answer was simple—the baron was a bad man, greedy and capable of making indecent suggestions to a helpless young woman. Even if true, this explanation failed to say why the baron's lust or avarice would lead him to add plainly wrong statements to Franziska's protocols. A pattern was emerging. Again and again Franziska would blame the mistakes and contradictions in her statements on the people who received them. In a similar way, witnesses who failed to recognize her as Anastasia did so for reasons of their own. Isa Buxhoeveden, she intimated to Grunberg, had turned traitor after following the imperial family to Siberia, betraying an escape plan in order to save her own life. A "guilty conscience" and self-interest led her to betray the family once more by refusing to acknowledge its sole surviving member.

She also urged Grunberg to seek the dress she had worn on the night of the massacre and left behind with the Tschaikovskys in Romania. How this was to be accomplished was left unsaid. This too would become a pattern: Franziska would exhort investigators to find things which did not exist. The object might change (a mysterious letter, a bracelet, petticoat, baptismal cross, the child himself) but the intent seems to have remained the same.

These red herrings would distract seekers, leading them into blind Romanian alleys and away from nearer and more dangerous discoveries.

II

The afternoon seemed quiet enough. The day had begun with rain but the sun had come out. Franziska took a walk and happened upon a clump of mushrooms which she picked at once, gathering them up in her skirt. Back at the house, she left them in the kitchen, but quickly sensed something was wrong. The lights were dimmed and two female guests had arrived while she was away. She wanted to wash her hair, to make herself presentable, but Grunberg led her toward the guests in the dining room. It was an ambush.

Franziska would later claim that she immediately realized that one of the guests was Princess Irene who was for some inexplicable reason introduced to her by a different name. More likely, she only knew that she had made a terrible error as she turned and fled upstairs to her room.

She stood at a window, back turned to the door, as "Aunt Nini" followed her up the stairs, urged on by Grunberg. Franziska's weeping was her only acknowledgement. She was determined not to talk to Irene or to let her get another good look at her face. It wasn't much but it was the least, the only thing she could do.

Irene would later write that she "saw immediately that she could not be one of my nieces. Even though I had not seen them for nine years, the fundamental facial characteristics could not have altered to that degree … she did not even answer when I asked her to say a word or give me a sign that she recognized me. It was the same when I asked her—not to leave anything out—'Don't you know me, I am your Aunt Irene'."

Discouraged, Irene went downstairs, gave Grunberg the bad news and left. Grunberg was mortified and then angry: a member of the Prussian royal house had been rudely treated under his own roof. The Prussian *Hausmacht* had collapsed, but Grunberg still felt the ancient deference of the functionary for his sovereign's family. He had enlisted the aid of a colleague, the police superintendent of Breslau, in approaching Irene so the humiliating negative verdict would doubtless be talked about there as well.

Irene's opinion was hard to discount. She had visited her sister's family in Russia often, sometimes staying for months at a time. Her "niece" had purportedly made the difficult journey to Berlin expressly to see her, after all. The failure left Franziska in an untenable position. No amount of mushrooms, sketches, or painfully retrieved shards of "memories" could make up for it. She would spend decades trying to explain it away. It was intolerably rude of Irene to allow herself to be sprung on her niece this way, hiding under false name, she would say. "Anastasia" could not permit herself to acknowledge her aunt under these circumstances. She would even claim that Irene had actually recognized her as Anastasia and had invited her to Hemmelmark.

Ernst Jannicke was summoned and seems to have arrived at Funkenmuhle at great speed. Grunberg was furious; the girl would have to leave his house immediately. Franziska was still upstairs, barricaded in her room. Jannicke had always had a way with Franziska. He convinced her to come out and led her downstairs past Grunberg and out to his car. It was dark by then, the headlights of the car fitfully illuminating the road back to Berlin. Franziska sat in the back, lost in her tears, the rich mushroom-bearing soil of Funkenmuhle still caked on her arms.

III

Franziska came to stay with the Jannickes, but it was only a temporary respite. The Nazi party was still very small in Berlin and Ernst was often called away to Munich and elsewhere. Mrs. Jannicke was unable to cope with Franziska on her own and said so. Franziska would have to find another place to stay before the month was out.

There must have been reconciliation with the Kleists, who arranged for someone (the mysterious "S") to pay her bills at the Westend Hospital in Charlottenburg. It seems that she had developed tuberculosis and was suddenly very ill. Tuberculosis was still the dreaded "White Plague" of popular imagination. Susceptibility was notably partial to certain families but the disease itself was a great leveler. Franziska's own mother would eventually die of it in a hut in Pomerania. Anastasia's uncle George had succumbed to it long before, in the lonely splendor of a villa in the Caucasian mountains. Franziska would spend the balance of 1922 and most of 1923 in the Westend Hospital, removed from scrutiny.

Franziska's illness did, strangely enough, have its peculiar benefits. It allowed her to spend the period following the Irene debacle in seclusion. The Westend Hospital was a private institution only a block away from the lush grounds of the Charlottenburg Palace. As a fee-paying patient Franziska must have enjoyed a degree of peace and privacy unknown in Dalldorf.

Outside the walls of the hospital, political intrigue and economic instability roiled Berlin. Some of the intrigue involved monarchists like Franziska's patrons. On October 10 the Duke and Duchess of Coburg hosted a mass "Germany Day" that marked the Nazis' first major expedition out of their Munich stronghold. A little over a month later the former kaiser remarried. His new bride, Hermine of Reuss, had close ties to the Nazis. Like many other Germans, the monarchists seem to have failed to grasp the radical nature of the party, and allowed themselves to be persuaded that its primary goal was to restore their privileges.

All this might have remained the preoccupation of selfish people in chilly drawing rooms if the bottom hadn't fallen out of the economy as well. The Weimar government responded to the Allied demands that it honor the heavy schedule of reparations stipulated in the Treaty of

Versailles by devaluing its own currency; if it had to pay off the victors it would do so in its now worthless marks. Hyper-inflation was set loose on everyday Germans, wiping out savings and paychecks simultaneously. When it reached its peak in November 1923 people were dying for want of food, heating fuel and warm clothing. Food riots became commonplace. The introduction of a new mark finally stabilized the situation, but the horrors of the economic abyss and the perceived cynicism of the Weimar government strengthened the hand of the radical parties of both the right and the left.

Franziska's term in the Westend Hospital spared her the worst of it, much as Dalldorf had done earlier. A photograph from around this period shows her looking heavier than she had looked in the photos taken at Dalldorf. A small Christmas tree, adorned with candles, sits on a table as Franziska reads a book nearby. A picture of the imperial family hangs over the bed. A radio, flowers, more pictures. She seems well cared for, content in her cozy retreat.

When she emerged in late 1923 she first seems to have gone to the Kleists' apartment before running off to live with Clara on Schumannstrasse. Altogether the Kleists were said to have taken her back four times, regularly calling the police to report her disappearances until someone finally told them that whatever else she might be, Fraulein Anny was of age and could come and go as she pleased. Franziska seems to have loathed the Kleists and the surprise isn't that she fled their apartment four times but that she kept going back to it. Perhaps it functioned as a last resort, a place to return to when all other options had been withdrawn.

Franziska had begun to wander. The following two years are frustratingly vague, marked by seemingly undirected back-and-forth motion between the apartments of friends. Clara was frequently her hostess. She stayed with the Jannickes some nights, and spent others in the home of Eva Wahl, a niece of Inspector Grunberg's.

Franziska passed quite a bit of time in the Schwabes' apartment. They had recently had a baby and Franziska had stood as godmother. She seems to have been particularly fond of the captain. Franziska devoted much time to the study of Schwabes' stock of Romanov photographs. She was learning the faces, the rooms, and incidental details which could be strung into the narrative she was creating in her head: the tsar with a cigarette holder shaped like a pipe; Alexei in a miniature sailor's uniform and the older girls in the uniforms of the regiments they were honorary colonels of—one a hussar, the other an uhlan—the tsarina's very own motorcar with its lucky swastika mascot on the hood; the tsarina's room strewn with hothouse flowers ... it was a haphazard catalog of people, places, and things she would mine in the following years.

IV

A ripple appears in the summer of 1924. It seems that people sought some sort of acknowledgement from Irene, despite her negative opinion. Clara continued to write, as did Baron von Kleist. Franziska herself wrote at the end of August:

"Must implore your forgiveness that I did not speak that time at Funkenmuhle. Everything came so unexpectedly and you were introduced to me as a strange lady, so that I lost all courage. I entreat you to bring me someplace else, they intend to put me in an asylum or a hospital. Love and Kisses, Your Anastasie."

What brought this on? All we know is that the appeal was ineffectual. Irene never responded and Franziska re-entered the Westend Hospital five days later and stayed until mid-November.

A representative of Irene's wrote the baron on September 21, insisting that he "refrain from the further sending of letters and requests ... It would be appreciated if you would influence your protegee and Fraulein Peuthert accordingly."

This chilly dismissal rattled the baron, who promptly jumped ship. Although Franziska gave no indication of missing the stability of her stop-overs at Nettelbeckplatz, the defection of the Kleist family left her in an increasingly precarious position.

V

The fragments gleaned from accounts of the period all take place at night—Franziska wandering the dark streets of Berlin, sitting up in cafes and resorting to sleeping on a bench in the Tiergarten, having a final argument with Clara before either flouncing out or being evicted on a winter night. The Berlin of Franziska's nocturnal ramblings was the city of the notorious *Die Wilden Zwanziger*, the Wild Years of cabarets, beerhall politics and often inexplicable violence. She seems to have threaded her way through it like a sleep-walker, or like someone with a higher purpose which keeps them self-contained, oblivious, and somehow safe.

Why did she endure in the face of almost total failure? No one was forcing her to continue to impersonate Anastasia. Her true identity was as yet unknown, making it an easy matter to melt back into Pomerania. The Schanzkowskys undoubtedly would have taken her in and shielded her from anyone who came seeking Mrs. Tschaikovsky. One thinks first of the difficulty of Franziska's role, the interminable questioning and nightmarish confrontations, but there had been real triumphs too. If she gave up, the kind of life she had come to love at Funkenmuhle would be lost. She would never again eat at a baron's table, summon a servant to fetch a cup of tea, or extend her hand for the kiss of a former officer. In choosing to persist, she surrendered to her wildest hopes and lost something of herself in return.

Franziska's foul temper had returned. The expectations of her new friends were so contradictory. On one hand they were a source of tension, always asking questions and springing unpleasant surprises. On the other hand, they were prepared to tolerate almost any rudeness from "Anastasia," a naturally imperious grand duchess who had suffered so much and was, like her mother, a bit unstable. Perhaps Franziska was beginning to guess who could be pushed and how far, and who might actually enjoy being bullied by a fiery "Russian princess."

The rages were never purely strategic though, and often alienated people when she needed them most. Her suspicions about the people she had drawn into her life goaded her as she walked along the dark streets, impulses and desires rising, overwhelming her calculations and constraints. The feeling of living in a waking dream didn't inspire much sympathy for the other people who hurried in and out of the scenes. It was easy to dismiss them, to feel that the disjointed movements of the dream would proceed without them.

The leave-takings were often sudden and spiteful. She constantly threatened to return to Dalldorf, although this seems to have been a bluff. Dalldorf would have led back to Neuruppin and she had no intention of going *there*.

Her relationship with Clara had become increasingly volatile. Clara had seen Franziska painstakingly practicing Anastasia's penmanship. She kept quiet about that, for the moment at least. The easy moments of whispering in each others ear would never return. Clara had moods of her own, and often scorned Franziska's pretensions.

Franziska's later supporters would later admit that Clara had a friend (never named, but seemingly female) in her building who also happened to be friendly with Mrs. Wingender, going so far as to depict the threesome of Clara, her friend, and Mrs. Wingender as a cabal which spread lies about "Anastasia."

The friends do seem to have talked amongst themselves, and to have shared certain information with the Schwabes. In late 1924 Captain von Schwabe loudly denounced Franziska, labeling her a "Polish vagabond." It seems likely that this rejection made Franziska even more reliant on the uncertain friendship of Clara Peuthert. The situation had become bad enough to attract the attention of local social workers, who expressed alarm at her deteriorating situation.

The final falling out, the result of an unflattering article about Franziska that appeared in the *Lokal Anzeiger* meant that she was well and truly stranded. It was January, too cold to wander the streets until dawn. She had no money, so the coffee houses and cafes which might be open at that hour were out. Somehow—Franziska would later remember sobbing in the hallway—she attracted the attention of the Bachmanns, a family of coal porters who rented rooms nearby. They took her in for a time, but had little to share. It seems doubtful that Franziska would have accepted their hospitality if she had had anyone else to turn to. Here is another point where the story might well have ended, were it not for the reappearance of Inspector Grunberg.

VI

Ironically, Franziska's fame had grown as her material fortunes declined. Although few of the Russians remaining in Berlin believed in her, they seem to have talked about her a lot. Speculation about who she really was, what she did, and what her motives might be was entertaining. Eventually this gossip spread further and many Germans became interested in the case, generally taking a more favorable view of Franziska's authenticity.

The demise of the Romanovs was tragic, but the war and its aftermath had destroyed countless families and stranded widows and orphans all over central and eastern Europe. The survivors had crowded the relief agencies and haunted the thoroughfares of all the major cities. The once fortunate provided pawnshops with a deluge of diamond brooches, silver cigarette cases, ormolu picture frames, and pearl stickpins—the detritus of a lost world, picked over by speculators and foreign visitors. Why, in the wake of all this, were people so interested in the plight of "Anastasia"? A lost princess, perhaps a lost fortune, secret migrations across closely guarded borders, priceless jewels sold in back alleys ... details which seem unlikely now seemed perfectly plausible to many Berliners in the Wild Years.

Some were particularly eager to believe. Her story gave the opponents of the Bolsheviks a chance to have it both ways: here was a testimonial from the Murder Room itself and, as the Ekaterinburg assassins had feared, a living banner to rally around. Franziska would have a far-right contingent among her supporters for years to come.

Some were hardline Russian monarchists who ought to have known better. Others were Germans who knew an opportunity when they saw one and were willing to at least give lip service to a restoration of the monarchy.

VII

It must have been a relief to be received back into Grunberg's household. It was too cold for Funkenmuhle so she stayed in his townhouse on Wilhelmstrasse, only about a block away from the Landwehr Canal and very near Schumannstrasse and the coffee houses of her recent past. It must have seemed solid, comfortable, and very safe.

Grunberg's own feelings were probably more ambiguous. His superiors had already instructed him to drop the matter. Captain von Schwabe had turned up and began working on the Inspector, spreading doubt. Their conversations "always made Grunberg very nervous." Still, the allure of the mystery held. Grunberg re-opened his investigation.

According to some, a humble stranger from Franziska's past appeared and presented someone with a photograph of himself before vanishing. Schwabe would later say he was the anonymous person who had visited Franziska at Dalldorf, and that the picture wound up in the hands of the Berlin police. Clara, unpredictable as ever, claimed to have had contact with the stranger too, but said he was the mysterious Serge, brother of Alexandre Tschaikovsky. She also claimed to have the photograph, which she sold to Harriet Rathlef-von Kielmann, soon to appear as one of Franziska's most committed supporters, for thirty marks. Harriet repeated the story but never produced the photograph.

Grunberg doesn't seem to have thought much of this, perhaps because he had managed to get in touch with the Crown Princess Cecilie, the wife of the kaiser's eldest son Wilhelm. A meeting was arranged for early June.

Cecilie had come to know the tsar's daughters during a 1911 visit to Russia. She had been young, fashionable, and easy to talk to, a favorite guest of the girls. In the meanwhile, Cecilie had heard of Isa Buxhoeveden and Irene's experiences and seems to have approached the meeting with caution, agreeing to drop in on "Anastasia" on her way to a concert.

At an earlier point in Franziska's life seeing the crown princess in full evening dress would have been a wondrous event, but it doesn't seem to have been one on this particular night. Franziska herself was simply, even shabbily dressed and plainly resented it. Little was said apparently. Franziska had developed a new approach to these hopeless "reunions." Instead of becoming hysterical she was now indifferent, cold, unyielding.

Failure was inevitable, she may have reasoned, but the damage might be lessened if she revealed nothing, and if she could later claim to have been struck dumb by her offended sense of pride ("this was really beneath my dignity").

Cecilie would later say that it was "virtually impossible to communicate with the young person. She remained completely silent, either from obstinacy or because she was completely bewildered. I could not tell which." Cecilie definitely stated that Franziska was not Anastasia and that she seemed more like a "Czechoslovakian maid" than a Russian grand duchess.

Franziska claimed to have been disdainful at being confronted in such a gauche manner. She also claimed that Cecilie had promised to return to Grunberg's townhouse after the concert, but never did. Did Franziska and Grunberg sit up in his tidy parlor until late that night, waiting for a visit that never came? He did at some point become very angry, much as he had after the meeting with Irene. Why? What did he think was going to happen? The intensity of his reaction seems to suggest that he had regained at least some of his confidence in Franziska, only to be disappointed and humiliated again.

He told Franziska that she would have to vacate her room before July 3, when the Grunberg family was due to go on holiday. The delayed departure was probably a concession to the fact that Franziska had no tactful Jannicke to come fetch her, that she really had nowhere else to go.

The interval before the deadline must have been awful. Franziska would later remember it as the "dreadful weeks that I spent after that [meeting with Cecilie]; it is a very long time since I have cried as much as I did then." She was becoming very ill and didn't want to resume wandering. The tuberculosis had attacked her arm, causing an open, throbbing wound.

There was a lot of talk about her now, but much of it was unfriendly. Grunberg himself remained unrelentingly hostile. He would attempt to disguise his disillusionment in a widely circulated statement: "I have reached the firm conviction that she must at least come from one of the highest Russian families, and that it is quite probable that she is of royal birth."

This was a face-saving gesture which would sustain disappointed supporters in the future; well, the argument went, perhaps she wasn't Anastasia per se, but she was someone special, no mistake about that. All the same, Grunberg's impatience to rid himself of his "royal" guest must have been apparent to all.

Chapter Six

I

There would always be saviors in Franziska's life. Franziska herself had created Alexandre Tschaikovski, a handsome figure with a stony face, a humble pauper but secret nobleman, who saved her from a lonely forest grave and carried her away in his hay-strewn wagon. Franziska might have wished for another Alexandre as she packed to go back to Dalldorf. Alas, she had killed him off and he was unlikely to reappear from the Bucharest cemetery where she had placed him.

But someone came, after all, and brought "Anastasia" back to life. That someone was Harriet Rathlef, a Baltic Russian sculptress who had settled in Berlin. Dr. Karl Sonnenschein, a noted philanthropist, had taken an interest in Franziska and asked Harriet to help her.

Harriet's intervention would change Franziska's life in a way she had never imagined. Observers have always wondered about the many German aristocrats, dethroned royals, and influential people who cared for Franziska over the years. Despite the setbacks, the Romanovs who labeled her an impostor, and her thunderous temper and ingratitude, someone was always there to pay the bills for hotels, spas, and hospitals and to look after her. Why?

Harriet Rathlef was a Jewish convert to Roman Catholicism and an Anthroposophist. This triple identity was complicated but not contradictory. Members of the Anthroposophical Society came from many religious backgrounds; Anthroposophy was not so much a religion as a way of looking at the world.

The people who came to care for Franziska were Anthroposophists who not only felt that Franziska was truly a grand duchess, but that she had a spiritual mission to perform for Russia and the world.

"By Anastasia the life side by side with this tragic fate, invites us to prepare for the future, to assist the coming epoch to help the Russian folk soul to a spiritual breakthrough," wrote Baroness Monica von Miltitz, a longtime supporter of Franziska.

"Her life is a life of Karma struggle in which her own fate only sometimes rings like a small bell," noted a German nobleman who would later put Franziska up at his castle. " ... there's an area in her that's free from Karma struggle. And when one can direct her there—meet her there—one stands before a pure and strong soul. It is the real spirituality."

Some define Anthroposophy as a spiritual science developed by its founder, Dr. Rudolf Steiner, an Austrian philosopher, in 1913. He taught that humans have not only a physical and soul life, but a life of the spirit. It is the spirit that lives on, stripped of its earthly associations, through different incarnations. He devised a system for communicating with these spirits, and believed that some of them had tasks to perform for humanity. The return of Christ was imminent, he taught; current events effected by an impending battle between light and darkness.

It is easy to brush off—an old maidish sort of occultism, full of disembodied spirits, lost continents, ether worlds, demons, and angels. This is not entirely fair; apart from founding the influential Waldorf Schools and inventing biodynamic farming, Steiner formulated a philosophy which continues to attract adherents. Members congregate at Dornach, Switzerland from all over the world. Colin Wilson claimed Steiner was, perhaps, the greatest man of the twentieth century.

Steiner's autobiography concerns itself with philosophy and art almost exclusively but features many photographs of its author in dramatic poses, like a portfolio of shots by an actor who could play character roles.

He was born in 1861 to a railway employee and a former maid named Franziska. Steiner had been awarded a doctorate in philosophy by the time he was thirty. He had come so far—a man proud of his humble origins, and an intuitive and persuasive scholar, attuned to shadings of epistomological meaning, well set for a productive academic life. It must have been hard to understand why he joined the Theosophical Society.

This was the movement founded by Helena P. Blavatsky, Russian mystic and author of tomes like *Isis Unveiled* and *The Secret Doctrine*, which merged Victorian spiritualism and its dark rooms and seances with the mystique of India and Tibet. There were secret Ascended Masters with names like Koot Hoomi who rang silver bells and caused letters from the astral plane to turn up in disciples' writing boxes. By the time Steiner joined, the Society was under the leadership of Annie Besant; he quickly became General Secretary of the German branch, but broke away when Besant proposed putting forward an Indian youth, J. Krishnamurti, as a reincarnation of Christ and expected Steiner to take on the role of John the Baptist in Germany.

A large number of like-minded seekers joined him when he formed the Anthroposophical Society. He was earnestly interested in his growing flock, and people at all levels of social and intellectual sophistication were attracted to him: "During the next three days I heard all the lectures Rudolf Steiner gave ... The figure of the teacher appeared to me immersed in a colored spirit-atmosphere," wrote a young medical student.

Members of the nobility were attracted as well. Prince Max of Baden and Prince Moritz of Saxe-Altenburg were his friends, and he became closely attached to the von Moltke family.

The Anthroposophy that developed during the life of its prophet was a distinctly German enterprise. Steiner thought that all the nations of Europe had a role to play in the upcoming battle between good and evil, but that Germany was the most philosophical nation, and had the greatest potential for both. World War I, and Steiner's marriage to a mystical Baltic German from St. Petersburg named Marie von Seivers, increased the urgency of his message. Russia was the nation of brotherhood, of raw spiritual stamina, but also chaos and fratricide. It would need a powerful intercessor.

Before his death in 1925, Steiner discussed "Anastasia" with devotees. He felt she was genuine. His opinion carried great weight.

"I am personally convinced, that she was real and the victim of occult powers. But her life served a very good purpose: the future civilization and culture will be the 'Russian' and her life prepared her for her future mission and incarnation. I was not able to investigate her karmic past but the fact, that she came into contact with Steiner and those around Steiner, give important indications," wrote a longtime member of the Society in 1999.

He also compared Franziska to Kaspar Hauser. Kaspar was for the West, "Anastasia" for the East. He was "the child of Europe," "Anastasia" the "child of Russia."

II

Kaspar Hauser literally walked into history May 26, 1828, when he turned up at a Nurnberg stable with a note for the riding master. The note asked that Kaspar be taken on and prepared for life in the cavalry. Kaspar himself said "I want to be a horseman like my father," and little else. The surviving drawings show a sturdy looking teenager with an open, friendly face. His behavior was eccentric, though, and eventually the police were called.

Once in custody, Kaspar laboriously wrote "Kaspar Hauser" on a piece of paper, but answered "I don't know" to all questions. He was never really seen as a criminal; early on his keepers, hardened as they might be to swindlers and lunatics, saw him as a special case. His story was not long in coming—since earliest childhood he had been held captive in a dungeon, alone, in perfect darkness, and on a diet of bread and water. Eventually he was taught to write his name and then set loose in Nurnberg, with the note and directions to the stable.

As unlikely as it might seem, many believed him and were captivated by his presence. "Innocence and goodness of heart are evident in all his doings and speech, although he had not the slightest idea of right and wrong, good and evil ... of passion and bad inclinations there was no evidence, apart from his newly awakened vanity." They treasured memories of his naive way of speaking and of his rather ostentatious unworldliness, his gentleness with all living things, and his ignorance of the purpose of money. This naivete was also used to explain his implausible tale: "some things which are unbelievable or enigmatic about his imprisonment and transportation to Nurnberg—certainly some things which are not true ... he often said things in his muddled, murky, gibberish way which were not what he intended to say."

Kaspar remained delicate and unpredictable, although he acquired some basic skills. Over time, other traits arose—he was fond of the fashionable clothes given him by some of his new friends, and sometimes said things he knew to be false.

The stress may have come to a head October 17, 1829, when Kaspar claimed to be the victim of a sudden attack by a man wearing a black veil. The assault produced only minor injuries and no witnesses. There seems to have been widespread local skepticism about the incident, which many felt was staged by Kaspar to attract attention to himself. His supporters rejected this possibility, saying that "the truth of the story is vouched for by the personality of him who tells it."

They had come to believe that Kaspar was the son of Stefanie Beauharnais, a step-daughter of Napoleon who had married into the ruling house of Baden. She had two sons, both of whom were reported to have died in infancy. Kaspar was supposed to be the elder of these, the rightful Prince of Baden, who had actually been kidnapped by people who wanted to see the crown go elsewhere. These conspirators had kept Kaspar in the dungeon and then released him for reasons never disclosed.

While these revelations created some excitement, it seems as if little of it reached Kaspar himself. He had moved to Ansbach, and was living an increasingly dreary life in the household of a schoolteacher named Meyer. Meyer had come to doubt the story of Kaspar's imprisonment and treated these romantic ideas with disdain.

It wasn't long before Kaspar became the victim of another mysterious attack as he walked in a public garden in Ansbach. Again, the assailant was a mysterious stranger who managed to stab Kaspar and escape without being seen by witnesses. Meyer himself was highly suspicious of the incident, calling it an "inadvertent suicide" when Kaspar died of his wounds on December 19, 1833.

Although it is impossible to rule out the chance that some fanatic had read of the claims made for Kaspar and was moved to assassinate him, it is hard to overlook the similarities between the fatal incident and the dubious attack of four years earlier.

Ironically, bloody undergarments from the "assassination" would yield the DNA that later eliminated Kaspar as a son of Stefanie Beauharnais.

Kaspar's mysterious death preserved his legend, making it a tragedy and giving weight to the whispers of dynastic intrigue and corruption. As it spun out over time, the image of the holy innocent destroyed by the dead hand of monarchy appealed to generations of idealists, particularly in Central Europe.

Literally hundreds of books and articles had been written by the time Rudolf Steiner picked up the story. He retained the essential elements and embellished them in his own manner, integrating Kaspar into his ornate cosmology by casting him as a leader in a war against the satanic forces massing for the final battle. Had he lived, Steiner believed, Germany would have been directed away from the path that led to the Great War and the political extremism which followed.

A web of similarities seemed to link Kaspar and Franziska. Like Kaspar, Franziska had suddenly appeared in the middle of a German city, confused and uncommunicative. Both had appealed to their keepers; Kaspar to his jailors, Franziska to her nurses—people who had seen many criminals and lunatics, and who were impressed by their good behavior, and specifically, their fine, white hands.

As time went on, both claimants would tell of the strange, isolated interludes that came before their emergence, although no one was ever able to find Kaspar's dungeon or Franziska's Sventi Voevosi Street hideout. Kaspar and Franziska were both presented as royal waifs kept from their birthrights by the machinations of their own families. They seemed younger than their years and aroused strong protective feelings in their followers. They were good with animals and shared a talent for gardening. Both were rather fragile, finicky eaters prone to nervous upsets. Some claimed that they possessed remarkable memories while others claimed that the traumas they had suffered left them virtual amnesiacs.

Most importantly, both figures possess immense magic for believers who continue to feel that their karmic missions influence the entire world. If Kaspar, alive and in his rightful place, would have led Germany to a cultural peak that would have prevented the rise of Hitler, then "Anastasia," rescued from dark powers, would have freed Russia from its terrible fate.

Kaspar Hauser

Chapter Seven

I

Harriet von Rathlef-Keilmann met Franziska for the first time on June 19, 1925, at Grunberg's townhouse in Berlin. It was only four months since Steiner's body lay in his studio in the Goetheanum. Harriet may have felt guided by his spirit as she stood looking at the woman Steiner had karmically investigated.

It had been Anastasia's birthday the day before, June 18, New Style. Neither Harriet nor Franziska remembered this important date. Franziska had other cares. The tubercular infection in her arm was worse. Soon the TB would metastasize, attacking her bones and joints. Her lungs were showing signs of pleurisy. In short, she must have felt wretched as she stood before Harriet. She was also on the verge of being homeless.

A Dr. Sonnenschein, the "poor man's friend," had apparently asked Harriet, because she was a kind person who spoke Russian, to help the mysterious waif.

"She was small, very thin, and appeared to be ill," noted Harriet. "She was shabbily dressed, like an old woman of the poor. When we approached to shake hands, I noticed that she had lost practically all her upper teeth, which made her look older than she really was."

But "her movements and her bearing were those of a lady of the highest social rank in Russia ... I was however, particularly struck by her resemblance to the Dowager Empress. She spoke German, but with a typically Russian accent. When I addressed her in Russian, I noticed that she understood everything ... She had an open wound in her arm, and I advised her to visit a hospital."

The next day, Harriet, accompanied by a friend, "Mrs. N.N.," took Franziska, "her eyes swollen with weeping," to St. Mary's Hospital. Grunberg refused to come down to see her off.

Dr. Ludwig Berg, the chaplain, received them at St. Mary's. Aware of Franziska's special status, he offered her a room in his private apartment on the hospital grounds until a bed became available in the hospital itself. A Catholic priest interested in making converts in the Russian community, he was a mystic too, having edited several books that attempted to merge Russian mysticism with Western practicality. He asked Harriet to make notes for him of everything Franziska said.

If there would not have been an "Anastasia" case without Clara, Franziska would not have physically survived without Harriet. Harriet was thirty-seven and had four young children, but she soon devoted herself totally to Franziska's care, even moving into her hospital room and administering injections. Her photograph appears in the book she would later write: bobbed hair, long chin, doleful eyes; she is a woman who understands sorrowful mysteries.

The reality in the Berlin hospital had nothing to do with palaces or tsars. "Indoors or outdoors, the July heat was unbearable. But, in this hospital, situated as it was in the airless wilderness of houses in the East End of Berlin, not a bit of ice could be obtained to make cooling compresses to alleviate the pain in the patient's arm, which was in-flamed right to the bone. Mrs. Harriet von Rathlef-Keilmann finally succeeded in buying ice in the neighborhood. The overworked sisters told us that the sick woman was very quiet and patient, never asked for anything, made no noise, generally lay with her face to the wall, the sheet pulled high so that she could hardly be seen from the other beds. As she would scarcely touch the hospital food, Mrs. Harriet v. Rathlef-Keilmann undertook to see to the greater part of her nourishment by bringing her light and appetizing dishes," noted a friend of Harriet's.

That Franziska was able to maintain the facade of being Anastasia under these conditions says something about her control and her des-perate need for an ally. Although Harriet would later claim that it took a long time for Franziska to confide in her ("slowly, slowly") it seems more likely that the pressure to fabricate tsarist memories began almost immediately.

Harriet soon read Pierre Gilliard, Anna Vyrubova and Lili Dehn's memoirs of life at court, sometimes aloud to Franziska. The books were a good starting point for factual information as Harriet looked for proof, explored memories, and noted physical resemblances between Franziska and Anastasia: deformed feet, a tiny scar on the forehead, the scar on the finger, possibly a cauterized mole on the shoulder.

She redefined Franziska in the process. Franziska became the "little one": "She was not a girl of twenty-five years, but rather gave the impression of being only seventeen. Since, for eight years after such a catastrophe and such experiences, she had been continually in the hospital, she had in some respects remained in a perpetual state of inexperienced childhood, such as is only conceivable in the case of royalty."

Interestingly, Harriet, much like Kaspar's tutors, would record that Franziska's supposed naivete had a less attractive aspect: "[She] was completely without any understanding of human nature. She believed most in those who constantly flattered her and were servile towards her."

Franziska, the former bookworm, could no longer read or write. She couldn't tell time or count. Later on, she left behind a ten mark note at a store, not realizing that she had change coming. Being royal, she was not used to handling money and barely seemed to understand its purpose. The girl who fled rural Pomerania for the paved streets of Berlin was, it turned out, really a child of nature and not a child of the town.

"In the spring, each bud and each fresh leaf on the trees pleased her, and she longed to be out of town. At times, I drove with her to the Wahnsee and to Potsdam. On such trips, she had eyes and ears only for those things which were happening in nature and for everything that bore in it the sign of spring." Harriet would write of later days, "She always took the greatest delight in flowers, and even during the time she was seriously ill, she always expressed a wish to have flowers at her bedside ... "

Harriet, already convinced, set about convincing others. She began by introducing Franziska and her case to prominent Anthroposophists. Danish Ambassador Herluf Zahle, the dashing "tall man" Franziska would have liked to see in court dress, sometimes paid her bills personally. He and his wife, Lillian visited Franziska several times a week. They interested their relative Carl Vett, an Anthroposophical lecturer in London.

Prince Frederick of Saxe-Altenburg attended Anthroposophical meetings in Berlin around this time and said that he and other young royals believed in "Anastasia." His father, Prince Moritz, was involved with Anthroposophy and soon hired a lawyer to investigate the affair. Over the years, other Saxe-Altenburg relatives would be supportive and Prince Frederick would introduce Franziska to other German royals, who welcomed her into their castles and contributed funds. Even today some of their descendants still believe in the "Anastasia" vouched for by Rudolf Steiner.

After only one week, Harriet contacted Ernst, the Grand Duke of Hesse, elder brother of Alexandra and thus Anastasia's uncle. Harriet included an x-ray, showing evidence of a head injury. This x-ray mysteriously disappeared, as did the injury because future x-rays revealed no trauma to the skull.

Ernst's secretary wrote back immediately. The grand duke knew the entire family had died in Ekaterinburg. Other claimants had appeared. It was all nonsense.

Harriet wasn't deterred. She brought in Zahle, albeit in a private capacity, and not as a representative of the Danish government. It was Zahle who kept the whole thing going, the Grand Duchess Olga said later.

Thyra, Duchess of Cumberland, the Dowager Empress Marie's sister, had recently told Marie about Franziska and the talk among the Russians in Berlin. Now Zahle contacted her brother, Prince Waldemar, and advised him that Franziska could very well be Anastasia.

Zahle was persuasive. An old servant, approved by Marie and Waldemar, was soon on his way to Berlin to see the strange woman and report back. If anyone should have recognized Anastasia, it was Alexis Andreivich Volkov. Volkov was Alexandra's personal servant and had followed the family to Tobolsk, where he pushed Alexandra in her wheelchair and saw the family at close quarters every day. He would have gone with them to Ekaterinburg if he hadn't been arrested by the Bolsheviks. Other servants were summarily shot, but the quick-witted Volkov escaped into the woods at the last minute and eventually made his way to Copenhagen, where he found refuge with the dowager empress.

Volkov and Zahle arrived on July 3, two weeks after Franziska was admitted to St. Mary's. In Berg's office, Volkov looked out of a window as Franziska sat in a garden. He didn't recognize her.

Volkov didn't return for two days. Was someone stalling? Talking to the old servant, trying to influence him before he saw Franziska up close? Whatever happened, the interval hadn't helped when he met Franziska face to face. No recognition. She didn't look like Anastasia and didn't even speak Russian. His questions had to be translated into German before she answered them.

The real Anastasia would have recognized Volkov, whom she saw often in Tobolsk. Neither Zahle nor Harriet seems to have thought of this, nor been troubled by the fact that Franziska failed to know him. But Franziska "recalled" the initials the Tsarina etched into the windowpane with her ring and Volkov wept.

"At first the attitude of the old servant was very cold and reserved," wrote Berg. "On the second day, however, he seemed to change his opinion, because he seemed very polite and was moved to tears when he left."

Volkov gave his true feelings in an interview: "on my first visit I wasn't allowed to talk to her and only saw her through the window, but it was enough to convince me this woman wasn't the killed Grand Duchess ... On the second day I found that Madame Tschaikovsky didn't speak Russian, only German. I asked her if she recognized me, she said no. I asked her other questions; the answers were unsatisfactory.

The behavior of the people with her seemed to me very suspect. They intervened at every instance, completing her incomplete answers and explained her mistakes were due to her illness ... I can affirm categorically that Madame Tschaikovsky has nothing in common with the Grand Duchess Anastasia. If she knows things about the lives of the Imperial Family, she learned them exclusively from books. Her memories are all superficial. One can prove this by the fact that she didn't know a single detail except those that have appeared in the press."

Marie lost interest after Volkov's visit. Harriet claimed the old man feared for his job if he told the "truth" to the dowager empress, who continued to believe that her son and his family were alive and hiding in a monastery in Russia.

Zahle went to Nicholas' younger sister, the Grand Duchess Olga next. Married unhappily to Prince Peter of Oldenburg, who gambled away her dowry and ignored her, Olga had lavished her affection on her nieces and had seen them every week. Anastasia was her special pet. Both shared an unconventional streak. Olga was an artist who hated the pomp of court. Anastasia was an impish tomboy and mimic. "I liked her fearlessness. She never whimpered or cried, even when hurt. She was a fearful tomboy. Goodness knows which of the young cousins had taught her to climb trees, but climb them she did even when she was quite small ... Anastasia or 'Shvipsk', as I used to call her, hated what she labeled 'fuss'."

All her life, Olga kept the small gifts Anastasia had given her—a silver pencil, a perfume bottle, an amethyst hatpin, and other trinkets.

Olga's first marriage ended during the war. Her second was to a commoner, Nicholai Kulikovsky. The couple and their two sons escaped Russia with great difficulty and now lived with Marie in Denmark. Olga heard Zahle out and wrote to Pierre Gilliard and his wife, Shura, Anastasia's nurse. She asked them to go "at once" to Berlin to see if the woman could be her beloved niece.

More controversy was on the way.

On board the *Standart* (l to r)—Olga, Anastasia, Olga Alexandrovna,
Marie, Alexandra, Nicholas

II

Another controversy had already appeared. Harriet was dismayed by Ernst's quick dismissal of "Anastasia" and compiled an annotated list of Franziska's scars which she sent to Hesse-Darmstadt via Amy Smith, the granddaughter of the Mayor of Hamburg.

Grand Duke Ernst was away from court when she arrived. She was received by Count Hardenburg, the Marshall of the Court, who listened with interest to Amy's account, at least until she revealed that Franziska claimed her "uncle" had come secretly to Russia in February, 1916 to urge his sister and brother-in-law to make a separate peace with Germany.

The issue of Ernst's "trip to Russia during the war" would occupy the partisans for decades. The rumors began while the war was still on, when the family ties between monarchs were the subject of many unfounded suspicions. Similar tales had once been told about Marie Antoinette and her brother, Joseph II of Austria. Franziska's supporters based their case on witnesses who claimed to have either had contemporary knowledge of the visit, or to have glimpsed Ernst himself in Russia in 1916. "What I don't understand is why everyone keeps talking about the Grand Duke's 'secret' trip. We all knew about it," claimed an aged Russian socialite.

If everyone knew about it, why was Franziska's knowledge so significant?

Others claim that Ernst's diary proves he was in France at the time. The matter remains a mystery, although a brief yet complicated sentence from the intimate correspondence of Anastasia's parents might contain a clue. On August 30, 1915, when talk of treason and of a secret letter between Ernst and Alexandra had already produced a scandal in the Duma, Alexandra wrote to her husband to complain of the lies that were circulating about Rasputin's access to the palace at Tsarskoe Selo: [They] *say he lives at T.S., as before they said we had Ernie here.*

For Alexandra, Ernst's wartime visit was a wild story told by her enemies, one with no basis in reality at all. If the idea of Ernst visiting in 1915 was ridiculous, the idea of him visiting in the calamitous year of 1916 was even more so.

Hardenburg bristled at this old piece of malice, so odd coming from an alleged daughter of the tsarina, and called Franziska a "mad impostor."

"Oh, they will all come when I'm dead!" Franziska "groaning with pain and in a high fever" sobbed, according to Harriet.

As it happened, the rumors provided an explanation for Ernst's opposition to her claim: he was abandoning his "niece" because her revelation tended to weaken his chances of regaining his throne if the political situation shifted back towards monarchy.

If only she could go to Copenhagen, Franziska lamented, all would be well. Her "Grandmamma" would know her, she cried, most certainly not expecting, or wanting, to meet the old empress, who would unmask her at once.

Franziska may have realized the futility of hoping for recognition. Sometimes she spoke to Harriet about getting a job and saving money. She would travel to Greece. Or spend the rest of her life in an Orthodox convent if she were denied her identity, as if anyone, Franziska included, could imagine her hiding away with nuns.

Baron Osten-Sacken, who had once come to Dalldorf with Captain Bulygin to translate Franziska's High German into Russian, was back. If he noted her much poorer German, he did not say so. Osten-Sacken was convinced now because Franziska had noticed his pipe-shaped cigarette holder and mistook it for one belonging to her "father." Osten-Sacken readily confirmed that his holder was similar to one used by the tsar, perhaps refreshing his memory by looking at the same photo, showing the holder in the tsar's hand, that Franziska had seen.

In a few years Osten-Sacken would marry Baroness Nina von Huene-Hoynigen, who attended seances about "Anastasia" held in the homes of aristocratic Anthroposophists in Berlin.

III

Tuberculosis was literally destroying the bone in Franziska's arm. Eventually, undeterred by modern antibiotics, the infection would cause her weight to drop below seventy pounds. She spent months in bed. The muscles in her legs withered, and she had to learn to walk again. The pain became so intense that Franziska required morphine every three hours.

Still, the questions about her "memories" continued. They would form the basis of Harriet's book, *Anastasia, The Survivor of Ekaterinburg*. The German title, *A Woman's Fate As The Mirror of World Catastrophe*, more closely spells out Franziska's special role. Harriet says that she did not probe, and that the morphine made the "little one" talkative. How else to explain the "recollections" that spooled out over the pages of her book, artfully expanded, re-worded and reconciled with later information?

Harriet upgrades the Tschaikovsky family, giving them a farm in Ekaterinburg. In Bucharest the women removed their kerchiefs, the men dressed in suits, and Alexandre looked good enough to be an officer. The child was born sometime in fall, when an Armenian named Sarscho Gregorian met a supposed grand duchess near the Dniestet River on the Romanian border.

Harriet, now claiming that "Anastasia's" head injuries had caused her to forget her Russian altogether, nonetheless noted that she had spoken Russian to the Tschaikovskys as they trundled across Russia in their peasant cart.

Another Russian Anthroposophist, Dr. Rudnev was now on the case. He had a poignant memory of seeing the grand duchesses with their parents at the Kremlin, on the day Russia declared war on Germany. Oh, yes, Franziska remembered—they were so young then, so unaware of what was to come. They had secretly thrown paper balls at the crowds massed below their balcony. All this, when the girls were actually hundreds of miles away, in St. Petersburg, on that remarkable day.

IV

Franziska was beyond caring about cigarette holders and paper balls when Gilliard and his wife, Shura, arrived in Berlin on July 27, only four days after receiving the Grand Duchess Olga's letter. Franziska's arm had swollen to a shapeless mass and she drifted, impaired by opiates.

Pierre Gilliard, the French language tutor of the Romanov children, had accompanied the family to Tobolsk, but was forcibly prevented from staying with them in Ekaterinburg. After the massacre, he assisted the Whites with their investigation. "But what about the children?" he had cried when he began to sense the scale of the atrocity. Once he returned to Switzerland he married Shura Tegleva, Anastasia's beloved nursemaid. In 1921 he wrote a book about his experiences in Siberia.

The Gilliards sat down beside Franziska and observed her. Her features were all wrong. He asked a few questions in German; Franziska mumbled vague replies.

Shura asked to see Franziska's feet. Here was a surprise. Franziska's right toe bent forward, forming a large bunion. "Her feet are very like those of the Grand Duchess," Mrs. Gilliard said. "The conformation at the base of the Grand Duchess' right foot was not so good as that of the left, and the same applies in this case." There was no sign of a scar, right through the foot, which would later be cited as an injury suffered at Ekaterinburg.

In the evening, there was a meeting at the Danish Embassy. Gilliard asked Rudnev exactly when he had been a physician to the imperial children.

No, no, Rudnev protested; he'd never looked after the children, but Professor Feodorov, a close colleague, had given him exact information about them.

Harriet was next. Hadn't she told Zahle that Rudnev had been the children's physician?

He told me so himself, Harriet said, and Rudnev said he must have been misunderstood.

Harriet doesn't mention the controversy about Rudnev. She must have been glad to escape the hospital. Franziska was cross, saying the visitors had made fun of her. Then she began hallucinating—Aunt Olga was in the hall, making fun of her, because she had come down in the world ... Harriet didn't seem to consider the possibility that Franziska had taken Shura, the woman she had seen, for Olga. That would happen the next day, when the Gilliards returned.

Franziska was less feverish and more alert, prompting Gilliard to ask who the woman with him was.

"She is my father's youngest sister," Franziska replied.

Gilliard, however, was troubled that Franziska knew "Schvipsk," Olga's pet name for Anastasia. Franziska had most likely learned it from Captain Bulygin, who had been given the name as a code word by Olga in his searches for the Romanovs in Siberia.

The Gilliards would be back.

V

Between them, Harriet and Rudnev had arranged Franziska's transfer to Mommsen, a private clinic where more intensive treatment was possible. At Mommsen, he operated immediately, "to save her life, and if possible, her arm, for the question of amputation was not remote." Under chloroform, he cut away the infected tissue, "and with a sharp spoon scraped out the purulent matter which lay between the muscles and the bones, from which [he] also took away some of the infected parts."

Franziska was "very anaemic and emaciated, like a skeleton covered only with skin, and without any fat whatsoever; in the lower left side of the left lung there are slight sounds due to pleurisy."

Zahle posted guards at the door of Franziska's room and Harriet prepared delicacies to tempt Franziska. She also continued to compile notes. As Franziska lay in bed, Harriet prompted more and more "memories"—coaching, some would call it. Sometimes Franziska sulked for days, like a cross child. The temper resurfaced, as it always would. Her moods were counted in her favor. Wouldn't an impostor show more gratitude?

Mr. and Mrs. Zahle came with gifts and flowers. A white kitten, Kiki, arrived to liven things up. In the meanwhile, Franziska and Harriet spent a lot of time looking at Romanov pictures. Why not? An important visit was approaching, the most important one so far. The Grand Duchess Olga and her husband were coming from Denmark, along with the Gilliards. Harriet, Zahle, and Rudnev had high hopes for the outcome of Olga's visit with the "little one."

Zahle was worried. Olga hadn't seen Anastasia since before the family was sent into exile. Would she be able to recognize the cheerful teenager in this emaciated, toothless woman? Had Olga, influenced by the negative reports, made up her mind beforehand? One had to spend time with Franziska, as he and Harriet had done, to really understand her.

On October 27, the very day Olga and the Gilliards arrived in Berlin, Zahle wrote to Count von Moltke, "I shall do everything possible to see that the Grand Duchess' visit lasts until she in my opinion has been able to form a true picture."

Olga must have hoped, as Irene had, that by some miracle Anastasia was alive. If not, why come to Berlin? The Gilliards must have also had some doubts about their initial negative reaction to Franziska.

"Heaven only knows if she is [Anastasia] or not. It would be such a disgrace if she were living all alone and if all that is true ... " Olga wrote to Shura. "If it really is her, please send me a wire and I will come to Berlin to meet you."

So here Olga was. She hadn't come at once, or at the height of Franziska's illness. Three months had passed since the Gilliards' first visit. Maybe they had all had time to think. Perhaps Zahle's success with Prince Waldemar had swayed Olga to finally make the trip over her mother's objections.

Zahle and Gilliard arrived first. For once, Harriet wasn't in the room when Gilliard sat down beside the bed. Gilliard now knew for certain that she was not Anastasia.

"Do you know me?" he asked.

Franziska had no idea who he was, having been too ill on their last meeting to memorize his face or voice. She knew that visitors were expected from Denmark, and Harriet had said that Shura was going to come, too. She hesitated "I know the face; but there is something strange about it, so I am unable to say who it is. I must consider it first."

What else could she say? Someone unknown to Anastasia would not be visiting. But who was he? Someone royal? She tried to recall photos but the faces were a sea. She closed her eyes.

"The visit and the excitement caused by it greatly fatigued the invalid. She looked exhausted, and lay impassive among the pillows. No proper conversation between her and her visitor was possible." Harriet was now in the room, taking notes.

"Please chat with me a little," he asked. "Tell me everything you know about your past."

"[Gilliard] did not know her as well as I had learned to know her; otherwise he would not have addressed her with this direct request," Harriet wrote, apparently forgetting he had known the real Anastasia very well. She was not surprised by Franziska's answer. "I do not know how to chat. I know of nothing I could chat with you about."

Franziska's temper flared "Do you think that if you had been nearly killed, as I was, you would have known much about your earlier life?"

After Gilliard left, Harriet reported that Franziska told Zahle that the stranger must have been her brother's tutor, Mr. Gilliard. Nudges?

But Gilliard had taught all the Romanov children, Anastasia among them.

The Grand Duchess Olga, accompanied by Zahle, arrived either later that morning or the following day. Franziska's face turned red, Harriet wrote, but it was not the emotional scene one would expect between an aunt and long-lost niece. There were no introductions.

Olga said that Franziska asked *Isst das die Tante?* ["Is that the aunt?"].

The women shook hands and chatted, using the formal *Sie*, not the familiar *Du* used with intimates. Olga spoke Russian, Franziska German, saying little. "They admired the cat Kiki, and spoke about illness," Harriet noted.

"I knew at once that I was in the presence of a stranger," Olga told her biographer. Later she would itemize the features that were so different from Anastasia's: the tilted nose, the forehead, the eyes, the eyebrows, and especially the big mouth Olga saw when Franziska finally lowered the blankets.

The grand duchess remarked that the interviews were made more difficult by Franziska's manner. She would not answer some of the questions and looked angry when those questions were repeated. Some Romanov photographs were shown to her, but no recognition showed in her eyes. "It was obvious that she greatly disliked Mr. Gilliard, and little Anastasia had been devoted to him." Olga's biographer explained.

The voice was different too. Franziska didn't understand English or French, languages Anastasia had used. She could not answer the "small, intimate questions" Olga posed, and did not know the pet name, "Mimi," of Anastasia's uncle, the Grand Duke Michael.

"Her attitude would have put anyone off," Olga said.

But Olga remained at the bedside. Fascinated, and perhaps touched by the plight of the invalid. Or perhaps transformed by Franziska's presence, a transformation others would speak of in the years ahead, when with a gesture, a word, the improbable Franziska would somehow convince visitors that here was someone special.

And maybe Franziska was transformed herself by Olga's kind, countrywoman's face that had no airs or graces about it. Olga loved to paint, rising early to get to her paint box. She enjoyed flowers, loved the two boys she had finally given birth to. Motherly and tender, Olga was moved by Franziska's dilemma. "Somehow or other she did not strike me as an out-and-out impostor," Olga would later say.

As time passed, Franziska relaxed. "I had the impression that she was getting tired of playing a part someone assigned her. She nearly admitted to me that some people always told her what to say on certain occasions. She did in fact admit that a scar, allegedly resulting from the blows to her head at Ekaterinburg, had been caused by her tubercular condition. I felt really sorry for the woman by the time I left."

Olga was ready to return to Copenhagen that night, but Zahle persuaded her to stay, just as he had told Count von Moltke he would.

Harriet made more notes that evening. Franziska was joyful, happy that her "aunt" had recognized her. Would everything be all right now? Franziska asked. "May I go to Grandmamma? There are plenty of good doctors who could dress my arm ... You must get a basket for Kiki, so that I can take him with me."

Was it just the same old game, the same responses to Harriet's nudges and cues? Was she caught up in Olga's warmth?

Harriet wrote that Franziska even said that "Grandmamma" would be displeased by Harriet's bobbed hair. What is evident is that Harriet did entertain some idea of accompanying Franziska to Denmark. Harriet the savior, the one who had brought about the recognition ... Harriet with her shorn hair, ushering "Anastasia" to a Danish reunion like Joan of Arc leading a reluctant Charles VII to Reims. The editor of her book would repeatedly describe her as Franziska's "unwearying guardian" and "courageous champion" in the text of the book itself.

Harriet was not going to go away.

While Olga sat at Franziska's bedside, her husband, Kulikovsky, Mr.Gilliard and an old army friend, Baumgarten, visited the Russians who knew Franziska. They quickly discovered the Kleists and the

Schwabes. An episode in which Franziska swore in Polish, her fascinated perusal of Schwabe's photos, and "vulgar manners" all came out.

Olga was back at the clinic at nine the next morning, to find Franziska "radiant," according to Harriet, but "apathetic" according to Olga. She had brought along photos of her little sons, Tikhon and Guri, which gave her an opening to ask about Franziska's son. The mythical child, the royal bastard, lost in Romania. Franziska "turned red and evaded the answer."

More questions, more photos that went unrecognized.

And then the subject of money came up, Franziska would later tell Zahle. She said that she revealed to her "aunt" that the tsar had put away twenty million roubles as dowry money for his daughters in England. He had repatriated his own foreign funds to help pay for armaments, but hadn't felt it right to touch the money that would assure his daughters' future security.

The money, Franziska went on, was in an English bank account, overseen by a Russian ex-banker with a short German name. "Aunt Olga," who had to earn spending money by selling her paintings, grew a little distant after she heard about the bank account, Franziska claimed. In her later testimony before the Hamburg court, Olga categorically denied ever discussing money with Franziska.

Harriet's book states that Olga recognized her "niece." All writers "for" Franziska have used Harriet's account of the visit. Olga said that it was "a complete fabrication."

Olga kissed a weeping Franziska good-bye as she left, and Franziska kissed her hand, according to Harriet. Olga denied any kissing— plausibly, considering Franziska's active tuberculosis. Before she left, Harriet informed Olga that she was worried Franziska would attempt suicide if Olga did not remain friendly with her.

That night, Zahle gave a dinner for the Gilliards and the Kulikovskys at the Embassy. It was a "tension-ridden" meal, with Zahle abruptly turning away from his guests and drumming his fingers on the table. At Kulikovsky's urging, Mrs. von Schwabe and Dr. Grunberg joined them after dinner. Olga heard about the "Polish vagabond" firsthand.

"I believe we have resolved this story," Gilliard said with satisfaction.

"You have been much too active," Zahle retorted angrily.

The Berlin visit should have settled things for Olga but, according to Harriet, Zahle claimed that Olga told him before she left that "My intelligence will not allow me to accept her as Anastasia, but my heart tells me that it is she. And since I have grown up in a religion which taught me to follow the dictates of the heart rather than those of the mind, I am unable to leave this unfortunate child."

Did Olga really say that? Her thank you letter to Zahle was politely negative, saying that she was sure the patient was "not the one she believes herself to be," but does mention "strange and inexplicable facts" yet to be resolved.

Perhaps Olga remembered the suicide threats. She wrote at least five polite letters to Franziska. All of the letters use the formal "you" pronoun *Sie* and the tone is friendly without being intimate. The *Sie* is significant. No aunt would ever use *Sie* when addressing a niece. Tellingly, in the German edition of a book in which the letters are quoted, the phrases are reworded to use "one."

Harriet answered the letters for Franziska and sent Christmas gift books for Olga's sons.

"Don't be afraid," Olga wrote. "You are not alone and we shall not abandon you."

"Thinking of you all the time."

"My thoughts are with you."

She also sent gifts: a handsome shawl, bought in Japan, and a hand-knit sweater which she could not wear "because I am in mourning for my aunt." My aunt, not our aunt. Olga did not expect Franziska to mourn Queen Alexandra, the consort of Edward VII, and Anastasia's great-aunt. Harriet noted that Franziska had "wept bitterly" at the news of Queen Alexandra's death.

On December 22, 1925, three days before Olga sent the sweater, she wrote to Princess Irene:

"It was pitiful to watch this poor creature trying to prove she was Anastasia. She showed her feet, a finger with a scar, and other marks which she said were bound to be recognized at once. But it was Marie who had a crushed finger, and someone who believed it was Anastasia must have told her this … For four years this poor creature's head was stuffed with all these stories, she was shown a mass of photos, etc., and I believe this whole story is an attempt at blackmail … [Kulikovsky and Gilliard] visited all the Russians she had once lived with, learning thereby a great deal that is significant … But in the present case most people have only one wish: to complicate the story or legend further."

Waldemar, Olga's uncle, was now paying for Franziska's hospitalization. It is another curious thing, because Olga never wrote to Franziska again and in January she issued a public statement saying that the woman in Berlin was not Anastasia.

"That child [Anastasia] was as dear to me as if she were my own daughter," Olga told her biographer. "As soon as I sat down by that bed in the Mommsen Nursing Home, I knew I was looking at a stranger. The spiritual bond between my dear Anastasia and myself was so strong that neither time nor any ghastly experience could have interfered with it. I don't really know what name to give to that feeling—but I do know that it was wholly absent. I had left Denmark with something like hope in my heart. I left Berlin with all hope extinguished."

But as late as the Fifties, when Olga had moved to Canada, she still thought of the strange Miss Unknown and admitted to a friend that family pressure had been a factor in her repudiation of the invalid.

Perhaps it could be summed up this way: strangers came to see Franziska. No one recognized anyone.

But Franziska was getting better. She would live. That is, perhaps, the only incontestable truth of this part of Franziska's life. It is this truth that mattered most to her, but no one realized it, especially not

Harriet, who had added another layer of myth to the story surrounding Franziska.

Chapter Eight

I

Beyond the sickroom, things were falling apart. Olga's involvement seems to have alerted the opponents to the seriousness of the case and the determination of Franziska's supporters.

Early in January Gilliard learned from Schwabe that Harriet and Rudnev were planning to publish a statement which claimed that Gilliard and Olga had recognized "Anastasia." Gilliard immediately advised Harriet that he would publish a categorical denial if the proposed pamphlet came out. Harriet wrote back on the 15th and begged him not to publish the denial. "If one really states in this brochure that you recognized the Grand Duchess in the invalid, then it's certainly not true," Harriet wrote, making a lie of much of her upcoming book.

On the same day, the *National Tidende* in Copenhagen wrote: "By way of a categorical denial, in order to settle the matter once and for all, we can disclose that [the] Grand Duchess Olga went to Berlin to see Frau Tschaikovsky, but neither she nor anyone else who knew Tsar Nicholas' youngest daughter, was able to find the slightest resemblance between the Grand Duchess Anastasia and the person who is called Frau Tschaikovsky … Frau Tschaikovsky leaves the impression of a poor highly strung invalid who believes in her story and is confirmed in the belief by the people around her. We hope that she can be freed from this idee fixe in the Berlin clinic where she is now being treated."

Olga's public denunciation gave others the green light. The opponents hinted at conspiracies by Communists, Jews, and Masons but never learned of the Anthroposophical involvement. They would always deny there was an organized opposition to her claim, but even in 1926 there was a loose alliance of people against her.

Markov of Dalldorf days denounced Franziska (again); the Grand Duke Kyril Vladimirovich, the contender for the vacant Russian throne, was against her. The Grand Duchess Xenia in England opposed her, as did the relatives in Denmark, with the exception of Waldemar. The Grand Duke Ernst of Hesse, totally against, was meeting with Pierre Gilliard, who encouraged the gullible Harriet to send him detailed notes about Franziska's utterances so that he could refute them.

Harriet hinted at "dynastic difficulties" and "perplexities and complications." Shades of Kaspar. His royal relatives had plotted against him too, or so his followers believed.

Soon Schwabe was on the lecture circuit, talking about "the Polish vagabond." He wasn't the only one. Constantine Savitch, former President of the Court of Assizes in St. Petersburg, went around Berlin speaking about the impostor. Gossip spread that Franziska was the common-law wife of a gangster from Riga, Tschaikovsky-Arbatschevsky. The Riga police ruled this tale out in February. The Russian Refugee Office tried to remain neutral; its head, Serge Botkin, never came out publicly for Franziska.

On the plus side, Kyril's brother, the Grand Duke Andrei started a private enquiry. He hadn't met Franziska, but seemed convinced. It was felt he worked with Olga's blessing, but Olga denied this, protesting that no one could stop him.

Andrei, too, saw conspiracy, but this conspiracy dated back to the abdication when other Romanovs, including his ambitious mother, had plotted to remove Nicholas. If they didn't want Nicholas, why should they want "Anastasia," who knew about these machinations? He would work doggedly on Franziska's behalf over the next few years, even before he met her face to face. Nothing seemed to faze Andrei, who would also claim to have Soviet documents about "Anastasia."

The Soviets took the threat of a tsar-in-exile seriously. They seem to have been most interested in the Grand Duke Nicholas, who was still popular in Russia. Soviet agents never ceased trying to kidnap him and even penetrated his "court" at Choigny, fabricating a monarchist group in order to draw closer to him.

Obviously Kremlin operatives would have taken a far more active interest in Franziska if they had thought that she was a surviving daughter of Nicholas II. Simply enough, they knew better.

II

The light picks up the white painted railing on the bed, an icon of St. Nicholas suspended from the top bar of the headboard. There is a nightstand nearby with a glass of water, little jars, and a bouquet of flowers. Harriet is hovering over the invalid—no make-up, face shining slightly from exertion, hands out, ready to do something. Franziska lies in a nest-like arrangement of pillows, blankets, a coverlet. She looks like an outsized infant until you study her face, canny and tight; this is how she looks just before she sees an outsider and pulls the covers up over her head.

The news from Denmark has been a blow, but Franziska's friends are keeping this from her, or so they think. Questions are being raised in a breathy, teenager's voice: "Is there a letter from Denmark? Has Aunt Olga written? Can I soon go to Grandmamma? Has Shura sent a line? I want to kiss Shura. I love her so! When we were small, Shura would have given her life for us!"

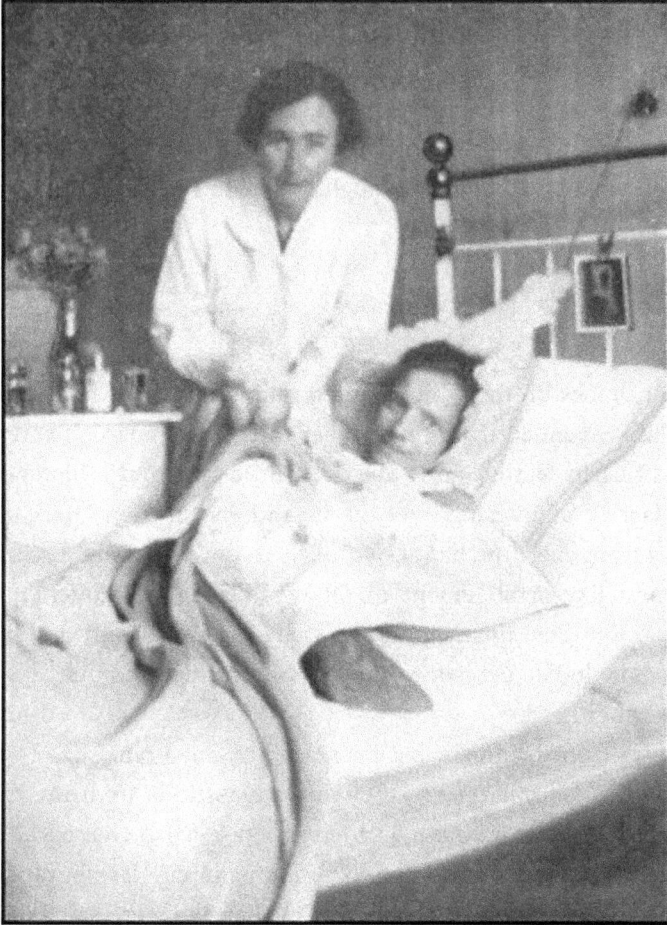

Harriet and the "little one," Mommsen, 1925

It would be useful to be accepted by the people in Denmark, but it is even more important to hold the loyalty of the people nearby. Franziska is busy practising her signature to send to Gilliard and asking these questions, keeping up the pretense.

There are drives out to the countryside too, in the ambassador's car. Franziska doesn't have to invent the joy she expresses to Harriet. Out of that room and moving at last. She drew the curtains around the booth in the Russian restaurant, after making a performance of bowing to all the waiters. It was an odd gesture but it worked. Harriet and an emigre writer and his wife were moved by its unexpected graciousness (don't you acknowledge everyone when you enter a room?) and by the tears she shed during a version of *The Black Hussars* sung by ex-officers and their wives. The closed booth, the weighty food, the song of the defeated regiment also hanging heavily, a dirge in the heart and in the stomach.

The writer and his wife notice her childlike concentration at an Orthodox mass, but outsiders see her crossing herself like a Roman Catholic, left to right. This gesture, as automatic as breathing, will trip her up later too. Word of it spreads, and she doesn't return to services.

Back at the hospital Rudnev and other physicians produce learned, earnest explanations of her memory lapses and lack of basic skills. The atmosphere of her airless hospital room seems trapped in the pages like a gaseous cloud. Harriet collects them, Franziska ignores them.

"I only want to get well," she tells a visitor. She also tells him that she doesn't seek recognition, going on to hint that she would be glad to live quietly somewhere if only her "relatives" would give her a quiet corner to live in and … perhaps an allowance? An allowance of any kind from the Romanovs was a fantasy, but one she would return to over the years: a secret grand duchess in a cottage or flat somewhere, discreetly banking a stipend from powers unknown.

Franziska's supporters would always oppose this vision of her future. How could the real Anastasia quietly creep away, willing to remain unrecognized in return for an allowance from her enemies? How could she be like Kaspar if she accepted money instead of her birthright?

This wasn't the only area in which their interests diverged. She had been cultivating a friendship with a masseuse, Frau Giesel, whom Harriet scorned as a flatterer and a "very excitable person." Franziska wanted a Clara around, someone a bit noisy and dramatic, someone who might tell her things the others didn't want her to know. When Giesel read in a newspaper that the Gypsies had kidnapped "Anastasia's" child in Romania, Franziska wept and wanted the imaginary child found. They must get him back from the Gypsies! She had fastened her baptismal cross around his little neck before leaving him with her husband's mother.

Harriet banned the masseuse from Franziska's room and lamented the "little one's" reliance on sycophants, even if the incident did provide her with a touching episode for her book.

III

With all the public fuss, the lectures and denials, it's no wonder that Franziska began to interest the press. "Anastasia" brand cigarettes appeared; the Riga tale made the tabloids; another article described her as "always a lady," a statement she had the wit to laugh at. An American journalist, Bella Cohen, wrote about her in the *New York Times*.

This was the turning point. Her story had largely been kept out of the papers until now, contained within the monarchist community. What would happen if her photograph appeared and old friends, fellow workers, and neighbors recognized her?

Harriet and Zahle knew it was time to get her out of Berlin. A *Kur* would do, a visit to a spa where the "little one" could regain her strength in the pure mountain air of Switzerland.

IV

Switzerland? Franziska wanted no part of this. Not only would she have to cross a border with phony travel papers Zahle had obtained from the German Foreign Ministry, but she would be far from Berlin, where she still had places to escape to.

Aware of the new publicity her case was receiving, Franziska must have feared unmasking at any minute. At least in Berlin there were old friends. At the very worst, she could get on a train bound for Pomerania. Who could prove it was Franziska who had incurred medical expenses under false pretenses? Anastasia could disappear, presumed kidnapped or killed by Bolsheviks. In Switzerland she would be stuck in a strange land, caught in any net her opponents chose to cast.

Prince Waldemar was still supportive. By some accounts, he paid 22,000 marks for her care. The mark had been stabilized; this was real money, a sum which could easily stretch into six figures in current U.S. dollars. Ordinary workers like Felix Schanzkowsky earned about thirty marks a week. Soon after returning to Copenhagen Olga noted that she had had a "very long conversation with my mother and Uncle Waldemar all about our poor little friend." Waldemar seems to have been unimpressed, and went on paying Franziska's fees at Mommsen.

At the very least, Waldemar's generosity attested to the importance her case had assumed. One result of this new status was the privileges that came with it, the special care and attention Franziska had come to enjoy. Harriet noticed that she was quite interested in fashion: "She is very anxious to be well-dressed."

Harriet continued to compile the helpful reports from Franziska's attending physicians. These had begun with Rudnev, included Doctors Nobel and Bonhoeffer and, later, Eitel and Saathof. Some were willing to discover previously unknown forms of amnesia or to credit imaginary head injuries in order to explain her "symptoms." The support of Waldemar and the advocacy of Harriet and Zahle must have played a part, as did the favorable reports of their colleagues. The more positive testimonials there were, the easier it was to add another.

Franziska reluctantly went to Switzerland. There was little choice in the end, if she meant to continue being "Anastasia" at all. Harriet accompanied her to Lugano, where Zahle had made reservations for a shared room at the Hotel Tivoli.

At first it went well, according to Harriet. She arranged a therapeutic regimen for Franziska: balanced meals, exercise (walking and boating); two hours daily of painting, reading, sewing; practice sessions so that Franziska could "recover" the languages she was supposed to have spoken as a Romanov. A British tourist volunteered to drill her in basic English.

Franziska must have spent hours hemming handkerchiefs, sketching the garden, and copying Russian and English letters as she worried about false documents and potential unmasking.

Back in Berlin the newspapers continued to write about "Anastasia." The public seemed fascinated, but the royals were urging Waldemar to cut the flow of funds. Zahle wrote to warn Harriet that without Waldemar's help, she and Franziska would have to leave the Hotel Tivoli. "...a shattering letter," Harriet noted, "everything is hopeless ... there is no money."

The invalid was beginning to rebel: "But of course we had to economise—I kept hearing that from my companion ... our financial worries were now so great that Mrs. Rathlef had to refuse almost all my wishes. We quarreled with each other a lot." Franziska said later. "I began to be suspicious of her and treated her just as badly as she treated me."

What had gotten into "Anastasia"? Harriet had seen her sulk before, but the behavior in Lugano was evidently something new. Franziska had come to expect a lot. "And then there were the extras," as she put it, or, rather, no money for any extras beyond the full board meals at the Tivoli. Harriet was a nuisance, but she had earned her keep by arranging special accommodations and winning over useful friends. Plainly those days were over and Franziska longed to be rid of her.

Franziska threw her stockings in Harriet's face and demanded she darn them. She complained to hotel staff about Harriet's neglect and about having to share a room with a "serving girl."

Harriet had had enough. In June she wrote to Serge Botkin, detailing "how dreadfully hard it is to deal with the patient, how she keeps running off, won't let her arm be dressed, has locked away all the dressing and ointments I need, and refuses to eat ... Either I get no answer at all or else she shouts at me to leave her in peace ... you know my position ... and all I have done for her ... She knows all that, yet somehow she does not feel one is trying hard enough to help her."

It's easy to picture how the tension must have built in the little room in the budget inn. Franziska makes it impossible for Harriet to carry out her nursing duties and then complains of neglect. The walls are thin. Franziska's hectoring can be heard by the other guests, fierce and grating. She even tries to enlist the staff on her side of the argument. Who knows when someone will complain and what the management might do? Harriet attempts to escape the room, but Lugano, like all resort towns, is a depressing place to linger without the price of a meal. All around are happier people, casually ordering multi-course lunches and planning day hikes.

Franziska wrote to her friend Giesel, the masseuse. It was a startling four-page missive from the hand of the "little one" herself, who only knew broken German and had forgotten how to write, having to practice for weeks to produce a simple signature.

It seems Harriet confiscated the letter and sent it on to Zahle. What was in it? At the very least it was a violent anti-Harriet screed, but it may also have spoken of some sort of escape plan, since Franziska would later insist that she wanted to travel alone to Berlin and live in a rented room with Giesel.

Zahle was astonished by the letter and made enquiries. Had Franziska written it herself? Osten-Sacken soon confirmed that she said she had: "She says that she wrote the letter to Mrs. Gisell [sic] herself, which I am not inclined to believe, because she wrote a card to you in *Fraktur* while I was on the balcony, as I wanted to see if she could do it. I explained to her that a letter to Gisell wasn't the right way, that she should have written to you."

The issue didn't go away. Months later, Franziska would claim she had asked a maid to write the letter for her; it had been a great embarrassment to ask for assistance from such a simple person. The idea that Franziska was not as helpless as she seemed and that she was willing to communicate secretly with someone they didn't approve of was obviously unsettling.

On June 9, Harriet wrote Osten-Sacken to say that she had to leave for Berlin immediately. Franziska does not seem to have been intimidated by the interception of the Giesel letter and the "quarreling" continued, apparently.

Osten-Sacken didn't turn up until the 18th, when he rather conde-
scendingly surmised that Harriet and Franziska had simply gotten on
each other's nerves: "One can sense the animosity they feel for each
other ... it was difficult to persuade the patient that Berlin, where she
wanted to go, was not the right place for her."

Franziska was well-behaved, perhaps hoping to turn him against
Harriet. She refused to accept any blame for the deteriorating situation, but Osten-Sacken noted that he knew differently, "for she had
written forbidden letters."

Harriet left the next day in a third-class railway compartment, vow-
ing to continue her efforts for the "little one." Franziska didn't even say
good-bye. Her attempt to establish a beachhead in Berlin with Giesel
had failed, but the failure hadn't cost her much. More importantly, her
complaints and outrageous behavior had allowed her to get away from
Harriet and Lugano. There was a lesson in that.

On June 21, Zahle telegraphed that Osten-Sacken should accompany Franziska to the Stillachhaus Sanatorium of Oberstdorf in the Bavarian Alps. "Money sent," Zahle noted, not saying who the benefactor
was. The luxurious Stillachhaus would be more expensive than a rented room in Lugano, but the gap had been met somehow.

The baron immediately escorted Franziska, reluctant and queru-
lous, on to the train to Bavaria. She was still insisting that she wanted
to return to Berlin and Giesel. It must have been a long trip for both of
them.

V

The Stillachhaus Sanatorium was nestled in what many Germans
feel is the most beautiful part of their country. It was an elegant spa
with every convenience and a spectacular view of the Allgau, a pano-
rama of flower-bedecked chalets tucked into the hills, belled cows in
fields, and tiny villages.

The *Kur* is still popular in Germany. After an operation or medical treatment, patients are often sent to a san in the country to fully recover their strength. Away from daily cares, the patients follow a regimen of exercise, special diets, rest, and careful diversion. The sans are more like hotels, with private accommodations and elegant dining rooms in idyllic settings.

Franziska had Room 22 all to herself. No Harriet, no lessons, no structured hours. She was free to be herself for long stretches of time, after almost a year of Harriet's hovering, listening, and watching.

"Here at Oberstdorf she is happy so far," wrote the matron, Agnes Wasscherleben.

Meals were regular and plentiful—cold cuts and bread for breakfast, dinner at seven. Hour long walks were prescribed morning and afternoon. All Franziska's visitors had to be cleared with Zahle "as long as I control the money for her care." He was still troubled by the letter to Frau Giesel, which he pointed out had been written without his "authorization."

Dr. Eitel quickly became a believer, saying he "would cease to believe in himself if Mrs. Tschaikovsky were not the Tsar's daughter." "Anastasia" was refined, if haughty sometimes—she made a scene when a letter was not promptly delivered to her—a condition that made him wonder if the Romanovs shared the "proverbial ingratitude" of the Habsburgs.

Dr. Saathof found she weighed forty-seven kilos (about 104 pounds), but said she still appeared weak and frail, looking older than twenty-five. Her arm was frozen at an eighty degree angle. There were still tubercular symptoms, an inflammation of the joints and her eyesight was poor. "Nervous, very correct, self-controlled and pleasant," he noted.

Franziska had "voids in her memory." She was still using a German illustrated journal with an article about Ekaterinburg as a visual aid. Saathof remembered her handing him the magazine as she intimated that "some parts of it are correct; but much of it is false. She herself cannot bear to talk of it at present."

"It would be impossible for anyone so ill physically, but who presents no psychopathic features, to sustain a false role without once deviating from there-from ... Our own observations ... all force us to the conclusion that Mrs. Tschaikovsky is, in fact, Her Highness the Grand Duchess Anastasia."

VI

At least Franziska could deviate from her role when she was alone. She could be herself as she wandered the nearby countryside, or shut herself in her room.

The door closed, she could be Franziska again, with her own thoughts. She could gobble her *Kotlett*, tear the meat, and not mind about the missing teeth or which fork to use. She could toss her clothes in anger or swear or cry. She could write imaginary letters to Felix and her mother.

But night brought terrors. She was always frightened at night, even thirty years later when a friend wrote that "she is always fearing dreadfully at night when she is alone."

She panicked and ran to her room when a patient choked on a fish bone in the dining room. She lamented her "family's" lack of interest in her. If only she could die, then she would be reunited with her loved ones!

Excursions helped. She accompanied her special nurse, Agnes Wasserschleben, to the cinema, where she critiqued the uniforms and horses in *The Tsar's Courier*. They toured local palaces where Franziska pointed out tsarist relics. She wanted a samovar. Yes, that was her dearest wish, to have a little flat with a samovar in it.

Franziska did not notice the detective who had begun to trail her on some of these excursions. He had been hired by the Grand Duke Ernst of Hesse.

VII

Franziska had been in Stillachhaus for two months when she had a visitor. Tatiana Melnik, *nee* Botkin, was the daughter of Dr. Eugene Botkin, who had died with the imperial family in Ekaterinburg. Tatiana's cousin was Serge Botkin, and her brother Gleb would eventually find his way into Franziska's saga as well. By some accounts, Zenaida Tolstoi had second thoughts and suggested that Tatiana (usually known as Tania), take a look at the claimant. Osten-Sacken also seems to have urged her to visit, although he also warned her that Franziska was suspicious of new faces and might well refuse to see her.

All these tantalizing clues, these strange stories, must have recalled the precious hours she spent with the tsar's children. Tania and Gleb hadn't known the Romanov children well, having only played with them a few times on the *Standart* when their father was ill.

Tatiana and Gleb saw them in Tsarskoe Selo and later at Tobolsk, and were thrilled to wave at the remote, magical royal children. Tania's memories of the grand duchesses were obsessively detailed, but the contact had been brief and superficial. The surviving Romanovs, always reticent about the Ekaterinburg massacre, do not seem to have felt obligated by Dr. Botkin's sacrifice and ignored his children, who had been left to find a way out of Siberia on their own. Perhaps "Anastasia" would be different.

Osten-Sacken, Tania and her aunt, Maria Debagory, arrived at Stillachhaus on August 27. "[Franziska] was most unpleasantly surprised when she saw two ladies had come with me," Osten-Sacken wrote, noting that she immediately ran to her room. He followed her there and hinted that the family of the visitors had been close to the tsar. Franziska refused to meet them. Maybe tomorrow.

That night, Tania glimpsed Franziska, who knew she was being watched, in the dining room. Oh, yes. The way Franziska held out her hand to the manager ... her walk ... yes, yes, she could be Anastasia.

In the morning, Franziska complained the Osten-Sacken that she hadn't slept all night, worrying about the identity of the visitors. Franziska probed a bit, and he told her the names of the two ladies.

After lunch he insisted they all go for a walk. Franziska wanted to show Tania a path. Ten minutes passed.

Tania initially saw no resemblance to Anastasia at all.

The invalid remained mute. As Tania studied her she covered her lower face with a handkerchief. This emphasized her eyes, "so blue and full of light."

As they walked along Tania told amusing stories in poor German. Franziska listened to her intently, face still half covered, as they walked along the path.

Quite suddenly, Tania felt certain that she was walking with the Grand Duchess Anastasia: "In her face I discovered features I had known before; but the mouth has changed and coarsened remarkably, and because the face is so thin, her nose looks bigger than it used to."

The resemblance, Tania said later, was only in the eyes. In her 1927 report to Serge Botkin, she surmised that "Anastasia's" mouth and nose had been "horribly" altered.

In the afternoon they met on the balcony for tea. There was stilted conversation about the area. What should Franziska talk about? She knew little about Dr. Botkin's children apart from the fact that they had followed the Romanovs into Siberia. She was still pretending not to know who Tania was. What now?

Tania produced a photo album, which Franziska took to her room. Tania found Franziska weeping over pictures of the imperial family.

"Did you know them from before?" Franziska asked in broken German. "When did you see me last?"

"In 1918."

"You do not recognize me?" Tania asked.

"No, with no sleep and nothing but thoughts, no sleep and nothing but thoughts—"

Tania hugged her. "My little one."

"That is what my father called me. *Malenkaya*."

A Russian word, one of Harriet's favorite endearments. It was so easy.

Tania was back that night to share more photos. Franziska wept again, put her head on Tania's shoulder, and stared into space.

Tania spent two weeks at Stillachhaus. Franziska listened while Tania spoke of the Romanovs by the hour. She emphasized her new disabilities: she couldn't read well, count, or tell time. She was like a child, like Kaspar, using primitive German to tell disjointed stories about her past.

Perhaps as they talked, Franziska began to sense how little time Tania had actually spent with the real Anastasia. Franziska didn't have to say much; any effort was fine for Tania, who eagerly listened to all utterances by "Anastasia," once so far away, so regal, now here, beside her. It was natural that she didn't want to talk about "the dead" but rather about "dancing, and nice, funny things."

When Tania left, she swore she would write to one and all to tell them that Anastasia was alive. Tania's pledge caused her much trouble. Everyone, including the Grand Duchess Olga and her own uncle Peter Botkin, felt she had made a fool of herself.

Gilliard said that Tania had "an excitable temperament" and showed a great "lack of caution where Mrs. Tschaikovsky was concerned." Tania had only been nine the last time she saw the actual Anastasia, he pointed out.

It was at this point that Harriet stated her intention to publish a book about Franziska in the coming fall. Serialized articles would appear in February 1927 in the *Berliner Nachtausgabe*. The "Schanzkowsky Scandal" was on the way.

Chapter Nine

I

Gossip about "Anastasia" had reached Stillachhaus. Tourists appeared and death threats came. A reporter from the *Berliner Nachtausgabe* turned up. Dr. Eitel threw him out, but Franziska heard about the incident. Getting rid of the paying guests who thronged Oberstdorf in hopes of seeing "Anastasia" wasn't as easy.

The police attention was the worst of it. Acting on information supplied by Baron Ludwig Knorring, a friend of Gilliard's, the Bavarian police issued an order for Franziska's expulsion based on the charge that she had given false information on the travel documents she'd used to go to Switzerland. This was a serious matter which confirmed all Franziska's fears about using phony papers. Zahle intervened with the Bavarian minister in Berlin, but it was a close call. She locked herself in her room and blamed Osten-Sacken for the row.

Her finances were becoming a problem. "It's very difficult to say if I can continue to care for her after the first of the year. Russians have only contributed six hundred marks," Zahle reported.

Franziska was sleepless now. Perhaps she knew the money was drying up again. She refused to eat and complained to Agnes Wasscherleben that everyone was against her, even Zahle. "I feel that after years of hard waiting, she can't endure much longer," Agnes wrote. "It's always the same yearning: to see her grandmother again—only to see, not to talk to."

Franziska's supporters were horrified at the prospect of Harriet's book.

"I can't have anything to do with this," Zahle said.

"... extremely detrimental to the invalid's case ... will nip in the bud any further communication with those people who are now hesitating," Osten-Sacke wired.

Harriet would continue with her plans.

II

As the snow fell, it must have been a strange Christmas for Franziska. Was she alone? Did Agnes Wasserschleben give her pretty handkerchiefs, a bottle of lavender water? Chocolates and bonbons from Eitel and Saathof? Flowers from the Zahles?

Did she join in when everyone sang *Heilige Nacht, Stille Nacht* by the candlelit tree? Did she think about Felix and her mother, the real Mama, so far away, but looking at the same stars and lighting Christmas candles too, while she reminisced about "Christmas at home, in Russia?"

And when New Year's Eve came, did she think about the Pomeranian blacksmiths who foretold the year to come by casting lead?

Quiet Stillachhaus, slumbering in the snow; Franziska, sleepless and terrified, creeping to the window to look at the dark fields. Alone now, not acting; toothless, shivering in her white nightdress. No one had to cast lead to tell her what was coming.

III

In January 1927 the Danish government ordered Zahle to drop Franziska's case. He also learned that Prince Waldemar would stop paying her bills on February 1. The Grand Duke Andrei was continuing his investigation but lacked the personal funds to undertake her support. Attempts to raise money from the Russian emigres fell short.

At the end of January Zahle went to Darmstadt to meet with the grand duke. According to Ernst, Zahle looked at photographs of the real Anastasia and photos of the "invalid" and admitted that there were fundamental differences between the two. Zahle also conceded that there were discrepancies in what she "remembered" and what Harriet and others reported. Ernst had no idea who Franziska really was, he said, but feared there was some sort of Bolshevik involvement behind the scenes.

All the same, Zahle agreed to pay Franziska's expenses for another month. She wasn't going to be left out in the cold; she was going to live in a castle.

IV

Castle Seeon in Bavaria was the seat of George, the Duke of Leuchtenberg, a distant Romanov relative. Although the duke befriended nationalists along the way, autocracy—the right of his extended family to rule much of Europe unhindered by elective bodies—was his unrelenting focus. Politics were very personal to the duke.

The period immediately following the Russian Revolution saw him in Ukraine, leading a German sponsored army dedicated to the restoration of the Romanov dynasty. If the Germans seemed sympathetic to the plight of his family he would back them, even if his family did not wish to be helped by the Germans, and even if his intervention became another factor which sealed their doom. From the Ukrainian capital of Kiev the duke peppered his German friends with urgent bulletins about various Romanovs stranded in the Crimea as their army set about looting the rich resources of Ukraine.

After the hostilities he holed up in the castle, where he became a patron of monarchist periodicals and of the fledgling Nazi Party. While he celebrated the holy days of the Orthodox calendar in his private chapel, he also delved into Anthroposophy and anxiously consulted spiritualists.

General Max Hoffmann stepped in. A master of intrigue, he had presided over the Treaty of Brest-Litovsk, the instrument by which the new Soviet government had traded away much of its lands in the west for a separate peace with Germany. It is said that the experience made Hoffmann a fanatic anti-Bolshevik, although it seems likely that he had loathed them from the start. By 1920 he had worked his way into the intersection of Russian emigre politics and German nationalism.

Hoffmann seems to have offered himself as a witness, insinuating that his role at Brest-Litovsk had given him inside information about Franziska's case. It was hinted that the concern of the kaiser for his relatives in Russia meant their fate had been a topic of discussion during the negotiations. Gleb Botkin would write that "[Hoffmann] was probably the best informed man in the world on what had actually happened to the various members of Russian royalty in the fatal summer of 1918."

The only problem was that he would not come out and say what this knowledge was. Some said that Hoffmann "could produce incontrovertible proof of the fact [of Franziska's identity as Anastasia], but for certain reasons preferred not to do so except in an extremity." Why these vital facts had to remain secret was never explained. The Treaty of Brest-Litovsk had been signed March 3, 1918, when the tsar and his family were still at Tobolsk. Anything Hoffmann might have learned about their situation would be very old news by the time the "fatal summer" arrived.

It also seems odd that he never actually saw Franziska, despite ample opportunities to do so. "I do not need to see her, as I know definitely," he told Harriet repeatedly.

According to the duke, it was Hoffmann who brought him into the case and convinced him to take Franziska in as a guest at Seeon. Hoffmann gave his word as a German officer that she really was the grand duchess.

Why? It seems to have been another murky gambit, a means of embarrassing the Bolsheviks or of creating a line of succession. The effort cost Hoffmann little personally, and not seeing Franziska gave him some wiggle room if she was discredited. The general seems to have had an intimidating personality, one capable of dominating the impressionable duke. The agreement was made.

Franziska herself seems to have been willing enough to fall in with her new nationalist friends. She made pious statements about the necessity of a Russo-Germanic alliance and praised Bismarck when the opportunity presented itself, although there are indications that she always held a little back, balancing her pro-German statements with avowals of her love of England and desire to eventually live there.

V

Harriet's first installment in the *Nachtausgabe* appeared February 14.

Back in Wedding, Frau Wingender was glad to get off her aching feet. She sighed as she opened the door to her flat. Her old varicose veins were acting up and the damp winter weather did nothing for her arthritis, either.

The table was set for *Abendbrott*: bread sliced. *Wurst* on a plate, knives placed beside the bread boards.

Doris was making tea. She was grown up now, a shapely blonde wearing an apron over her wool skirt. It was chilly in the *Stube*, but the kitchen was warm from the coal stove.

Mrs. Wingender sank down in a chair and unlaced her shoes before opening the newspaper. "Going out tonight?"

Doris had a boyfriend; maybe, soon, a fiance. She smiled to herself as she buttered bread and her mother leafed through the *Nachtausgabe*. Perhaps by Easter they'd celebrate the engagement ... a small party in a restaurant ... she'd need a new dress for something like that ...

Doris, Kind, kuk doch mal an!

"Doris, look child! Look at this!"

VI

Two days later Zahle sent a telegram, ordering Franziska to leave for Castle Seeon at once. Even then, Franziska had her conditions. She would only go if Tania Botkin accompanied her.

Zahle quickly obtained a visa for Tania. Her expenses would be paid and while she was at it, perhaps she could find out what Franziska needed for the journey. Anything, if it would just get her behind the protective walls of Seeon. It turned out that Franziska needed morning dresses, a parasol, a rain umbrella, and playing cards.

VII

Living in a castle might have been the pinnacle of Franziska's achievement so far, if she hadn't been forced to go there for safety, much as in medieval times when the lord's serfs and other dependants flocked behind the walls for protection against marauding armies.

She was certainly familiar with castles, which dotted the German landscape. Some were crumbling ruins, testaments to duchies and royalty whose days had passed. Some, like the castle at Butow, recalled mythic eras, old stones for dreamers. A few still housed the dukes and princes who had lost their power after the war.

Franziska was not impressed with Seeon. Perhaps she reminded herself that her ancestors had once consorted with princes. She knew precisely how to behave when she arrived with Tania and Lillian Zahle. There was still snow on the ground. Inside, the thick walls and dark corridors seemed filled with shadows, ghosts.

"I hope you will be happy at Seeon," the duke said. He was a tall man with silver hair and a straight back, the effect of which was somewhat diminished by his slight lisp.

Franziska turned to him and held out her hand "Good night."

She waited for the duke to leave, as a courtier attending a grand duchess would be expected to do. The duke looked at her "as if seeing her for the first time." He opened his mouth and closed it. "Good night."

Duke George lived at Seeon with his wife, Duchess Olga, *nee* Repnin; his eldest daughter, Natalie Baroness Meller-Zakomelski; youngest daughter Tamara; and his son Dmitri and daughter-in-law Catherine. The family members would argue, dividing themselves into pro- and anti-"Anastasia" factions as the visit wore on.

Castle Seeon also served as a refuge for Russians of a kind already known to Franziska. There were former officers, and old women of small and carefully managed means. They were piano teachers, unmarried daughters of naval officers, and language teachers who had lived at the edges of the imperial feast. They may have once seen the real Anastasia on a distant balcony or at a particularly grand patriotic assembly; in some ways they were the women Clara had pretended to be. They were willing to believe, perhaps because having "Anastasia" in the house provided some excitement, perhaps because the growing faith of the duke was proof enough for them.

Franziska was given a spacious room on the second story, with views of the lake and garden. For now, Franziska barely spoke to the duke and refused to meet the duchess. Servants brought meals up to her room. She particularly enjoyed roast pork, "a little more elegantly prepared than usual," a maid would remember. She and Tania spent days at a time tucked away, talking. Tania suited the ambience of Seeon perfectly. Even though she was young, she seemed as out of step and full of regrets as the older Russian women.

Franziska lay on a sofa, complaining about headaches, Harriet, and the newspapers. She continued to display her helplessness to Tania. She could now count to twenty-five, and tell playing cards apart once more. Progress. She got lost in the corridors as she scurried back to her room, having "entirely lost her sense of space and distance," Tania noted. Her German remained bad, even as she spoke "normal" German to the maid.

"I will not stay here until Easter," Franziska revealed. "I am tired of living at someone else's expense. I want to go to a convent or a free clinic!"

When she said that she wanted to go to "Grandmamma in Denmark," Tania finally told her the truth: the family in Denmark thought she was an impostor and wanted nothing to do with her. Franziska had already pieced this together herself, but displayed the appropriate panic and disbelief: "I want to see my Grandmother! I will prove it, I will prove it!"

Tania continued reminding Franziska of Russian things, showing her a medallion, for instance, that her husband had been given when he was a patient in the hospital at Tsarskoe Selo. Franziska stored the memory. She was good at that, according to Irina Lamosey, the duke's step-granddaughter.

Lamosey now lives in Canada, but has fond memories of Seeon and her stepfather, Dmitri, and the duke, a kind man and a wonderful grandparent. She was only ten years old when Franziska lived at Seeon, but she recalls seeing Franziska in "a long brown caftan," and the stories her mother, Duchess Catherine, told about their remarkable visitor. "People would come, old generals, and ask, 'Do you remember you had a—say, for instance, a little white china dog?'

She didn't remember, but the next person who talked to her would say, 'She said she had a white china dog in Russia!'

We grew used to this kind of thing."

As much as she might disparage Harriet, Franziska had come to appreciate the presence of a personal assistant. They could serve as a source of information, a shield against the curious, and an intermediary who could tell others when Franziska needed something. Franziska broadly hinted at this when she observed that Tania had become like a "proper lady-in-waiting." She would cling to Tania, trying to keep her from returning to her family, even after Tania's children became ill and needed their mother. It might be that Franziska took Tania's departure after two weeks badly; they would never be as close again.

Nurse Wasserschleben from Oberstdorf came to care for Franziska. Maria Baumgarten, an elderly Russian lady, and Vera von Klemenz, a piano teacher, were also helpful, as was Faith Lavington, the English governess to Dmitri and Catherine's children.

Franziska passed by a new visitor in the corridor outside her room without a second glance. Colonel Anatole Mordvinov had been an aide-de-camp to the tsar and knew Anastasia well right up to the time of the abdication. He had sat up with the grand duchesses the night they learned of Rasputin's murder. The duke hoped Mordvinov would recognize Anastasia in his mysterious visitor. He didn't: "I came here so hoping to find my grand duchess ... and what did I find?"

Franziska accused Mordvinov of having a guilty conscience, just like Isa Buxhoeveden.

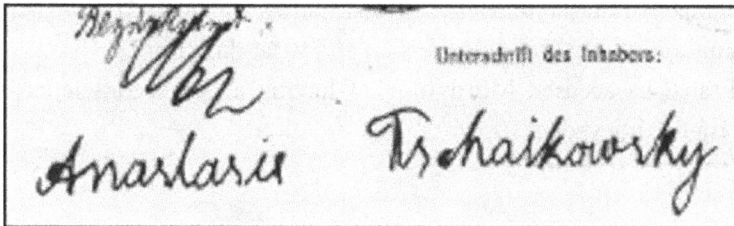

Identity photo on the *Personalausweis* issued to
Franziska at Seeon in 1927, with her reluctant
"Anastasie Tschaikowsky" signature below.

VIII

The *Berliner Nachtausgabe* published their first volley on April 1, 1927: "The woman rescued from the Landwehr Canal on February 17, 1920, who calls herself Anastasia Tschaikovsky ... is, in reality, Franziska Schanzkowska, unmarried, born on December 16, 1896, at Borowihlas ... We will communicate the details to our readers in due time."

It was six weeks after Harriet's first article appeared.

The Wingenders hadn't rushed to the *Nachtausgabe.* There were things to consider. Would they get in trouble? Would the police get involved? What would happen to Franziska?

They had known Franziska was back with the Russians. The neighbor of that Peuthert woman had found out all about it, and passed the word on. There had been rumors after that: Franziska was living with a baron; Franziska was seen in a Russian restaurant; Franziska was being treated at a private clinic.

Doris and her mother shook their heads as they re-read the story in the *Nachtausgabe* and looked at Franziska's familiar face. How she must be laughing at the higher-ups!

While the Wingenders pondered what to do, Detective Knopf went through the files of missing women at the Berlin police headquarters. It didn't take him long to discover the 1919 *Polizeiabmeldung* of one Franziska Schanzkowsky and to match the handwriting on the document with the claimant's "Anastasia" signature. The only problem was that the records said Franziska had disappeared January 15. Knopf had a call to make at Neue Hochstrasse 17.

IX

On March 15 Doris Wingender sat down in the office of the *Berliner Nachtausgabe*. The editor had been expecting her.

"I know who this 'Anastasia' is."

Doris took a breath, crossed her legs, and went over the agreed facts: when Franziska had first come to them, when she had left, what she was like, and when she had returned to their flat in August 1922. Yes, she was certain the "grand duchess" was their former boarder. She had recognized the picture at once.

"We saved her papers, of course," Doris went on. "In case Franziska came back and wanted to go back to work. We wouldn't throw her papers out! She was supposed to go back to Friederikenhof in March and a person needs papers if they want to work. My mother has them all carefully put away in a wardrobe."

She watched the pen gliding over the paper. The hard part was coming up.

"Maybe the papers would be worth something to the *Nachtausgabe*."

She felt her face turn red. What if they didn't offer money? What if they called the police? But Knopf had said not to worry.

"The papers would be of much interest, Fraulein Wingender. I will call the stenographer in, shall I?"

Doris signed a contract with the paper. In return for 1500 marks, Doris would hand over the documents Franziska had left with her. She would also travel, at the *Nachtausgabe*'s expense, to Bavaria to identify Franziska in person. Five hundred marks would be paid upon publication; the remaining thousand would be hers after she identified Franziska face-to-face.

There was no mention in the contract of the clothing which Doris had kept after trading her blue suit for it during the "missing three days." It wasn't until March 29 that Knopf, having obtained the items from either the Wingenders or the newspaper—this was unclear—

showed the Kleists the camel hair coat, the lilac dress, and the embroidered underwear. The Kleists recognized the garments immediately.

What could be more conclusive than this? Despite assertions that Ernst of Hesse was behind the Schanzkowsky "legend," none of Franziska's supporters ever succeeded in explaining away the clothes.

X

On March 22, exactly a week after Doris signed the contract, but before the appearance of the unmasking article, Detective Shuricht, hired by Harriet, sat down in the Schanzkowsky cottage in Hygendorf.

Knopf had already been there. He had found Mrs. Schanzkowsky, ill, and with a "hostile stare," lying on the sofa. Walter, Juliana ("Mariechen"), and Gertrud all recognized Franziska in the photos Knopf showed them.

Mrs. Schanzkowsky gave him her only picture of Franziska and described her daughter's fine manners and the affected speech she sometimes liked to use.

Walter had not been pleased by Knopf's visit. The neighbors had gossiped about Franziska after she disappeared. The police in Butow suggested Franziska could have been murdered by Karl Grossmann but Walter wasn't mourning: "She was too good for work, our fine sister."

He wanted nothing to do with her. Yes, sure, she was a grand duchess. "And I'm the Emperor of China!"

That was Walter—moody and abrupt. Knopf left money for him and his sisters, Juliana and Gertrud, to travel to Berlin to identify Franziska. They hadn't gone anywhere, though. The family sent a friend, George Witte, to Berlin to ask their own questions.

Maybe Mrs. Schanzkowsky had given Walter a talking to by the time Shuricht visited. Harriet's detective was impressed by the three Schanzkowskys. "Family makes impression of good, honest people— not cunning. The mother says they should send Franziska to Hygendorf—she would recognize her."

They again identified recent photos of the "little one." They had last seen her when she worked at the Butow brewery. Mrs. Schanzkowsky stated under oath that she recognized Franziska's photos. She wished only to see her Franziska before she died, she said. All the Schanzkowskys present signed a protocol dated March 22, 1927.

Gertrud had married a farmer, Ellerik, who wanted nothing to do with this Anastasia-Franziska business. Where would it all lead? Would Gertrud be forced to go to Berlin? They weren't getting involved in this nasty business: *Raus! Raus!* Get out, get out—or else!

Shuricht fled to the brewery in Butow, where Franziska had washed bottles. Sure, they remembered Franziska up to her elbows in soap, rinsing bottles and setting them out to dry.

Knopf had ended up feeling sorry for Franziska, coming out of this background. "A heap of misery," a woman with an inferiority complex who had wanted to better herself. An uneducated woman wasn't the same as a woman who couldn't be educated, he said.

"You would understand why the mother doesn't come to her daughter if you'd been there," Knopf would tell the Duke of Leuchtenberg, "or why the daughter won't return there, even to visit her dying mother."

XI

The duke had just arrived at the apartment he maintained in Paris when he was given advance word of the *Nachtausgabe* series that was on the verge of publication.

In articles dated April 5 and 6 and titled "The Unmasking of the False Grand Duchess Anastasia," the paper would print everything: Franziska's suicide attempt, her background, the story of the missing three days. Her *Polizeianmeldung* was reproduced, as were three pieces of paper given to Mrs. von Schwabe by the mysterious man, supposedly Serge Tschaikovsky, along with the suggestion that some of the fragments matched Franziska Schanzkowsky's handwriting.

Perhaps most damning of all were three photos of Franziska, show-ing her in 1915, 1921, and 1925 captioned "The Changes of the Face of the Tschaikovsky/Schanzkowski Woman." For many it was impossible not to see that all three photos were of the same woman.

The duke believed the story at once. A reporter from the Scherl Verlag, which owned the *Nachtausgabe*, appears to have been his source. "There seems to be no doubt," he sadly wrote the Grand Duke Andrei, who had also received a letter that day from Serge Botkin. Botkin had felt the Franziska Schanzkowsky identity was "distinctly probable."

Zahle's position was shaken. Over the years, he would continue to support Franziska, often covertly, but in the spring of 1927 he was forced to sign a document stating that he no longer believed in her.

Leuchtenberg headed home at once, only to find a policeman standing at the gates of his castle. The constable had wanted to con-front Franziska but the duchess had put him off. Leuchtenberg wa-vered.

Franziska remained in her room. It was said that she was oblivious to the commotion, but how could she not have known about the po-liceman? Or failed to have sensed the agitated atmosphere at the castle, the looks and whispers of the servants? She had been ready for some-thing terrible ever since she learned about Harriet's publishing plans. Now she could feel it, growing closer and closer as she scurried to hide in her room. She put herself to bed. She would refuse to get up. If they wanted to pack her off to jail, or to Hygendorf they would have to lit-erally drag her out of her bed.

On April 4, Doris, accompanied by Knopf and a reporter named Fritz Lucke, met the duke in Munich. They were expecting Franziska to be brought to them that evening on the pretext of a dental ap-pointment. After the identification they planned to take her back to Berlin.

The duke was plainly nervous. "My dear gentlemen, the Invalid senses something. She used to walk in the park and sometimes even joined us at breakfast; now she lies in bed in a very nervous condition, fearing something unexpected is going to happen. We expected to send her to the dentist in Munich on Monday, but unfortunately the dentist was at Seeon on Sunday. Tomorrow, however, gentlemen, my wife and children want to attend a dance recital by Pavlova. Mrs. Tschaikovsky was looking forward to coming along, as she said she'd seen her dance in Russia. But today she stated she felt ill and wouldn't be able to go."

"She knows," Knopf told the duke, "this woman, this Franziska Schanzkowsky, knows since February 1920 that something could happen at any moment. She always tried to protect herself from having her photograph taken. She was always very ill when Russians who knew the Imperial Family or former officers wanted to visit her. This woman cannot treat the world, and you, Highness, as idiots. If she won't come to Munich, then the confrontation must take place at Seeon."

The discussion went on until late in the afternoon. Finally the duke reluctantly drove the *Nachtausgabe* team to Seeon, where a "Bavarian guard" stood in front of the door.

The confrontation took place the following morning. A cold, rainy day, full of thunder and unnatural darkness. People in the corridors. Franziska covered herself with a nest of blankets. She would remain silent, say nothing. The only defense.

The duke tiptoed into her room, stammering nervously: "A lady who knows you wants to—to say hello."

Suddenly Doris Wingender was in the room! "Good day, Franziska. How are you?"

Franziska, forgetting her resolve, shot up in bed: *Dass soll rausgehen!* Get her out of here! Out! Out!

She had never acted this way with a visitor before, no matter how much she might have resented them. The witnesses were transfixed.

"Out, out!"

Doris stared. It was Franziska all right.

"Out!"

Doris left, but Knopf remained behind. "Good day, Miss Schanzkowsky! Your family asked me to give you their greetings. I was in Hygendorf a few weeks ago. Walter, Juliana, and Gertrud are well, but your mother is very ill and wants to see you before she dies."

Franziska said nothing.

The duke interrogated Franziska at length the day after the confrontation. Details are lacking, but she seems to have held up under questioning. What did the duke really think of her identity? He would continue to shelter her, but even under prodding, never produced a statement that unequivocally expressed a belief in her identity as Anastasia.

Franziska needed an injection to help her sleep that night. Somehow she was still in the castle, not in Munich or Berlin, under police custody. As she drifted off to sleep, she made a point of playing her role, suddenly babbling that she wanted to compare the inscription on an icon to the handwriting of "Uncle Mischa," the tsar's brother. Could Wasserschleben get this for her? She must see the handwriting of her uncle!

On April 9 the story of the confrontation appeared in the *Nachtausgabe* and Doris Wingender received her thousand marks. Franziska's reaction to Doris was another element of the story never really explained by her supporters. Franziska herself said that she wanted Doris to leave because her "father" would never have allowed a cheap blonde like Doris to appear at his court.

It had all been such a nasty shock. "A woman without culture, without morals," Tania Botkin moaned. "That damned Polish woman!"

The duke showed Franziska the *Nachtausgabe* stories. Much of it was scorn directed at "The Polish peasant ... the factory worker ... the German maid." If she became Franziska again she would always be tainted by the awful caricatures. Perhaps for the first time, Franziska realized how others had always seen her—if they had noticed her at all.

XII

Franziska fasted through Lent, and on Easter, a week after the confrontation with Doris, dined with the Leuchtenbergs and attended the chapel at Seeon. She apparently took Communion and made confession, although not to the Leuchtenbergs' regular priest, but to a visiting officiant.

Her lack of familiarity with Orthodoxy caused talk. She excused her ignorance of the ritual by saying that she had not gone to church much since leaving Russia. Actually the Romanov children had been imbued with religion. They prayed regularly, went to services, collected icons. Films made during the 1913 Jubilee show them kissing an icon with a graceful self-effacement that seems to contain the essence of Orthodox piety. Anastasia herself was a girl to whom the different regional styles of decorating an iconostasis were a significant matter.

Madame Marie Hesse, widow of the Tsarskoe Selo palace commandant was an Easter guest at Seeon: "I noticed she made the Catholic sign of the cross, sometimes mixing it up with the Orthodox way. She said she didn't know to which religion she belonged now. At communion she was completely lost … "

XIII

Prince Felix Youssoupov was the next visitor. Married to the tsar's niece, Irina, he was best known for his involvement in the murder of Rasputin. His denunciation of Franziska to the Grand Duke Andrei would perhaps be the most hostile of Anastasia's family members: "I claim categorically that she is not Anastasia Nicholaevna, but rather an adventuress, a sick hysteric and a frightful playactress. I simply cannot understand how anyone can be in doubt of this. If you had seen her, I am convinced you would recoil in horror at the thought that this frightful creature could be the daughter of our Tsar … All these false pretenders ought to be gathered up and sent to live forever in a house somewhere … "

After this run of hostile witnesses Franziska began to blame others. Youssoupov! Well, he had killed Our Friend and had tried to kill her as well. The duke was to blame for the Doris affair, and Harriet for just about everything else. She even fired Agnes Wasserschleben in a fit of rage.

The English governess, Faith Lavington, now attended to Franziska. She kept careful notes in her diary about Franziska's stay at Seeon. "She had been wild ALL DAY and finished up in a screaming gale of passion … Nothing seemed too bad or too far-fetched for her to say … the duke, the duchess, Tamara, all, all had their reputations simply played away from them. She positively dissects people and leaves one without a word to say."

The Leuchtenbergs continued to put up with their mysterious guest's awful behavior. Grand duchesses could behave any way they pleased, it seemed. Franziska was beginning to lose control, but this continued to work in her favor; "Anastasia" had been through so much.

But the most important test lay ahead.

Chapter Ten

I

A Thursday morning writing class. The students have been asked to give an opinion about the young man in the photograph. It's a studio shot from the mid-Twenties, with a muted background and a swath of curtain. The subject stands beside an ornately carved chair. He's dressed in his best, with a cravat, and a handkerchief draped out of the breast pocket of his suitcoat. The face is grave, with a high brow and enigmatic eyes.

Who is this man?

"He has just finished law school and will soon take his place in the family business. He's up-to-date, accustomed to well-appointed surroundings."

"He's serious, with a ramrod, straight posture. He's older than he looks and is off to war. He's having this photo taken for his parents."

"He looks as though he has lots of money, at least more than average for the period. Upper crust, a bit aloof, but photos can be deceiving. Clothes maketh the man."

"This guy reminds me of my father when he was in the Polish infantry. Serious, little or no bull about him. This is serious stuff—getting my picture taken!"

Everyone is surprised when the identity of the young man is revealed: Felix Schanzkowsky, a miner.

Felix Schanzkowsky

"A miner?"

"No!"

Felix Schanzkowsky, Franziska's brother, would be the ultimate judge of her new identity.

"I consider the most dangerous moment to be that of the Schanzkowsky family's recognition of the patient," Andrei had written Serge Botkin on April 8.

"If the police were to believe in this recognition, they could issue a new passport on the spot, and at the request of the Schanzkowskys, settle her in that family's place of residence, which would be equal to killing the patient. If, however, the police were to become doubtful, the case is saved."

Felix was complicated, difficult to know. Like Franziska, he was bright. Poverty had ruled out higher education. Felix had to support himself, and if his brains counted for little without an education, at least his strong back earned him twenty-six marks a week at the Rubbeck Mortar Mine in Ammendorf, a small town near Halle.

Some writers have referred to Felix as a "communist miner," but Waltraud von Czenstkowski says her father wasn't interested in politics, that he preferred to keep to himself.

"I wish I had known him better," Waltraud says. "But my parents divorced when I was a teenager and my mother was so bitter about him."

Waltraud was sixteen or seventeen when her father told her about his sister and her life as "Anastasia." She says the Schanzkowsky family took an oath of silence about Franziska, never mentioning her name. "He didn't know where Franziska was later on. He had no way of finding her."

Harriet sent Detective Shuricht to interview Felix in Ammendorf on April 28, 1927. Felix was cautious. It had been over a month since detectives had turned up in Hygendorf. Felix would certainly have heard about their visits, but he said he'd only read about Franziska in the *Rotefrontkaempfer*. It appears that the Schanzkowskys had decided on a strategy of some kind concerning Franziska, and were cagey now.

Felix impressed Shuricht as having the most intelligent expression of all the Schanzkowskys. They talked about the languages Franziska spoke, the fiance who died in 1915, her childless state, the fight with Gertrud. Shuricht showed Felix photographs. The passport photo didn't look like Franziska at all; she was never so thin, or ill looking, but the earlier hospital picture—yes, that could be Franziska. Felix had decided to leave a little opening.

He told Shuricht how close he and Franziska had been, and praised her soft, small hands. At last a good word about Franziska.

In the end Felix agreed to go see the lady who might be his sister, after being reassured that his lost wages and travel expenses would be covered.

II

Felix put the trip off, giving illness as an excuse, but at last, on May 9, Harriet picked him up at the train station in Munich. He would not be going to the castle, but to a nearby inn in Wasserburg. Franziska's determination to stay in bed had thwarted a confrontation in Munich, but this time Franziska wouldn't be able to hurl herself under the bed-clothes. She had no choice but to leave Seeon for the meeting with her brother.

Harriet said that it was her idea to invite Felix to come to Wasserburg "in order to completely make away with the Shantkovski myth." Her writing is terse: "he said to me that he would say nothing but what his mother had written to him. It was clear to see from his whole manner that he was not unprejudiced."

Harriet apparently told him he wouldn't be held financially responsible if he identified his sister and that she could remain at Castle Seeon, although it seems unlikely he believed this.

While Harriet drove Felix to the inn at Wasserburg and hid in some nearby bushes, Franziska passed through the hall at Seeon and nodded automatically at a young man lingering by the door before stepping out into the sunshine. Soon it would all be over.

In the Biergarten of the inn, Felix waited with Dr. Voller, Harriet's lawyer. People were coming along the path. Felix knew her at once. Thinner, older, expensively dressed and surrounded by strangers, she was still his Franziska. The old man touched her elbow. A woman whispered in her ear. Felix rose.

"Do you recognize her, Herr Schanzkowsky?" the duke asked.

"That is my sister, Franziska."

The duke stammered "Go and talk to your brother."

"She told an aunt of mine who'd come along, 'I don't want to see him, I don't want to talk to him'," Irina Lomasey recalled. "'Go and talk to him', my aunt said and she did. They went for a walk together and how alike they looked from the back, my aunt said."

Franziska and Felix would remember this time for the rest of their lives. Walking alone, together, but not touching. So close once, and here they were in a beer garden in Bavaria, just out of earshot of Russians who thought she was the Grand Duchess Anastasia. It was the last real conversation Franziska would ever have, the last time she told the truth to anyone.

And then? We only know what Waltraud says, that Franziska asked him not to identify her, that she didn't want to work in the fields or as a maid again. Felix agreed to lie.

Voller had already drawn up a statement for Felix in which he declared his recognition of his sister, but Felix refused to sign it. Strangely, it wasn't until the next day that he signed another statement. By then Franziska was safely back at Seeon. Felix must have spent the night at the inn.

"There exists a strong resemblance between my sister Franziska and the lady with whom I have been confronted, but my sister had no scars whatsoever. Also, plaster casts shown me do not correspond with my sister's feet. The manner of speech of Mrs. Tschaikovsky ... also does not correspond with my sister's, nor does her general manner of expressing herself, nor her voice. My sister's face always had a healthy expression and did not look so sick as Mrs. Tschaikovsky. My sister never had a wound on her arm. She could talk only Polish, Platt and good High German. My sister always had good teeth. During the days' [sic] consulting, I spoke with Mrs. v. Tschaikovsky repeatedly. There would be absolutely no doubt that Mrs. Tschaikovsky did not know who I was. From the expression on her face one could clearly see that she did not know me. My sister Franziska sent in 1920—my birthday card—14 days late. My sister wrote saying she had too much work to do. Personally I cannot imagine that my sister Franziska is still alive, because she was very attached to me and surely would have written to me.

"I am signing this with a clear conscience. [sgd.] Felix Schanzkowsky"

"Witnesses: Harriet Rathlef, Dr. Voller."

III

Later that month, Felix took time off work and went to Berlin, where he visited Fritz Lucke, the reporter who'd written the Schanzkowsky stories. While Felix was there he stole several protocols "where the child was mentioned."

It says something about Felix that the idea of his sister having an illegitimate child disturbed him. It was as if he had to rehabilitate the image of the "Polish vagabond."

Harriet should have realized that Felix would hardly have cared if he didn't believe that "Mrs. von Tschaikovsky" was his sister, but she forged ahead. There were so many other things to do.

IV

Until her death in the Thirties, Harriet would devote herself to the "little one" and her cause. She continued to work to refute the Schanzkowsky identity. Her friend Gertrud Spindler made fruitless attempts to locate the Tschaikovsky family and the child in Bucharest. Harriet took on the Wingenders, making a great fuss about Doris' 1500 marks. Pierre Gilliard became a villain, allegedly paid by the Grand Duke of Hesse to discredit "Anastasia" because of the story about the 1916 "peace mission."

The "opposition" remained adamant that "Anastasia" was Franziska. Gilliard had published an article against her in *L'Illustration*, noting that

Dr. Kastritsky, the dentist who had treated the imperial children said that Franziska's teeth differed from Anastasia's. Dr. Bischoff of the University of Lausanne did comparison tests using photographs of Franziska and the tsar's daughters. He firmly concluded that Franziska did not match the photos of Anastasia. Supporters would claim that Bischoff had been furnished with a photo of Olga rather than Anastasia, but Bischoff had measured the features of all the grand duchesses and felt equally sure that Franziska wasn't Olga, Tatiana, or Marie either. Harriet insisted that Bischoff had used too few photographs.

In May Harriet accompanied by a friend, Miss Grabisch, visited Clara Peuthert, who had moved to Hufelstrasse 22. The two arrived just as Clara came puffing up the stairs, lugging her shopping. She carried an odd wooden contraption, which divided the food into compartments. Potatoes here, butter there. The fourth floor walk-up was tidy, with even a few pieces of good furniture.

"You are Harriet Rathlef!"

Harriet denied that she was Harriet as Clara put her groceries away.

"So you're not Harriet Rathlef. Fine, then."

Miss Grabisch handed over thirty marks from an "English friend" who wanted to thank the good Miss Peuthert for looking after the grand duchess. Clara pocketed the money. So they wanted to know about the grand duchess?

"The grand duchess is a liar and a swindler," Clara announced.

"What did the little one do while you were out selling newspapers?" Harriet asked.

"This I could prove to you right away. She studied to be a grand duchess," Clara laughed, producing a practice sheet of Russian and German characters in Franziska's hand. "The grand duchess is a swindler. She is no grand duchess! Her mother recognized her!"

Mrs. Wingender was the next subject of investigation. It was slaughter time and Mrs. Wingender was helping out at the home of her daughter, Mrs. Wypyrsqock. Not a nice scene: the small place was filled with the mess of sausage making, said Karl Siebert, the detective sent by Harriet. Even the beds were dirty. You couldn't get further away from a castle than this.

Franziska's shoe size, teeth, and scars were discussed, dates argued about as the women dashed back and forth, rinsing entrails, stirring the pot of blood for the *Wurst*, wiping the table, in a steamy kitchen filled with the smell of blood. It was a scene Franziska would have been familiar with, a scene not ideal for pondered, careful falsehoods.

Mrs. Wingender told Siebert about the jewelry she had bought from Franziska, and the trip to the offices of the *Red Banner* to denounce the Kleists. The stolen "AR" panties.

"But she wasn't a bad sort, our Franziska. Brought us potatoes from the country, apples too. Pious, you know? Didn't go to church much, but I still have the rose cross she gave me. And the *Nachtausgabe*? That was my story. Doris was too young, but we sent her."

"Disgusting surroundings," noted investigator Siebert. "Mother-in-law, maid and child slept in one room."

V

Is it any wonder Harriet consulted psychics that summer? In July Osten-Sacken sent her protocols of a seance in Konigsberg, followed by another which purported to give the name of the house in Bucharest where "Anastasia's" child could be found. He said the child had two brown spots on his lower back. He described the house and street in Berlin, where in mid-September 1920, the "Polish peasant Shantskowsky" was killed in a row with the pimp "Long Lulatch" who was now in Canada. She was buried as "unknown" in a graveyard at Predanze. This fantasy revealed one truth at least: everyone wanted the "Polish peasant" dead, if not turned into *Leberwurst* by a sex murderer, then done in by Mack the Knife.

The Grand Duke Andrei was apprised of these explorations but remained cautious: "To accept this material as a basis would be dangerous and undesirable..."

As elusive as this evidence was, it seems to have been the bright spot of the summer. A graphologist hired by Harriet said that there appeared to be more similarities between the handwriting of Franziska and Mrs. Tschaikovsky, than between the latter and the real Anastasia: " ... from a graphological point of view, many items tend to make it possible that the handwriting of Tschaikovski and Shantskovski might come from one hand ... "

VI

Felix had saved her and as soon as the ground felt solid under her feet again, another young man came forward to comfort her.

Gleb Botkin, the older brother of Tania, had left Vladivostok with his sister in 1919. Later he immigrated to the United States and settled in New York, where he earned a precarious living as a writer and illustrator.

Like his sister, Gleb had been enthralled by the imperial family and the golden world of Tsarskoe Selo. He also treasured the few memories he had of his days with the royal youngsters on board the *Standart*. Like Tania, he was haunted by an image of Anastasia laughing at the Botkin children as she hid behind a curtain, by her droll eyes that looked at you sideways.

It all went in a flash. The jumble of people who accompanied the Romanovs into exile at Tobolsk was crowded into the Kornilov House, recently appropriated from a prosperous merchant family. Across the street was the focus of all attention—the Governor's House, enforced residence of the Romanovs themselves. The occupants of the Kornilov House were divided between those who were allowed to visit across the street, and those who were not.

The Botkin children were "nots." Isa Buxhoeveden remembered that they "were not allowed into the Governor's House on the plea that they were not the Imperial Children's usual playfellows, as they had never been invited to the Palace, either at Tsarskoe Selo or at Livadia."

They spent a lot of time sitting on windowsills, Gleb would later say, hoping to catch a glimpse of the imperial family on the balcony, at a window, or exercising behind the tall fence which enclosed the garden of the Governor's House.

Dr. Botkin was just as enthralled. The tsarina's diary recorded his spending Christmas 1917 with the imperial family—and not across the street with Gleb and Tatiana, one notices. He told his children many stories about things said and done in the Governor's House, but their own exclusion must have been a disappointment. Did they resent being so thoroughly left out? It's hard to tell about the more cautious and observant Tania, but Gleb seems to have minded very much.

If Gleb couldn't cross the street, at least his animal drawings could. Dr. Botkin carried them over in his bag, with some secrecy, for the entertainment of the children.

The drawings are innocuous at first glance, but it is easy to imagine why Dr. Botkin was eager to conceal them from the guards. It would be interesting to know what the girls made of them. They illustrate a parallel universe, one also convulsed by civil war, where bears battle monkeys, and autocracy triumphs after considerable bloodshed. Misha, Gleb's protagonist (and, one suspects, alter ego), is a bear cadet who liberates his hometown from revolutionaries and berates his elders into upholding an absolute monarchy. In one of the leaves he strikes a monkey commissar bearing a remarkable resemblance to Kerensky with a riding crop. They are dark, surprisingly cynical tales, full of grit and anger at an ineffectual older generation.

VII

Gleb arrived at Seeon days before the Wasserburg confrontation. Franziska refused to see him but he glimpsed her, Rapunzel-like, gazing out of a window.

"Strangely symbolic were the surroundings in which I met the Grand Duchess Anastasia for the first time after her supposed death.

Castle Seeon was some thousand years old and had been a fortress of robber barons, a monastery, and a ducal palace ... it possessed one of those famous torture cages too small for the prisoner to either lie down or stand straight or sit in a natural position ... There were salons decorated with all the splendour of the First Empire ... The garden was overgrown with flowers and old lilac trees whose fragrant blossoms reached the second story windows ... "

It was a fitting place for Sleeping Beauty. Gleb came as a reporter for the *Herald Tribune*, but he also wanted to believe, as his sister had. When he saw the distracted way Franziska had nodded to him on the way to the Biergarten, he immediately recognized before him, miraculously alive, Her Imperial Highness the Grand Duchess Anastasia Nicholaevna of Russia.

Gleb had in fact come to hate most of the surviving Romanovs. His father had died for them and now they sought to deprive "Anastasia" of her rightful identity and fortune. Both he and Franziska would become anathema for the Romanovs, and both became increasingly eccentric as they aged. But in 1927 they were both still young; Franziska dressed in white, fitted with new dentures, Gleb with slicked back hair and a seductive *tres suidisante* look. And here they were in a castle in Bavaria. What could be more romantic? Gleb was smitten.

It's not certain how they actually met. One author said that Gleb came across Franziska in the garden. He just happened to have his old drawings with him, and how revealing it was that she could tell the difference between the drawings he had done in Russia and the ones he had drawn later. That the drawings were dated didn't seem to matter.

Gleb himself wrote that Franziska finally allowed him to be brought up to her room. Naturally she was in bed, covered up and clutching the same old hanky. She looked "tired and nervous" but Gleb saw in her "the adored little Princess of my childhood, the bewitching Anastasia."

Franziska was eager to please, but she refused to discuss the past. Even the words "Tsarskoe Selo" caused her to wince. "It would be criminal to ask her anything likely to stir up painful memories in her mind."

He later observed Franziska watching a storm: "Her finely carved features acquired an ephemeral quality in the weird glow of the almost uninterrupted lightning. And her blue eyes stared in the distance with an expression wherein profound sadness blended strangely with a sort of solemn joy. What thoughts, what emotions, did that magnificent display of nature's noble anger provoke in her? I wondered. What did she perceive in those heavy clouds? What messages did she hear in the thunder which scattered through the mountains in a thousand echoes?"

Franziska and Gleb only spent a few days together at Seeon; short enough for Gleb to remain enthralled, and for her to be on her best behavior. She had been awful before the confrontation with Felix, arguing with the duchess, slamming doors, flinging insults, and causing dissension in the usually easy-going household.

At this point she seems to have begun to draw Gleb in. It was a tactic she would develop over time, this recruitment of new allies. She opened by lodging outrageous allegations against her current patrons, making the new friend feel the recipient of her most secret confidences. Having learned what monsters the other supporters were, the new confidant had no qualms about working against them, feeding Franziska information, and helping her carry out plans they might oppose. Often there was the additional lure of some benefit down the road: perhaps the Romanov fortune or the memoirs that would answer all the questions and sell many copies.

"She has only two dresses and very little lingerie, all of it quite old," Gleb reported. "She mends every little hole and repairs her dresses over and over."

Actually, the Leuchtenbergs had been more than generous in this and many other respects: "Three dresses arrived from Munich, having been altered, and the Sick Lady has cast them ... entirely forth from her room, refusing to even look at them ... her dresses lie outside the door upon the ping pong table ... her new fur coat hangs in the cupboard," Faith Lavington wrote in her diary.

He would claim that the Leuchtenbergs failed to show enough "respect" for Franziska's "proud and sensitive nature." He claimed the duchess became more "respectful" when he gave her money and asked her to be kinder to Franziska, much as he might have bribed a negligent innkeeper.

Gleb was preparing the ground to get Franziska to the United States. He saw how unpopular she was becoming and knew that the duke had a gentleman's agreement with the Grand Duke of Hesse to turn "Anastasia" over to Knopf if witnesses definitely identified her as Franziska Schanzkowsky. Moreover, the police in Hesse-Darmstadt began to "exercise every effort to force on Anastasia the passport of the demented Franziska Schanzkowsky ... With such a passport, Anastasia could be locked up in an insane asylum for life because Franziska had been officially adjudged incurably insane."

Complicating this was the Romanov fortune, which the family supposedly did not want "Anastasia" to inherit. Yes, the money. There it was again. Gleb claimed that Franziska mentioned it first, saying that she didn't want it for herself, as she supplied him with the particulars. The account was in the name of a man with "not a Russian name, but a Germanic name—a very short name ... a one syllable name ... "

But it wouldn't matter soon, she reportedly said; once ten years had passed the money would be distributed to the legal heirs. Did she really say this? A deadline had never been mentioned before.

Like Harriet, Gleb now had a mission. But his mission did not involve Harriet and in fact ran at cross-purposes to her own. He wanted to restore "Anastasia's" rights himself, on his terms, in America.

She'd have lots of friends in America, he told Franziska.

It was the day before Gleb's departure. "I could find no words to express my feelings. I only kissed her hand and said, 'I am so happy to see you again' ... She gave me a long, eager look. I had the sensation that she was reading in my eyes all I wanted to tell her but did not know how to say. At last she parted her lips to say something, but instead suddenly began to sob. In a moment, however, she regained control of herself. 'It was all so dreadful', she whispered, as if apologizing for her tears."

Franziska performed brilliantly. Worried about Felix, exhausted from nerves, she knew exactly what to say and how to say it, how to hold out her hand, how to weep. Tears came easily. It was like a scene from a silent movie: the longing eyes, the weeping, the castle with the dark dungeons and the fragrant garden.

Gleb vowed to return, and to bring Franziska to America.

VIII

As summer wore on tourists flocked to Seeon to catch glimpses of "Anastasia." There were reports about her from the Soviet Embassy in Japan—she was the deranged Polish mistress of a soldier in Ekaterinburg who had taken her to Romania; there was interest from the Pope.

The Leuchtenbergs held a birthday dinner for her on Anastasia's birthday. Franziska was less pleased when the duke brought a hypnotist, Dr. Ostry, to Seeon. Dr Ostry tried, but could not hypnotize Franziska.

"I can't tell you if she is the daughter of the tsar or not," the duke said. "But so long as I have the feeling that a person who belongs to the tight circle of my society needs my help, I have a duty to give it."

Franziska was back to being difficult. Privately he noted that "She certainly has a bad character when she lets herself go."

Bad character or not, Franziska was taking piano lessons from Vera von Klemenz. Klemenz started Franziska on the beginner's book and thought that she had played the piano before. But it was difficult with her poor arm, and understandable when Franziska gave up the lessons.

Klemenz was reporting Franziska's effusions regularly to Harriet: "I am so happy when I have flowers in my room. At home we always had so many flowers … I have always been tremendously fond of perfumes, even when I was a child. My sisters were fond of perfumes too … "

And so on. Franziska tried her best, but people were still bothering her about those letters she had written. Apparently there was another one from Oberstdorf, asking someone to buy slippers for her. Osten-Sacken wanted to know if she had written the letters herself. Zahle said it was "important" to find out.

They consulted Agnes Wasserschleben, who protested that "She couldn't possibly have written letters, she could only after much practice copy words that one wrote for her ... When she hasn't practised, she can hardly manage to sign her own name. For instance, at Trautstein where she had to sign for a Bavarian visa for Seeon, one had to copy out her name, which took a lot of effort on her part to copy it."

Osten-Sacken and Zahle still plainly had their suspicions.

IX

In the meanwhile, Gleb was working on her behalf. He had hurried to Berlin to meet "that prostitute" Doris Wingender in a cafe, where he gallantly stole the *Nachtausgabe* contract from her purse. Anything to help.

"['Anastasia's'] innocent martyrdom had hardly been surpassed—nor often equalled—in the long annals of human suffering," he wrote.

He had an audience in the States. The Twenties were a snobbish era. More than one debutante had traded her father's money for a lordly marriage and a title; thriftier socialites concocted new genealogies. Jacqueline Bouvier Kennedy's family, for instance, promoted humble ancestors to the French aristocracy.

Gleb, poor and struggling, was soon visiting with a Romanov princess, Xenia, who had heard about Franziska from Margharita Derfelden, the widow of the head of the dowager empress' guard detachment.

He became a frequent visitor at Xenia's estate in Oyster Bay, Long Island. Xenia, a daughter of the Grand Duke George and a great-granddaughter of Nicholas I, was Anastasia's second cousin and an occasional playmate. Xenia herself had left Russia in 1914, just before the war broke out. At eighteen she married William Leeds, the son of industrialist William B. Leeds. While many Romanovs struggled in Europe, Xenia lived in luxury. Gleb was persuasive; Xenia agreed to invite Franziska to live with her, so that the family matter could be settled with a minimum of fuss and publicity.

He was jubilant: "I had at last found at least one member—other than the Grand Duchess Anastasia—of the Russian Imperial Family whom I could respect, trust and faithfully serve ... in truth how wonderful and moving it would be, I mused, to have these two lovely princesses, Anastasia, 'the Little One', and 'Little Xenia'—together defying the hosts of their bitter enemies."

X

At Seeon, people felt sorry for Xenia, who clearly didn't know what was coming. Perhaps she heard the rumors. Months of wrangling and indecision followed Xenia's initial agreement.

America! Franziska expressed fear and resentment: "Why must I go away from Europe ... because my family will not give me just a little to live on in some tiny corner," she cried.

She was furious at Gleb, who was already writing about her in the New York papers, but what could she do? She knew she wouldn't be welcome much longer at Seeon. The duke was ill, beginning to suffer from brain cancer. The family would not want her around once he was gone.

Another significant witness was on the way. Felix Dassel, a former captain in the 9th Kazan Dragoons who had been wounded in the leg in 1917 and found himself a patient at the little hospital associated with Anastasia and Marie at Tsarskoe Selo.

Dassel and a friend, Mr. Bornemann, turned up at Seeon in September. Dassel wrote down his memories of the hospital, which the duke dramatically locked up in his safe. He admitted hearing about

Franziska in 1922 but said he'd been unconvinced at the time, feeling that the story was a fantasy, a trip to "Utopia."

Naturally Franziska refused to see him, although Dassel heard her voice, shrill and angry, through an open window. It was not a voice he knew. She was still upset about the confrontation with Doris Wingender, her ladies told him nervously. She didn't want to see anyone, and certainly not Dassel, a Russian from "over there." She knew who he was, having been shown photos of him at "her" hospital.

The duke declared that Franziska was "probably" Anastasia, but seemed as anxious and frightened of her as the fluttering ladies were. He had managed to talk Franziska into receiving the visitors, however.

It was all very dramatic: "Why didn't I die with all my dear ones? I would have been spared the suffering, the agony I feel now … I was a child there and so proud of our hospital. And now—alone, ill, and I have nothing—no bed, and now I can't see anything because I see almost nothing when I am upset … Everything dances before my eyes …"

Franziska was steadier when she met him the next day. He deliberately fed her misinformation about the hospital; she corrected him. Miss Baumgarten became the messenger, passing on notes and further details. The clincher came when Franziska identified a photo of Colonel Sergeyev, whom the Grand Duchesses had nicknamed "the man with the pockets," because he had defied protocol by speaking to them with his hands in his pockets.

Bingo! Only the genuine grand duchess could have known that, Dassel said. The real recognition came, he said, when he looked into her eyes: "Now I look at her, look at her, look and search … with closed eyes, I return to the past. Very plainly, I see Marie, I see Anastasia … I am lying in bed … then come the laughing eyes of the little Princess … And now quickly back to reality, to the person opposite me, the unknown, wounded woman. I stare at her and see exactly the same eyes, laughing and childlike once, now nervous and haunted … Now I know! … the eyes of the Tsar! Yes, his eyes! Hasn't anyone noticed that her eyes are the eyes of the dead Emperor? Very unforgettable, and her nose reminded me of her father's too …I don't understand myself …why didn't I recognize her at once?"

Dassel's recognition would be touted for years. In fact, Dassel had been a visitor at the Kleists' when Franziska lived there. She had stayed in her room, but both Dassel and Gerda von Kleist admitted he had visited quite frequently. Franziska had heard all about "the man with the pockets" and the rest of it from the Kleists.

Dassel may have had a political motivation to recognize "Anastasia" as well. He was at Seeon on the behalf of the Jungdeutsche Orden, a paramilitary, pro-Hitler, anti-Semitic, and anti-Bolshevik group of 500,000 members. Many of them backed "Anastasia," believing that she could play a role in the fight against communism. "I am very glad to have an ally like the Jungdeutsche Orden," the duke wrote Harriet soon after.

Before Dassel and Bornemann left Seeon, Franziska asked Bornemann if he could get her a passport in a name other than Tschaikovsky. "She seems to hate this name," her visitors noted.

The name must have been a burden, so close to the despised "Schanzkowsky." Many of her supporters would add a "von" to it, perhaps feeling that it wasn't enough of a name for "Anastasia" to shelter under. It might even be that Franziska was planning some sort of a new identity, an escape, if things got as bad as it seemed they might. Nevertheless, she rose at six in the morning to bid farewell to her new supporters. Dassel would return later in the fall to take her on drives in the countryside.

This must have been before his articles ran in the *Tagliche Rundschau* at the end of October. He couldn't have visited Franziska after that because he was in jail. He was arrested for embezzlement the very week his series appeared.

Franziska's mood swung after he left. She accused Miss Baumgarten, her faithful messenger during the visit, of trying to poison her. Miss Lavington took over and reluctantly began to give Franziska English lessons. Out came the nursery rhyme books. Franziska, an excellent mimic, repeated phrases by rote. Lavington, unaware of the

Lugano English lessons, soon claimed Franziska knew English and could speak it if she chose. The operative words were "if she chose." The idea was that "Anastasia" was refusing to speak English much as she refused to speak Russian. Why she would balk at using English was another question, one that seems to have gone unasked.

Eventually Franziska would speak English more or less fluently, with a strong Slavic accent and a peculiar syntax which sometimes made her difficult to follow. Was this really the language of a woman who had spoken English since earliest childhood? It would later be admitted that Franziska's English was not the English one would expect to hear from a Romanov, particularly one trained by by the grand duchesses' expert tutor, Sydney Gibbes.

Did Miss Lavington really believe she was instructing "Anastasia"? Although she would later testify to her belief in the claimant, her diary contains hints that suggest her feelings at the time were rather ambiguous. Later much would be made of a suggestion there that Franziska was "laughing up her sleeve" at her supporters at Seeon.

Perhaps the knowledge that she would soon be gone from Seeon allowed Franziska to really let herself go. After Dassel's second visit she fell into moods that Lavington described as "straight from Dante's purgatory." Tensions were building.

The opposition wanted to have Franziska jailed for impostiture. The duke had so far been successful in keeping Franziska out of the hands of the Bavarian police, but who knew how long that would last? The Grand Duke of Hesse would soon start legal action against newspapers which claimed he had paid for the unmasking by funding Knopf.

"I should tell you of my deep conviction that certain people in Europe are bent on destroying her," the Grand Duke Andrei wrote to Serge Botkin in December. "The motive of [the opposition] remains unclear to me. In what way does the patient actually represent a danger to them? ... All this reminds me of the famous Kaspar Hauser case; everything is secret and unclear."

Now the police wanted Franziska brought to Berlin for interrogation. It was time to hustle her out of Europe altogether.

XI

Franziska's departure from Europe in January 1928 was a frantic flight to escape the police interrogations in Berlin. The logic behind it was rather curious: if her supporters really believed in her, why run away from the controversy?

Why, as Gilliard pointed out, did Leuchtenberg and Andrei not confront her with her mother and former workmates? Had they really believed, they should have been happy to finally refute the "Shantkovski myth" themselves. It might have been a bit undignified to be inspected by brewery workers, but what was dignified about skipping town with the police at her heels? The answer may have had more to do with her supporters' fear of Franziska's reaction than with the certainty of their belief.

As it was they hustled her out of Germany as soon as the American consul issued a six-month visa for Franziska under the name of Anastasia von Tschaikovsky, with the proviso that Princess Xenia and her husband would be responsible for her support while she was in the country.

Xenia was on a Caribbean cruise at the time but quickly sent her daughter's governess, Agnes Gallagher, to escort Franziska to the *Berengaria*, where first class tickets waited for "Miss Gallagher and niece." Franziska was ready to leave as soon as Miss Gallagher arrived. Her behavior had become unbearable for her hosts. She ate Christmas dinner with the family, but accused them of planting the silver wishbone in her food. She refused to see Dr. Nobel of Stillachhaus, suspected Miss Lavington of nefarious deeds, and wanted nothing more to do with Felix Dassel. The rages her panic produced were running out of control; the Sick Lady had become a madwoman.

Franziska and Miss Gallagher, accompanied by the duke, left Seeon early in the morning of January 29. Miss Lavington was up to say goodbye to Agnes Gallagher, but not, apparently to Franziska. Duchess Catherine, the mother of Irina Lomasey, had come to believe that Franziska was a bearer of the evil eye, and made a point of staring her down from an upper story window in order to counteract any malignant spell she might cast: "If you curse my husband, my child, or this my household, then may this curse return upon you forever." Miss Lavington herself noted that "It was very curious that the Sick Lady looked earnestly up at our windows when going—was she mentally saying goodbye? or was she surprised not to see the windows lined with attentive spectators, we shall never know. Anyhow, she is gone, and I sincerely hope she will be a happier woman in America."

Before boarding the train in Munich, Franziska bought a new all-white wardrobe and picked up the visa from the United States consulate. It might be that Prince Waldemar and Zahle contributed toward the new clothes while Xenia paid for her passage.

Franziska and her entourage arrived in Paris on the 30th and checked into the Hotel du Paris with great secrecy. The Grand Duke Andrei was waiting to finally see the woman he was convinced was Anastasia. He was determined that none of the Romanovs or former courtiers living in Paris would get a chance to meet Franziska, which suited her plans as well.

The duke had to beg her to even see Andrei. Later that day, it was the expected scene: Franziska in bed, lower face covered. The stakes were high and she wept. Andrei gazed at her for a few minutes and then ran out of the room. "I have seen Nicky's daughter, I have seen Nicky's daughter!"

He would eventually write that he "was even more struck by the general family resemblance which is some respects is of almost more importance than a personal likeness."

What does this mean? Is he hinting that he did not really think Franziska looked like Anastasia? He had been troubled by the photograph of Franziska Schanzkowsky and by the evidence of Doris

Wingender. He followed Harriet's line and disputed the various plaster casts and photo comparisons produced by the opposition, but seems to have been most encouraged by Felix' denial at Wasserburg. Still, that disturbing photograph remained, as did the mystery of the missing three days. Was that why he was afraid to let other knowledgeable witnesses see her in Paris? Or did Andrei attach so much importance to the emergence of a Kaspar Hauser-like Anastasia that he was taking no chances with relatives who might be involved in a secret dynastic plot?

Princess Lili Obolensky, a lady-in-waiting of Alexandra's, did try to see "Anastasia," but was told she was too tired to receive visitors. Franziska claimed the princess had been disloyal to the imperial family.

Before leaving, Franziska convinced Miss Gallagher that she could speak French by ordering breakfast in the hotel restaurant, and left some change behind, for good measure. Franziska had ordered breakfast many times in the polyglot Leuchtenberg household, so this wasn't much of a challenge.

Franziska did get to meet another princess before she left Paris. The ballerina Mathilde Kschessinska had been Nicholas' mistress before his engagement to Alexandra. Since married to Andrei, she ran a ballet school and supported herself, Andrei, and their son, Vova. Mathilde and Andrei accompanied Franziska and party to Cherbourg the next day and presented Franziska with a potted plant. Franziska was pleased, as Anastasia would not have been. Mathilde had been anathema to both Alexandra and the dowager empress. It is unlikely that the real Anastasia would have received her father's ex-mistress. Mathilde said Franziska had the tsar's eyes.

XII

Finally the duke, Miss Gallagher, and Franziska rode to Cherbourg. It was the moment of leave-taking. Franziska whispered to herself in German, "I'm so afraid, I'm afraid."

The duke wept on board the *Berengaria*.

"All this is the fault of Harriet von Rathlef," Franziska said before she went to her cabin.

She was leaving Harriet and the Anthroposophists, right-wingers, and assorted monarchists behind in Europe, striking out alone in a strange country, but the faithful Harriet would continue to work on the "little one's" behalf.

Chapter Eleven

I

Franziska went to her cabin and stayed there. Her ship had begun life as the *Imperator*, the kaiser's favorite liner and the pride of the German merchant marine. Seized as a prize by the Allies after the war, she had been bought and renovated by Cunard. Fitted out with vast domed skylights, potted palms, and what looked to be miles of marble, gilded tracery, and molded plaster, she was the flagship of the line in one of the great eras of transatlantic travel.

The cold, wild waters of early February might explain why last minute passage was so readily booked on her. All that finery meant that the *Berengaria* had a tendency to "hang on the roll;" the weight of her upper decks made her slow to right herself in heavy seas. Passengers with more options had stayed away.

War and poverty would have made a crossing on the *Imperator* an unattainable dream for Franziska, but if she had somehow managed it, she would have ridden out the storms as a third class passenger in the bowels of the ship, perhaps muttering a mild oath as she rolled back and forth on a narrow metal bunk in a cabin full of shipmates she had come to loath.

As it was, she stayed sealed up in her gilded box of a stateroom, attended by Miss Gallagher and a discreet Cunard steward. Her voyage was only one leg of an odyssey which began with Franziska literally one move ahead of the police. Now she was safely aboard, but her fear of strangers and "imperial dignity" effectively prevented her from enjoying the amenities of the ship. The Palm Court, domed dance floor, and Pompeian Baths went unexplored.

She was also being watched day and night by Miss Gallagher. Franziska had evidently learned a lot from the lessons in Lugano, from Miss

Lavington, and from Castle Seeon in general. She impressed Miss Gallagher, who later remembered her telling stories about the perils of her life as "Anastasia;" a Russian doctor who deliberately used a dirty needle on her, and a box of chocolates which she implied had been poisoned by some unnamed enemy. Money was on her mind; she mentioned forty million roubles in a tsarist bank account she meant to recover, but only for the sake of her missing child.

While Franziska's ship pitched and rolled across the Atlantic, the Grand Duchess Tatiana spoke in "perfect Russian" at a seance in the home of Dorothy Caruso, widow of the tenor: "We are all here. We send you our love and kiss you ... " there was a sound of someone blowing a kiss. "Anastasia wants you to know the person who is on her way to America is not she. You must tell Aunt Xenia this."

Those on the earth plane worried about Franziska too. On February 4, Andrei wrote Olga to inform her that he had recognized "Nicky's daughter" and to lament that Olga had not. "What thoughts are going to haunt her in that distant country? God alone knows, but they will be terrible ... "

II

Fog prevented the *Berengaria* from docking. Gleb Botkin, accompanied by thirty fellow reporters and a Mr. Foley, agent to the composer Sergei Rachmaninoff, hired a cutter to go out to the befogged ship. Once aboard, Gleb went directly to Franziska's cabin, leaving his restive colleagues behind. Gleb beamed at Franziska in her new, "quite becoming" dress. The steward had already trundled off her trunks, but the arrival of two agitated men must have made the cabin suddenly feel crowded; stale too, from all the meals eaten and uncomfortable hours spent there.

The other reporters jostled and yelled in the passageway. What was this? Gleb expressed horror at the bumptious enthusiasm attending Franziska's arrival in New York, but it is hard to see who else had the precise knowledge of her sailing and the motivation to tip off the press. Stirring up a fuss meant his exclusive story would get much wider play. Under his indignation is a sense of excitement at being an insider, one who can pass through locked doors and close them behind him.

Franziska could hear the reporters outside her door, wanting to see her face. A reporter or two had shown up at Stillachhaus and Seeon, but that had been nothing like this. She hesitated.

"Your Imperial Highness!" Gleb bent over the hand of his "grand duchess."

III

The immigration service extended preferential treatment to Franziska, rubber-stamping her papers in the privacy of her stateroom. The fog held, and the reporters sailed off to file stories ("Lost Daughter of the Tsar Hides on Ship in Bay"). Gleb and Foley bunked down in cabins lent them by the captain.

In the morning, Gleb conducted Franziska down the gangway. Fifty reporters were waiting when she finally made an appearance, trembling and silent, wide-brimmed hat set low, face hidden in the collar of her full-length fur coat. Flashbulbs exploded. Some observers yelled impertinent questions: "Are you a grand duchess or a fake?"

Gleb stayed at her side as she climbed into the car that would take her to 48 Park Avenue, the residence of Annie Burr Jennings.

IV

Annie Burr Jennings would play an important role in Franziska's conquest of New York, serving as her hostess during much of her stay. Born in San Francisco in 1855, her father was Oliver Burr Jennings, an early director of Standard Oil. Gleb would remember her gift for telling a story couched in the "picturesque and juicy speech of an old New Yorker." Never married, she owned an apartment on Park Avenue and the Sunnie Holm estate near Fairfield, Connecticut, where she maintained a staff of over forty. The house servants wore livery. Thirty gardeners tended the grounds, which were often open to the public.

She enjoyed a good joke but looked self-consciously regal in an eighteenth century gown worn at a fancy dress party. That was the crux of her uniquely American dilemma; she was eager to demonstrate her kinship with Aaron Burr, and equally eager to dress up as Marie Antoinette. Franziska would come to refer to Annie Burr Jennings as a "peasant." Gleb described her as an "elderly lady typical of her kind."

V

Franziska carried herself with aplomb and appropriate mystery, at first only answering questions through Miss Gallagher. Asked how she had enjoyed passage on the *Berengaria*, she replied that it was a clean ship, but not nearly as nice as the *Standart*. The weather, she admitted, had been a bit rough.

In the weeks that followed, Miss Jennings' many friends and relatives came to the apartment to have a look at the "grand duchess." It was Nettelbeckplatz all over again, with the difference that many of the Americans believed at once. Millionaires and socialites bowed and curtseyed, sometimes kneeling to kiss her outstretched hand: "Your Imperial Majesty!"

Mrs. Derfelden was convinced by Franziska's superior "carriage" and sobbed as she kissed her hand: "Your Imperial Highness!"

Franziska managed to remain on her best behavior. This move to New York had been her plan, her deal with the fates. It was she who had convinced Gleb, and encouraged him to set it up. If she had left it all to Harriet and the duke as they had wished, where would she be now? In jail? In Hygendorf? The rages and suspicions had been left behind with the Bavarian police and the Detective Knopf.

Here she had a large, bright room of her own, filled with flowers and objets d'art. When she wasn't resting or receiving worshippers she was following Miss Jennings on a circuit of cocktail parties, dinners and dances. She visited a Broadway movie house with Gleb, and enjoyed a nocturnal tour of Times Square. Like many Europeans, she was amazed by the abundance and informality of American dime stores. Rumors circulated that Franziska would marry a rich bachelor, perhaps Miss Jennings' nephew, Oliver.

An odd thing was happening. The Franziska Gleb would describe was quite different from the "little one" Harriet had carefully cultivated. Gleb's "Anastasia" is more playful, more daring. The words he puts in her mouth show a certain bravado, a boastfulness. He was quick to note that Anastasia wasn't always a nice little girl, that she could be obnoxious and cruel too.

According the Gleb, her memory was "amazing." The problem was that she resented being questioned and "often gave nonsensical and untruthful answers" or refused to speak Russian purely out of spite. He spoke of adherents like Harriet who "totally misrepresented" her as a "paragon of all virtues and a most truthful person" in order to "provoke more sympathy" and to explain her inconsistencies. As it was, Harriet's child of nature seems to have really taken to Manhattan.

Gleb was often there. He had made a point of denouncing Franziska Schanzkowsky in order to contrast her with the enchanting "Anastasia" in her costumes of white silk and whispery chiffon. A little flirting; it was easy for Franziska. Gleb simply believed, and found his "grand duchess" beyond ordinary standards of conduct. Unlike most of Miss Jennings' friends, he was her own age, and did not treat her like a backward child. For all his deference, there was a bit of a rogue about him. He was impetuous, not above lying or rifling a woman's purse if it furthered the cause. For Franziska Gleb's devotion must have drawn her a step deeper into the waking dream, a step away from her secret self.

Gleb neglected his wife and five children to spend time with "Anastasia": duty calling. When he and Franziska went to the movies, he gazed at her profile in the dark. Franziska splashed perfume on him, Gleb wrote, and graciously asked him to simply call her Anastasia, not Imperial Highness. She invited him for dinner and did not ask Miss Jennings' permission. She boasted that she told Miss Jennings that the *Mona Lisa* in her apartment was a fake. She had climbed up on a chair to inspect the picture for herself: "I have a flair. I can always tell a copy from the original."

They were both fascinated by royal gossip. Franziska had lived among people who were obsessed with it, and had learned a great deal. They spoke in German, which must have been a relief. She was picking up English quickly, but it was still a struggle.

She begged him to stay true even when she turned on him, Gleb said.

They quickly had a disagreement.

VI

Gleb wanted her to meet the composer Sergey Rachmaninoff, who had provided logistical support and now wished to see the enigma for himself. Franziska balked, Gleb persisted. He was aware of trouble brewing beyond the sanctuary of Miss Jennings' apartment. The press was not overwhelmingly receptive to Franziska's claim. There was even some suggestion that after the initial excitement skepticism was gaining ground. Miss Jennings and her friends were oblivious to the doubters, but there was no guarantee that their interest would last.

The Grand Duke of Hesse had issued a denunciation and the Russians who had settled in New York were generally unfriendly, some accusing Franziska's friends of hiding her from competent witnesses. Gleb himself claimed to be "extremely eager to have her receive the people who wanted to see her," particularly if their endorsement lent prestige and financial support to the cause.

Franziska's objection was that Rachmaninoff was in some abstract way a traitor to his emperor, a charge she could conveniently extend to almost any Russian over the age of ten. Gleb pressed; she grumbled but gave in. Rachmaninoff was widely known as a contributor to Russian charities. His support could mean a lot.

The composer turned up at the appointed hour. Franziska was up and apparently dressed when his arrival was announced by the "well-nigh desperate" Gleb. When he came back with Rachmaninoff he found that "in the intervening minutes [Franziska] had lain down on her bed and covered herself up to her nose in blankets," gazing up at them with "eyes full of tears."

Rachmaninoff had never actually seen the real Anastasia, but Franziska seems not to have known this. "All three of us froze in utter embarrassment ... After a few minutes of unendurable silence Rachmaninoff tip-toed out of the room."

Franziska's ghost-written autobiography would say that "I happened to be not very well and was in bed. When I saw that Miss Jennings had come with him, I simply could not talk to him; he only stayed for a few minutes. He was certainly disappointed, and Gleb was even more so." The pall of that awful scene seems to hang over the evasions.

Although Gleb says that Rachmaninoff "accepted the whole incident in a most charitable spirit," he remained unsure of Franziska, even while eventually contributing $250 a month toward her expenses.

VII

In photos Xenia's face is clear, pale oval, somewhat inscrutable under a cloche hat. Her parents had been estranged, and Xenia and her sister Nina spent the war years with their mother in England. She had loved her father, an amiable man who had done his best to pull his cousin Nicky out of the deadly spiral of 1917, and then tried desperately to rejoin his family abroad. He was executed along with three other grand dukes on January 28, 1919, in the courtyard of Shpalernaia Prison in St. Petersburg.

Xenia was still a teenager when she married William Leeds and became the wife of an heir to a vast fortune. Perhaps this was the element which set her apart from her relatives and made her susceptible to Gleb's advance work. She had experienced so much grief, yet had so little experience of life. Her losses were great, but the terror, uncertainty, and poverty of revolutionary Russia were shocking stories, and not something that had to be lived through and learned from.

At long last, Xenia returned from her cruise and went to Park Avenue to see the mysterious stranger who might be her kinswoman. Gleb found positive evidence in the fact that Franziska did not "retire to the sanctum of her bed and cover herself up to her nose in blankets" when confronted with Xenia, but it seems clear that he kept the visit a secret until the last moment, perhaps to cut off Franziska's lines of retreat.

Annie Burr Jennings' drawing room was full and Franziska seemed to be holding court. Xenia watched from the doorway and saw a small woman with a large mouth said to be disfigured by rifle blows, her dark hair loosely fixed in an old-fashioned bun. High heels, white dress … up rose the arm, wrist gently bent, fingertips suspended in the air, slightly drooping … the impersonal smile, the slight nod of acknowledgement as Franziska accepted homage.

Xenia was impressed by her manner, much as Tania Botkin had been. Both women were agitated when introduced. Little was said, but she and Franziska kissed on parting. It had been a remarkable success, although Franziska later told Gleb that she could not read Xenia's dark eyes.

VIII

Franziska soon moved to Kenwood, the Leeds' fifty-three acre compound at Oyster Bay, Long Island. This transfer seems to have taken place in early March. She had a suite of rooms there, diligent servants, and plenty of privacy. Kenwood contained a stable, tennis court, and a private beach along a stretch of coastline studded with replica Italian villas, French chateaux, georgian manors, and medieval castles.

The Long Island afternoons may have seemed as long and golden as those legendary summer days in the Crimea, but this too was illusory. In less than two years Black Monday would hit and for many, Long Island would be a short, vivid party which ended badly. In 1928 though, Seeon must have seemed musty and far away, a place which could be safely forgotten.

At first all went well. Mrs. Derfelden was an attentive lady-in-waiting. Xenia brought Franziska two small parrots from the Caribbean. It was true that Xenia didn't recognize her cousin "visually," but she was impressed by the way her guest simply seemed to be Anastasia, without discernible acting. They spoke English together. Xenia made a lot of promises. Had Franziska, older, more experienced, and purportedly senior in rank, gotten the upper hand? Xenia promised to take "Anastasia" to Denmark herself, and to personally usher her into the presence of "Grandmamma." She also promised that no other Romanovs would visit while Franziska was at Kenwood, although why "Anastasia" chose to shun close relatives was puzzling. Even Xenia's sister Nina only saw Franziska once or twice, and briefly at that. Gleb himself soon disappeared from the scene—had Franziska tired of him?

Franziska said a few Russian words to her birds while Xenia was listening, convincing Xenia that she knew Russian but preferred not to speak it. Xenia, haunted by her father's death, understood. Franziska seems to have sensed this and played on it.

When Xenia began to tell her of her own experiences at the beginning of 1920 Franziska became "horribly upset" and said "to think all of you led such happy lives then. Do you know what I was doing in 1920?" She described how she and Tschaikovsky "had to cross every frontier unobserved by the authorities, and to do so were often forced to walk for miles through uninhabited regions. All of that in the middle of winter and with Anastasia barely able to stand on her feet. One story she told me about roaming in a forest with hungry wolves howling on all sides, really made my hair stand on end. It is hardly possible to imagine what she has suffered—poor thing."

Seeing Xenia's little daughter Nancy wearing a sailor suit made Franziska weep because the outfit reminded her of Alexei. "Please," she begged, "don't dress her like that."

When Franziska saw strange young men playing tennis, she opened the window and heard Russian. The faces looked familiar from photos and it didn't take much sleuthing—a word to a servant, a little question—to deduce that the tennis players were Romanovs. She was sobbing in her bed when Xenia walked into the room. At first Franziska refused to tell her what was wrong. Then, in anguish ... Xenia had broken her promise ... "Anastasia" had recognized the voices of her Romanov "cousins."

She also introduced red herrings; this time it was a missing green bracelet she'd still had when she arrived at Dalldorf. She'd written a letter in English to Princess Irene but a Russian man had come to Dalldorf and taken it away. Faced with Franziska, who "remembered" so much, and was so obviously traumatized by the family tragedy, Xenia believed. They had pitied Xenia at Seeon as one must pity her now, so generous, so unprepared for whom she was really dealing with.

The "two lovely princesses" might have gone on this way, but not everyone believed in "Anastasia" at Kenwood. William Leeds would come to refer to Franziska as a "scurrilous hoax." Gleb painted Leeds as a vulgar, tipsy denizen of Long Island. Others remembered him as a sportsman and a close friend of Edward, the Prince of Wales.

Although he initially seemed prepared to tolerate his wife's guest, his marriage would soon break up, and it was rumored that Franziska's presence had hastened the split.

"He did not like me and I did not like him," Franziska would later say. Actually she seems to have hated him, describing him as being "like a little dwarf, with brown eyes."

She made him out to be the Caligula of Long Island, hosting wild parties on his yacht with dancing girls and "thirty boys, with thirty boys, with thirty boys. Thirty. Thirty boys!"

Tensions were building at Kenwood. Xenia, aware that Franziska was not "normal," accepted her limitations and tended to indulge them, even or perhaps especially when Franziska became agitated and wild. Sometimes "memories" brought on screaming and pounding on walls: "I went through all that, and now they will not believe I am Anastasia!" Sometimes she ranted about the turncoat "relatives" she meant to execute once she had returned to Russia and wrested control from the Bolsheviks. Inevitably, she began to turn on Xenia, "quarreling" with her, as Gleb later put it. Xenia was drawn into the storm, and her husband quipped that he was "thinking of spreading nets on the treetops around the house to prevent our ladies from killing themselves when they start jumping out of windows."

The strain of being "Anastasia" twenty-four hours a day was beginning to tell. The "Shantkovski myth" had crossed the Atlantic. It seemed as if all of New York had read about "the poor, uneducated, tubercular and hysterical German-Polish girl with the plebeian name of Franziska Schanzkowsky" and the tsar's wealth Xenia was going to help her obtain. To make matters worse, a rather irreverent film loosely based on Franziska's case called *Clothes Make The Woman*, starring Eve Southern and Walter Pigeon, premiered on June 3.

The sisterly feeling between Franziska and Xenia had become strained. Xenia retreated from her volatile guest and was often away. Franziska would later remember feeling "deserted" and made peevish references to Xenia's absences ("I didn't see much of Xenia ... Xenia, so far as she showed herself at all ... Xenia, of whom I had recently seen little"). It was beginning to sound like Tania Botkin all over again: the initial confidences and hours spent cosseted in Franziska's room, engrossed in "memories." Eventually the new friend wearied of Franziska's intensity or simply had to get on with life and left her feeling rejected. Franziska, who had once gone for strolls along the beach, played with little Nancy, and taken occasional meals with the Leeds, was now largely secluded in her suite, often absorbed in truculent silences.

Franziska departed the Kenwood on August 8, six months after arriving in Long Island. She had nowhere else to go.

IX

How did this come about? The visa Franziska had obtained stipulated that Xenia support her for six months. That condition had been met, but surely Xenia hadn't automatically tossed her "cousin" out.

Xenia would be tight-lipped about the final rupture with "Anastasia," saying only that "there were so many lies ... and then someone mixed up all the cards." In her autobiography, Franziska stated that "On 8 August I left the house in Oyster Bay, though I had never thought of leaving it like this." Gleb's account of her last days at Kenwood revolves around a complicated tale of intrigue about the tsar's money and the introduction of a lawyer, Edward Huntington Fallows, into the action.

The theoretical fortune of the tsar was a fantasy that lay somewhere between discovering a sunken treasure ship and winning a lottery. Inside the drab exterior of a modern bank sat an undisturbed mountain of Russian gold. For the right person, uttering the right word to the clerk at the desk, the vault would spring open, revealing an ancient legacy instantly convertible into palladian mansions, diamond tiaras, and luxury motorcars.

Similar legends would attach themselves to the fortunes of the deposed monarchs of Romania and Yugoslavia after World War II. In one, Michael, the son of Karol II of Romania, went once, sometimes twice, a year to a particular Swiss bank to ask about his late father's special account. Each time he was politely asked for the code word; every time he tried a new one. He never managed to guess the correct word and was thus locked out of the account forever.

The hidden bank account was a boon for Franziska's supporters. It provided a facile answer to those who wondered why "Anastasia's" family refused to acknowledge her—they wanted all the money for themselves. It was said that Olga refused to accept her for this reason, and that the Grand Duchess Xenia had similar motives as the executrix of her brother's will. Beneath them seethed a mass of other Romanovs, relatively poor but accustomed to great wealth, who might benefit when the legendary vaults opened.

Franziska had talked about "the money" with the Kleists, and supposedly mentioned a "dowry fund" of five million roubles for each of the tsar's daughters (a total of 160 million in current U.S. dollars) to Zahle and her aunt Olga. The money was either in an English bank or in the Bank of England proper, and was controlled by someone with a short, Germanic name, a name that might also function as the password to the account. Perhaps the name was Peter Bark, she would later allow. He had been one of "Papa's" financial advisers. Zahle is said to have made some tentative inquiries, but no record of this was ever found in the archives of an English bank.

As we have seen, Franziska also told Agnes Gallagher of a sum of forty million roubles that was being held for her, perhaps in a separate account.

Decades of research into the tangled financial affairs of Nicholas II and his daughters have shed some light on these claims. According to a former minister, the daughters did have an English account codenamed OTMA in 1914, but this account had been one of the first to be repatriated and applied to the war effort. It had served as a reminder of the duty of patriotic Russians in time of war. The tsar demanded that the rest of his family follow suit, which partly explains their financial difficulties after the Revolution.

The amounts mentioned by Franziska were a problem too. Russian grand duchesses were furnished with impressive dowries, but one million roubles were nearer the mark. Recent estimates of the total prewar foreign investments of Nicholas, Alexandra, and their five children range between twelve and seventeen million roubles, a bit short of the twenty million allotted for the dowries, let alone the forty million mentioned to Miss Gallagher. To date, no accounts belonging to the Russian Imperial Family have ever been found in England, corroborating the denials of generations of bank directors.

The money in German banks was another matter. Russia's status as an enemy nation meant the tsar was unable to retrieve the substantial sums his family had invested in Germany. There was a catch to the German money, though. The funds sitting dormant in the vaults there had been decimated by the economic chaos of the postwar era and retained only a fraction of their original value.

The existence of the tsar's fortune had not particularly interested Franziska's European supporters. Zahle seems to have been satisfied to consider her knowledge of the account another piece of evidence in her favor. Franziska had likely heard the persistent stories of a lost Romanov fortune from the monarchists in Berlin. People often inflated the figures, wrongly assuming that since the tsar had been an autocrat, the vast gold reserves which backed the Russian economy had belonged to him personally. The phantom millions became another thing she was expected to discuss regretfully along with the "recollections" of Rasputin and Finnish cruises.

X

Gleb had been active in the meanwhile. He had continued giving interviews and writing about Franziska for the *New York Herald Tribune*, putting a good face on his exclusion from her life by saying that he was bowing out now that she had been "restored into her own circle." He had also been writing privately to the Grand Duke Andrei, who wanted fifty thousand dollars to take Franziska's case to court in Europe. "It will be impossible to avoid a litigation in court ... [she] will have to start court action in order to wash off herself the humiliating label of 'impostor' ... on this account I am corresponding with a prominent German attorney in Berlin, who after investigating the case, has arrived at the conclusion that it will be comparatively easy to win such a litigation."

Gleb felt that court action could be avoided if Xenia kept her promise to resolve the matter by taking Franziska to Denmark to be recognized by the dowager empress. Xenia was not hurrying to fulfill his expectations, however. It had been a rash promise; her aunts had no intention of allowing her to impose Franziska on their ailing, aggrieved mother.

Gleb consulted Edward Huntington Fallows in early June. Fallows was a corporate attorney with a flourishing practice in Manhattan. There was, according to Gleb, a Romanov cabal intent on depriving Franziska of her rightful inheritance. They were interested in more than just the secret bank account; against all dynastic logic, he swore that the Romanovs continued to reject "Anastasia" because their acknowledgement of her claims would automatically make her the head of the House of Romanov, and a cruel autocrat once the monarchy was re-established in Russia.

On July 12 he sent a Special Delivery letter to Franziska, urging her to begin the process of claiming the money supposedly sitting in the Bank of England before time ran out. Xenia apparently failed to pass the letter on to Franziska. Gleb would claim that this meant that Xenia was now a part of the plot to defraud "Anastasia," but Xenia said that she was only trying to avoid upsetting her sensitive guest.

Gleb's interference created tensions at Kenwood. Xenia had been quoted as saying that she would spend all the money necessary to secure Franziska's rights, and the media had mistakenly taken this to mean that she would help Franziska claim the money. Gleb had added to the furor by publishing a provocative article about the matter—he refused to say where this appeared, only that the editor had been reluctant to run it. The Leeds hadn't bargained on this sort of publicity when they took Franziska in, and were appalled. "We are not trying to get any fortune for her and we are not trying to prove she is the the Grand Duchess. No one is interested in that," William Leeds told a reporter.

Xenia wrote a careful letter to Gleb: "I am extremely apprehensive as to the advisability of the course you propose to take, for many reasons too long to write." She returned his letter to Franziska and said she would be "much obliged" if he would let her know when he could come to Oyster Bay to discuss their differences. Gleb responded by publishing an article claiming that the Grand Duchess Xenia coveted the secret bank account.

Nerves must have been frayed when Gleb turned up at Kenwood on July 22. His description of his meeting with the Leeds has the feel of bad film noir—a night scene at the Kenwood boathouse, with threats, tears, whiskey drinking, and villains who suddenly unburdened themselves in blocks of unwieldy exposition. He claimed that the Leeds conveyed an offer from the Grand Duchesses Xenia and Olga to support Franziska for life if she would renounce her claims and quietly return to Europe. The Leeds upped the ante by offering to return Franziska to Europe and support her themselves, if the first offer was for some reason unacceptable.

Xenia strenuously denied any talk of an offer from the grand duchesses, saying that her aunts were far too negative about Franziska to ever consider giving her money. She may well have offered Franziska a return passage to Europe, but it seems highly unlikely that the Leeds offered much more than that. Gleb himself admitted that "to be entirely fair to Princess Xenia is to state that she denies having ever offered to help Grand Duchess Anastasia in the latter's struggle for her rehabilitation; that she does not believe in the presence of a fortune in the Bank of England; that she had never told me that the Grand Duchess Xenia and Olga admit in private the fact of Anastasia's identity."

It seems that Gleb did actually make contact with Franziska on July 31, and that she agreed to become involved in the quest for the bank account. Gleb and Franziska were playing for time though, and obscuring her real intentions from the Leeds. Miss Jennings and Sergey Rachmaninoff, the only people Gleb knew who might support Franziska in suitable style, were both traveling in Europe. It was agreed that Franziska ought to try and string her stay out for another four months. The plan was a difficult one to implement; Franziska called Gleb the following day to report that she was unable to keep from quarreling. Hold on, Gleb counseled, but returned to Kenwood on the 6th for an "emergency" visit. The Leeds had finally laid down the law, perhaps aware of Franziska's delaying tactics and dreading months of further conflict.

Their obligations to her had been fulfilled. Franziska could return to Europe or go with Gleb as she wished, but she would have to make her decision in the following forty-eight hours. Europe meant Germany to Franziska, who lacked the necessary visas to go anywhere else. Germany meant the Berlin police. Franziska refused to return to Germany.

XI

Gleb and Fallows turned up on the 8th to remove Franziska from Kenwood. Franziska was ready, with her "meagre" belongings (birds, white dresses, furs, silver slippers, relics of the imperial court, etc.) packed. "All servants having disappeared as if by magic," Gleb carried her bags himself. Franziska would never see Xenia and William Leeds or Kenwood again. "She was leaving, penniless, the luxury of a millionaire's home, the protection of an Imperial Princess, and facing fearlessly an unknown future, because she could not, under any circumstances be untrue to herself or deny her identity."

Fallows' car, stuffed with Franziska's possessions, raced away. Franziska was in a strange mood. She urged Fallows to drive faster and faster, until they were stopped by a policeman and he had to talk his way out of a speeding ticket. They crossed into Queens and then took the Queensboro Bridge into the heart of Manhattan.

Chapter Twelve

I

Franziska's arrival in Manhattan seems to have been ill-prepared for. She was temporarily sequestered in the hot, dusty studio apartment of John R. Colter, a colleague of Gleb's. The following day would be eventful. Franziska signed papers assigning Edward Fallows her power of attorney, and made out a will with bequests for Gleb and his children. Collecting her signature had not been easy. Gleb and Franziska spoke German among themselves as Fallows and a notary waited. "Anastasia" first claimed that she did not know how to write her name in Roman characters, and then that she had forgotten how to spell the ending.

"What food for her enemies," Gleb thought as Franziska handed back the document signed "Anastasi." Gleb mumbled some "embarrassed explanations that the Grand Duchess was very nervous and for reasons unknown to me refused to complete her signature."

Her nervousness was genuine, born of a reluctance to produce evidence which could be used against her in a fraud trial. She lost no time in trying to steer Fallows to Romania, in search of her missing son.

Hetty Richards, a friend of Miss Jennings' who had been part of the original welcoming committee, stepped into the lurch, agreeing that it was unthinkable that "Anastasia" should have to tolerate the dog days of summer in Manhattan and offering to put her up in a suitable hotel for six weeks. They arranged for a Madame Schiveree, Hetty Richards' former French governess, to serve as Franziska's companion for the first two weeks of her stay. The following day Fallows drove her back out to Long Island, where she became a guest at the exclusive Garden City Hotel. At first things seemed to go smoothly enough. In order to avoid unwelcome attention, she was registered under a pseudonym,

185

one which would follow her for the rest of her life: Anna Anderson, or more formally, Mrs. Eugene Anderson.

The second element of Franziska's registration at the hotel is a bit surprising. Gleb introduced himself around as Anna's brother so that he could visit her in her rooms unchaperoned. He and Franziska apparently went to some lengths to maintain the ruse.

He would later write that "Anastasia and I were now forced to reverse the usual practice: in public we now found ourselves obligated to call each other by our first names, for otherwise nobody would have believed us to be brother and sister. More than that, we discovered that there were several Germans among the hotel's employees, which made it necessary for us, when talking in German, to address each other with the familiar 'thou' [*Du*] rather than the formal 'you' [*Sie*]."

It is astonishing that the normally cautious "grand duchess" would allow this. The subterfuge would have been interpreted as an admission that something illict was going on, and could have led to a hasty expulsion from the Garden City Hotel, perhaps after a humiliating interrogation by a hotel detective. Discovery would have also come as a boon to Franziska's opponents ("She was caught living with a married man who was calling himself her brother! Imagine!").

Elsewhere, Gleb goes out of his way to demonstrate his knowledge of Franziska's bedroom. There were two beds, one which Franziska lounged on during the day, and another which she occupied at night. There was a portrait of Louise of Prussia over one of the beds, and a radio thoughtfully provided by the Richards. It is clear that he spent a great deal of time there. Were they having an affair? Miss Jennings would claim to have seen a startlingly familiar note from Gleb to Franziska; she and Edward Fallows differed on many subjects, but they both seem to have been certain that Franziska and Gleb had been lovers at the Garden City Hotel. Interestingly, Gleb's wife never met Franziska, even though she lived only minutes away in Hempstead. In old age, Gleb would attribute the success of his forty-seven-year "idyllic" marriage to the fact that both he and his wife had been "free to love others."

The young Franziska had been strongly attracted to the sort of romance implicit in films with titles like *Tsar's Courtier* and *Waltz Dream*. Gleb may have fallen somewhat short of the ideal—he had no uniform, and Franziska was obsessed with uniforms—but he was handsome and doting, with a faint glow of the *Standart* still upon him. There must have been a core of sincerity to Gleb's effusions about the "bewitching Anastasia;" he was proud of their intimacy, and willing to devote himself single-mindedly to it.

Gleb spread a story, certainly false, that "Anastasia" had had access to a secret archive known only to the emperor's immediate family, and that this archive contained the answers to many of the mysteries of Russian history. Unsurprisingly, all the revelations tended to cast the Romanovs in a bad light or to undermine their legitimacy: "In other words, the present Romanovs have not a drop of the Romanov blood," and so on.

There was talk of death threats too. Early on there had been a rumor of one based on the account of a servant of a friend of Miss Jennings who had claimed to have overheard a menacing conversation between two men on the subway. Gleb felt himself in danger—"mysteriously threatened," whatever that meant. All the more reason to stay in Franziska's cool, secluded bedroom as the indolence of summer wore into fall.

Gleb had managed to interest an unspecified publisher in the possibility of bringing out "Anastasia's" memoirs. She was given a thousand dollar advance, and she and Gleb sporadically worked at producing a manuscript. It was a doomed effort as Franziska was the "dullest and most injudicious of authors," whose dictations were "void of any sentiment, indeed of any life," and who refused to submit to any kind of editing or ghostwriting. It seems doubtful that she ever really meant to present a written narrative her enemies could dissect at their leisure. Franziska had learned that it was possible to collect an advance without delivering a book, and that there were people who would be eager to help her write one. This was a lesson she would draw on soon.

Since Sergey Rachmaninoff had taken over the cost of Franziska's maintenance in mid-September, the flow of largesse ran unimpeded. She pleased her new friends by officially authorizing Edward Fallows to sue anyone making unlawful use of her name or image in motion pictures on September 24. This latest maneuver was probably in response to films being produced in Europe. A French one claimed she was a gangster's girlfriend. Striking closer to home was a German production, *Anastasia, The False Daughter of the Tsar*.

Miss Jennings returned from Europe and duly contributed a thousand dollars towards her expenses in early October. Franziska's difficulty writing doesn't seem to have prevented her from signing "Madame Anderson" to bills for her room and board, laundry charges, telephone calls, and room service. It is easy to imagine them eating these meals, Franziska peckishly, Gleb more enthusiastically. As they eat, classical music plays on the radio. Sometimes they make a game of guessing the names of the pieces. Franziska has a good ear, and Gleb is surprised at how often she guesses correctly.

Occasionally visitors turn up, mostly on legal errands. Their visits brought out a strange "mischievousness" which seemed designed to show Franziska's lack of respect for the proceedings and to keep Gleb on edge. She might make horrific grimaces behind the backs of her guests or say insulting things about them in German. "Seemingly restless, she would pace the carpet, shuffling her feet and then, while passing me, and unobserved by others, press her finger on the back of my neck, giving me a terrible electric shock."

A disquieting note was sounded on October 12, when Gilbert Kennedy, a British attorney hired to research the missing bank account, wrote Fallows to tell him that he could not find any evidence of the money Franziska claimed was in England. "We are not giving up, but it looks doubtful."

II

A drama was taking place far away. The following day "Grand-mamma" died after a long illness. Franziska seems to have met this loss with relative calm. It may have been a relief, a truly catastrophic confrontation forever averted. Gleb reports that Franziska had been "extremely depressed," although it would have been difficult to separate her reaction to the death from her response to what came next.

Twelve of the relatives who had gathered in Copenhagen for the funeral signed a document entitled the "Declaration of the Russian Imperial Family Concerning the Tschaikovsky Affair." There seems to have been two documents, one of which was released to the Associated Press from the Court of the Grand Duke of Hesse the day after the death of the dowager empress. A duplicate issued forth from Copenhagen October 16, and read as follows:

"For us, the nearest relatives of the Tsar's family, it is very difficult and painful to reconcile ourselves to the fact that not a single member of that family is still alive. How gladly we would like to believe that one of them, at least, had survived the murderous destruction of 1918. We would shower our love on the survivor ... But in the case of the lady in question our sense of duty compels us to state that the story is only a fairy tale. The memory of our dear departed would be tarnished if we allowed this fantastic story to spread and gain credence."

It was signed by the Grand Duchesses Olga and Xenia and by Xenia's six sons (including the Oyster Bay tennis players, Dmitri and Rostislav); her former husband, the Grand Duke Alexander; her daughter, Princess Irina, and son-in-law, Felix Youssoupov, and the Grand Duke Dmitri Pavlovich. They cited the statements of Pierre Gilliard and Sophie Buxhoeveden in addition to the reports of criminologist Bischoff and the former imperial dentist, Dr. Kastritsky.

Franziska's adherents would spend decades disparaging the Declaration. They pointed out that only some of the Romanovs assembled for the funeral had ratified it, and hinted that this indicated a tacit acceptance of Franziska's claim. Actually, some of the non-signers, the Grand Dukes Kyril and Boris, for example, were known to hold negative opinions in the matter but chose not to get involved. The same deep rifts which had doomed the dynasty prevented them from acting in unison here.

It has also been pointed out that only one of the signers (Olga) had actually seen Franziska, but it is hard to fault them there. Franziska would have been unlikely to have agreed to see all of them, and wasn't easy on witnesses when she did allow a viewing. She often refused to answer reasonable questions or to let them get a good look at her. Franziska's allies also had a tendency to claim that dissenting witnesses had actually recognized Franziska but refused to admit it, out of greed or weakness. Olga, Gilliard, Shura, Buxhoeveden, and Volkov had all been tarred this way, which did nothing to encourage future witnesses.

Gleb's response was immediate and intemperate. It read, in part:

"Twenty-four hours did not pass after the death of your mother … when you hastened to take another step in your conspiracy to defraud your niece … the wrong which Your Imperial Highness [is] committing pales even the gruesome murder of the Emperor, his family and my father. It is easier to understand a crime committed by a gang of crazed savages than the calm, systematic, and ruthless persecution of one of your own family."

There were two copies of Gleb's document. One was sent to the Grand Duchess Xenia in the form of a personal letter on October 18. The second went out to the Associated Press ten days later, the same day that Fallows issued a warning that "any person or corporation libelling or slandering Grand Duchess Anastasia will be held by her legally responsible."

Franziska's European supporters greeted these utterances with anguish. The Grand Duke Andrei moaned in a letter to Tania Botkin, "All is lost … Does she realize what he has done? He has completely ruined *everything*."

Tania herself broke with her brother: "Gleb's methods are so different from what I could endorse ... how can I know what my name will be made to stand for?"

The Duke of Leuchtenberg implored "[She] will destroy her chances for recognition and commence to play a 'dirty role'. That expression I think she will understand. Tell her, *in my name*, I beg her not to do it."

What did Franziska herself make of all this? Gleb said that she approved of his counter-attack, but adds that her moodiness had reasserted itself. At times she "truly became a miniature Ivan the Terrible—as Princess Xenia had nicknamed her." The idyll was over, the easy days of slandering long dead Romanovs were gone. Gleb's impulsiveness had cost her the active support of both Princess Xenia and the Grand Duke Andrei, and all the respectability they had conferred upon her claim.

The aftermath of the Declaration saw the rising influence of Miss Jennings, who bustled back into Franziska's life late in the fall. It was she who arranged Franziska's move into a private cottage on the grounds of the hotel and hired a servant/bodyguard to attend her. Had Miss Jennings gotten an eyeful of the dangerous habits Gleb and "Anastasia" had fallen into, and moved to protect her?

Gleb says that Miss Jennings wished to adopt Franziska in some extralegal sense, and to leave her the bulk of her sizeable estate. He encouraged her generosity. "What she does need is true, motherly love. If you can regard her as your daughter with whom you could never become angry, whom you would forgive anything," he pleaded. There are enough references to Franziska's special status as a ward of Miss Jennings in Edward Fallows' papers and in the news clippings of the period to suggest that there was some truth to this.

Franziska had acquired a taste for luxury, but no sure way of securing it. She must have longed for her own nest-egg, for money that was unconditionally hers. Since the Copenhagen Declaration had ended any idea that the Romanovs might be embarrassed into settling with her, two possibilities remained. The first was the chance that Edward

Fallows might actually discover a fortune in a European bank. Perhaps Franziska believed the emigre stories; many well-informed people did. It is clear that she approached the prospect with extreme caution, though. It was a dangerous way to go, one that threatened to become a criminal matter at every turn.

Next came Miss Jennings and her talk of making Franziska an heiress. There was a lot to gain. Miss Jennings was a brisk, active woman, but she was over seventy. One never knew. Life could be pleasant in the meanwhile; shopping at upscale stores, plenty of white dresses and perfume. There was no personal risk either. If Miss Jennings did leave money to her, it would be to Anastasia von Tschaikovsky or Anna Anderson, not the Grand Duchess Anastasia, per se.

Perhaps the two strands were never wholly separate. Miss Jennings was not the Duke of Leuchtenberg, with his limitless tolerance of those from his own "tight circle." She was a Yankee woman, sensible and even thrifty in her own peculiar way. It might be that Franziska felt obligated to announce her intention to some day pay her benefactress back, and to demonstrate her sincerity by taking the necessary steps to retrieve her "fortune."

The break-up with Gleb came at the end of the year, when Franziska moved back into Miss Jennings' apartment. Maybe she had grown weary of him and his plans. Perhaps Miss Jennings didn't approve of the relationship her "daughter" had gotten herself embroiled in. There was Mrs. Botkin and the children too. They had seen very little of Gleb in past months and presumably needed him at home. Gleb himself said that he had come down with 'flu, and that Franziska had resented his absence while he recovered. A note to Fallows written by Franziska on January 4, 1929, tends to suggest otherwise. Here Franziska comes very close to admitting an affair:

"I cannot see you on Tuesday because I have to go to Garden City, but I can see you on Wednesday, January 9 ... I do not wish you to bring Mr. Botkin with you for I do not want to see him. There have been several occurrences which never should have been and which cannot be permitted to happen again. Therefore, I have somebody else in mind and will replace Mr. Botkin on the board."

III

It was not until December 1928, and shortly before she returned to Annie Burr Jennings' apartment that Franziska signed the affidavit Fallows had drawn up in August:

"I, Grand Duchess Anastasia Nicholaevna, youngest daughter and only surviving child of the late Emperor Nicholas II and Empress Alexandra of Russia, do hereby declare that after our family had left St. Petersburg and were in exile in Ekaterinburg in Siberia, very shortly before the deaths of other members of my family, my father told my three sisters and myself that before the World War in 1914, he had deposited in the Bank of England five Million Roubles each for my three sisters and myself ... In 1925, when I was in Berlin, the Danish Ambassador Zahle, at Berlin, whom I had told of this deposit of monies, made official inquiries, and very shortly afterward informed me that there were monies on deposit for my sisters and myself in the Bank of England, but that the Bank was unwilling to state the amount."

All this was bad enough, but on February 7, 1929, Franziska signed another document, also drawn up in August, which formed the Grandanor Corporation. Grandanor, an acronym for Grand Duchess Anastasia of Russia, was incorporated in Delaware on February 9. The idea was that interested Americans could invest in Grandanor and receive a guaranteed five-to-one return on their money once "Anastasia" recovered her "inheritance." The funds paid in would support Franziska and cover Fallows' costs as he worked on her behalf in Europe. Franziska had in effect become a corporation. Even if she died, Grandanor would proceed. There may have been simpler, less expensive ways of researching Franziska's claims, perhaps by enlisting British and German lawyers to look into them on a contingency basis, but

Fallows' background was in corporate law, and a corporation was what he formed.

Why did Franziska, with her wariness of signing legal documents, agree to Grandanor? The simplest explanation is that she saw it as a necessary evil if she was going to continue to live in the United States. It seems significant that she signed the document on the 7th, the day before her visa expired. Fallows had written to James J. Davis, then the Secretary of Labor, asking for an extension of the visa on the 5th, but had not yet gotten a response. Franziska did stall for as long as possible. The January 4 note seems typical; here she attempts to throw someone off the board while dodging the papers that would make the corporation a legal reality. Eventually she realized that she could find herself with an expired visa and no attorney if she did not sign, and relented.

There may have been more to it than that. Dominique Aucleres, a French journalist writing in the Fifties cryptically noted that "Because of Gleb, [Franziska] became the object of blackmail." A puzzling scrap, one not enlarged upon. Who was blackmailing Franziska? And why? Franziska's relationship with Gleb was a weak point, but who was exploiting it? While it seems highly doubtful that either Miss Jennings or Fallows blackmailed her in the legal sense, the circumstances surrounding her stay at the Garden City Hotel may have made it more difficult to play the imperious grand duchess with her increasingly impatient American advisers.

At some point during her American stay Franziska heard from real blackmailers as well. The kindly, coal-heaving Bachmanns, who had taken her in after her final break with Clara, now threatened to write about her if she did not pay them off. Nothing is known of the weeks she spent with these people, who liked to sing in their courtyard, or precisely what they intended to tell the world, but the Jennings' lawyer, Wilton Lloyd-Smith, was certainly aware of them. Significantly, Franziska who said such vicious things about her believers, was always careful to praise the Bachmanns as good, "simple people." She never criticized the Wingenders either, despite their public betrayal.

Perhaps, like the Wingenders, the Bachmanns knew her real identity. The threat posed by the Bachmanns was at the very least a reminder of those endless nights in Berlin, when she walked among the destitute and slept wherever she could. At worst it was a direct threat to her shining new existence, to the barrier of fur coats, imperial relics, and attorneys she had heaped up against the memories of this discarded life.

It was a perilous time, complicated by Grandanor and the risks of attracting rich and powerful investors with fraudulent statements. Franziska was capable of controlling any of her supporters in a face-to-face situation, but would always be hampered by her inability to take the long view. This would not be the only occasion she found herself tied up in an arrangement she sensed was unwise in order to satisfy a short-term need—a visa, a place to stay, ready cash.

Franziska had become not only the mythic figure of Anastasia, but a corporation.

It was all out of her hands and she knew it.

IV

Edward Fallows' memo of February 6 lists himself as President, Curtis J. Mar as Secretary-Treasurer, and "Anastasia Nicholaevna" as Vice-President. Fallows would receive thirty-three dollars a day to cover expenses and provisions were made for additional funds as needed. Twenty percent of the subscriptions would go to administration. Mr. Mar would keep Miss Bidwell in Fallows' office informed of all expenses.

Fallows, the chief treasure hunter, would get twenty-five percent of all proceeds. Ten percent was set aside to cover legal fees and to repay loans taken out by Fallows. Another ten percent went to investors, with a guaranteed five-fold return on their initial investment. Thus if Franziska had ten million dollars waiting in the Bank of England, she would receive $5,500,000; Fallows would get $2,500,000; $1,000,000 would repay legal expenses and retire loans; and the final $1,000,000 would be split among the investors.

This was only one of many possible pay-offs, they felt. Who knew what American real estate owned by the tsar might turn up? There was property in Germany and Finland and perhaps a British hunting lodge as well. There was indisputably money in the Mendelssohn Bank in Berlin—Dr. Paul Kemper, a director of the Bank, confirmed that "several million roubles" had been deposited by the tsar and remained in its coffers. Inflation had reduced the sum to about £25,000. Unfortunately for Fallows, the Bank knew about the Franziska Schanzkowsky allegations and believed them. Grandanor would never see a pfennig of this money.

It would not be enough to merely find the money; Franziska would also have to demonstrate that she was the rightful heir to it. This entailed presenting convincing evidence of "Anastasia's" survival and identity, deposing people who had known her, and locating new witnesses. Fallows' faith in his client seems to have led him to underestimate the difficulty and importance of this task. He would not spend much time on the phantom child and quickly delegated the "Shantkovski myth" to Harriet, whose book was soon to appear in the States.

His involvement would bring together the European Anthroposophical supporters, who had not given much thought to the earthly legacy of the tsar, and the American element, which seemed to think of little else. Fallows would enjoy his European years, forming new friendships, living in hotels and traveling extensively on the Continent.

Countesses and baronesses, minor dukes and assorted members of the nobility confided in him. Many were Anthroposophists who hoped for a restoration of monarchism, and a return to traditional values and *Kultur*. Fallows would become involved in Anthroposophy himself, to the point of equating "Anastasia's" mission with Kaspar Hauser's.

He also left a record of his work in a bulky archive of thirteen boxes of uncataloged letters, affidavits, diary entries and manuscripts. The archive was donated to the Houghton Library at Harvard by his daughter Annette. It might have fascinated Henry James, this detritus of a drama so reminiscent of his own novels—a naive, idealistic American seduced and ultimately undone by the ambiguities of the Old World. Whether Fallows would have wished his records to be so public is debatable, but later seekers into Franziska's mysteries would have much to thank him for.

V

Documents and Grandanor money in hand, Fallows sailed to Europe in February and conferred with Arthur Gallop, a partner at Freshfields, Leese and Munns, solicitors to the Bank of England. It was a cordial meeting in the ancient financial City at the heart of London. Gallop expressed a desire to be as helpful as possible, but noted that regulations meant that "here you must take every step of the way yourself, as the Bank of England is a Government institution and we are not permitted to disclose the existence of a deposit except to an accredited depositor."

He went on to advise Fallows to "Go to the Court of Chancery, and get an order that your client is Anastasia and then come to the Bank and we will open our books."

Fallows came away much encouraged, although it must have taken some wishful thinking to do so. He seems to have willfully overlooked the scope of Gallop's disclaimer. Gallop had told him that banking law not only prevented him from discussing the particulars of the account, but also from disclosing whether the account even existed. William Clarke, a former Financial Editor for the *Times*, tactfully noted that Fallows "was not the first, or last, foreign visitor to make such a mistake. London's international bankers can still say 'no', or give nothing away, without offense better than anyone I know." The suggestion that Fallows seek to get the Court of Chancery to rule that his client was Anastasia ought to have given him pause as well.

Anastasia's British cousins had kept out of the fray, but remained banked up at the edges of it like a row of thunderheads, far away yet potent. Their silent disavowal was a force not even Harriet or Zahle would attempt to challenge. The failure of the British Royal Family to make a firm offer of asylum to Nicholas and his family after the Revolution had led many to see them as cold, stingy people, but they were people who could recognize one of their own, and who would not tolerate the embarrassment of having a relative rely on newspapermen for support. It was also far more difficult to claim that they were influenced by a desire to share in the missing fortune. An appeal to the Court of Chancery would be a risky undertaking, one which Fallows never made any real plans toward in the years to come.

VI

Fallows moved on to Berlin, setting up an office in the sumptuous Bristol Hotel. He found an assistant and translator, Helene Noeggerath, who would become a close friend.

He quickly immersed himself in Franziska's world. Advertisements were placed in newspapers, seeking new witnesses. He and Helene visited the Berlin police and learned that the police did not feel that Franziska had been murdered by Grossmann after all. On a more encouraging note, they had no proof that Fallows' client was Franziska Schanzkowsky and considered the matter closed.

Harriet von Rathlef was soon on the scene with a "working plan" that reshuffled the minutiae of Franziska's life before and after Dalldorf. Harriet, so quick to sense dishonesty in others, had become a master manipulator of dates, dental histories, and earring styles. The "working plan" was energetic but contributed nothing new to the cause.

The latest clue seemed to be the confused statement of a Mr. Kreukenberg, who claimed to have aided Anastasia in Romania. There was a lot of vivid detail—gypsies, a string of pearls, even a sister of Anastasia's alive in Istanbul—but the story petered out, another dead end.

VII

While Fallows was thus immersing himself, the famous jewel box of the dowager empress was finally opened in London: "Some lovely things," according to the laconic diary of George V. Another witness said that "Ropes of wonderful pearls were taken out, all graduated, the largest being the size of a big cherry. Cabochon emeralds and large rubies and sapphires were laid out ... "

Anastasia's aunts, Olga and Xenia were the chief beneficiaries of the hoard, although much of it wound up with Queen Mary, who purchased the pieces at what were reputed to be bargain prices.

"As the daughter of the last reigning Emperor of Russia, those jewels were mine. They belonged to me! Such things I would never wear, but I could have used the money," Franziska said later.

VIII

Franziska didn't need any of this money in 1929. Annie Burr Jennings was looking after her very well, taking her to the opera and to cocktail parties as well as lavish functions at the old Ritz-Carlton and the Waldorf. Eligible men like Cole Porter and "Black Jack" Bouvier, the rakish father of the future Jackie Kennedy, were attentive escorts. She had a charge account at Altman's department store and bought dresses, wraps, stoles, shoes, and lingerie, all in white, spending thousands on clothes at a time when the average American worker earned about $1500 a year.

Miss Jennings enjoyed displaying the "Grand Duchess Anastasia," whom she "called a daughter." Gossip about Franziska's place in Annie's will had spread. It was an odd sort of mother-daughter relationship, though. Neither ever forgot who Franziska was supposed to be. Although Annie had a large staff, she waited on Franziska personally, carrying trays and taking dictation. Harriet's book, flowery as it was, noted that Franziska "sulks and mopes and displays with the utmost arrogance the consciousness of her social superiority." Her new "mother" would see these traits soon enough. Later, Gleb would complain about all this coddling: "Miss Jennings supports the Grand Duchess, spending fantastic and unnecessary sums on her, accustoming her to luxury, and making her almost laughable by exaggerated attentions."

When Franziska and Annie tired of Manhattan, they went to Sunnie Holme. Liveried footmen served at dinner and three cooks prepared sumptuous meals. Franziska could wander meticulously maintained grounds that included goldfish ponds and an Indian garden with a log house and totem poles.

While at Sunnie Holme Franziska posed for Haley, a local society photographer. The images are full of light, flowers, crystal. She is seen perched on the arm of a chair or standing in front of an ornate mirror, dressed in modish white—a drop-waisted dress in satin and chiffon, and a filmy coat with an enormous fur collar. She never quite forgets herself, though. Her mouth is tight, and her chin remains buried in her collar. It must say something that she carefully preserved these glamorous images of herself up to the very end, despite her many losses of "precious goods" along the way. When she took up painting as an old woman and made a self-portrait, she depicted herself as a young woman wearing the vast, fluffy collar of those halcyon days.

Beneath the facade, Franziska worried. There was no Gleb to discuss things with, or to serve as a distraction. She voiced petulant complaints about Fallows in far-away Germany; he was spending Grandanor money on the high life in Berlin, and was even said to have a mistress there.

Curtis J. Mar was brought in, both as an adviser to Miss Jennings and as a collaborator in yet another attempt to write Franziska's memoirs. The rest of the Jennings family backed the memoir project enthusiastically. Walter Jennings told Franziska she could "make millions" by telling her story. Unlike Franziska's European supporters, the Jennings felt that she should not only cooperate with her lawyers in seeking her fortune but should also seek other means of supporting herself and repaying her backers.

The project was complicated by the advance Franziska had already collected for the book she and Gleb were supposed to have written; a letter threatening to halt the publication of Harriet's book in the United States was required to clear the way. Another publisher was found and Franziska received a second advance. Throughout April and May she went daily to Mar's office, where she dictated her "memories" to a secretary.

Ultimately this book fared no better than the first. Her dry, unedited statements gave little away, becoming only a bit livelier when she used the manuscript to attack her friends and enemies.

In July, Miss Jennings and Franziska moved from Park Avenue to an apartment on Fifth Avenue and East 70th Street, overlooking Central Park. The bright, busy world Franziska had become a part of shuddered violently on October 29, 1929, when the stock market crashed and took much of the wealth and glitter of the era with it. Franziska and Annie seem to have been left largely unaffected by the disaster, and continued their rounds of shopping, visiting, and theatre-going.

Late in the fall, Sergey Rachmaninoff was successfully treated for chronic facial pain by Franziska's old enemy, Dr. Kastritsky. The condition had been agonizing for someone who earned much of his living as a concert pianist. As it was, one of Franziska's backers had come away with great respect for the professional skills of one of her most vocal scientific detractors. Rachmaninoff, never truly convinced of her authenticity, would never give her money again.

IX

In the fall of 1929 Fallows began attending seances. Eliza von Moltke, widow of the general, had begun receiving messages from her dead husband via Rudolf Steiner long before. Steiner was gone but the messages still came, dramas of light and dark, of the Karma of history. It was a struggle to preserve the civilization of Goethe, Bach and

Brahms, a secret war against the vandalism of National Socialism. The belief in "Anastasia" would flower over the years, enmeshing her in deepening layers of myth and hope.

It's easy to imagine the scene after the lights were on again; the shadows clinging to the edges of the high ceilings, the table decked with *Kaffee und Kuchen*, silver spoons clinking against Rosenthal china, the rise and fall of the voices, muted, exultant, conspiratorial. An American lawyer elbow-to-elbow with German aristocrats and the remnants of Franziska's Russian believers: Dr. Rudnev, Harriet, Baroness von Huene-Hoynigen, Baroness von Beck, and Prince Frederick of Saxe-Altenburg. All united by the messages from the dead, the possibilities and spine-tingling evidence of "A's" identity.

It was a German quest now.

Chapter Thirteen

I

Fallows returned briefly to America in 1930 and met a cranky Franziska, whom he tried to pacify with a promise that she would be recognized within a year. The main purpose of his trip seems to have been the collection of further funds from Miss Jennings. When Franziska later complained about his spending in one of her manuscripts, he would state that while he had gathered twelve thousand dollars in advances during the first year of their corporation, Franziska herself had opened an account in the Guaranty Trust of New York with a balance of $2950. Back in Europe, he sent Franziska pictures of the British Royal Family and tried to dredge up new investors for Grandanor: "I am going to speak to you about one of the most tragic fates of a woman seen in history," he wrote in a forty-two page letter to prospective backers. "In its tragedy it appeals especially to women of the world … "

He was having an exciting time in Europe while Franziska began to stew in Manhattan and Connecticut. By February he was in Paris. He had drawn up a wishlist budget for Grandanor: seventy-five thousand dollars for travel, investigation, the deposition of new witnesses, and various expenses and court costs.

II

While Fallows became more immersed in the drama of "Anastasia" and the evil forces arrayed against her, Franziska continued to brood. An article in the *New York Mirror* at the end of March had labeled her a "Royal Fraud" and "the most astonishing hoax of the century," noting that "prominent Americans have been victimized."

At least some of Miss Jennings' friends were either disappointed by, or skeptical of the "grand duchess." One who met her in her Connecticut finery said that Franziska had "thick ankles and wrists and looked anything but patrician ... "

"The manners of the young woman ... were said to be strictly proletarian. When she did not like the ways things were going, she would remove her store teeth and otherwise behave in a manner not to be tolerated in anyone, let alone royalty ... The woman was generally moody, uncouth and disagreeable."

This fragment comes from a reporter who talked to people in Fairfield after Annie Burr Jennings had dropped Franziska. Her moodiness may have been exaggerated but the detail about the false teeth seems too bizarre to have been invented. One thinks of the dentures belonging to Gleb's father, which investigators found in the forest surrounding Ekaterinburg. Only dire circumstances, an investigator noted, would separate a man from his dentures.

Was this the actress stepping out of her role, taunting the audience with her true face? Or could she truly not help herself? There is simply no way of knowing. One is left only with an image of Franziska, a flash of an eye, the red blotches she was supposed to have inherited from Alexandra rising on her face as she pops her dentures out at Miss Jennings' table. The stunned silences, the humiliation of her hostess, the amazement of the hovering footmen. And the talk ...

The audience that counted still believed: "All was pardoned because her terrible experiences were thought to have made the young woman return to atavistic principles."

Miss Jennings had brought in a new lawyer, Wilton Lloyd-Smith, a classmate of Edmund Wilson and F. Scott Fitzgerald at Princeton. They had all been in the Triangle Club of 1916, and Wilson would record seeing him at bawdy class reunions in the following decade. He and Franziska collided almost immediately. Lloyd-Smith was relaxed and irreverent, not much impressed by her "imperial dignity." He was also Miss Jennings' lawyer, not Franziska's or Grandanor's. The proliferation of lawyers points up a problem documented in the Fallows

Papers. As time went on, it was becoming increasingly difficult to sep-arate the interests of Miss Jennings, Franziska, and Grandanor itself. There would also be disputes later as to whether Grandanor actually functioned as a corporation, but documents indicate that a number of people, Mrs. Hugh D. Auchincloss and Mrs. Auguste Hemingway among them, had contributed funds, presumably with the expectation of a good return.

It is no wonder Franziska started inching toward the breakdown which would follow in a few months. The mood swings resurfaced; she was either traipsing around with Miss Jennings or being rude to her, making silly accusations and refusing to leave her room. It was Castle Seeon all over again, but without the kindly Duke of Leuchten-berg or Zahle to smooth things over.

Gleb had denied his intimacy with Franziska when asked by Fal-lows. Perhaps in response to this accusation he published a strange, self-serving article in the *North American Review* on February 9, 1930. Gleb said that he could now write frankly about "Anastasia" as he had "officially and actually" withdrawn from the case, and went on to spell out, yet again, the basis of her claim. He affirmed her authenticity, but there was an arch, provocative tone to the piece which must have star-tled her friends ("Madame Tschaikovsky, who, having had her day of fame ... "). Elsewhere he feigned disinterest and was quite wounding about Franziska, who had "never been very pretty," and who could "also be an enfant terrible, and what seemed just naughtiness in child-hood can be very trying in a grown up person."

Grandanor wasn't mentioned, but he suggested that "Anastasia" was sure to win her court case if it actually came to be litigated, even if she was "penniless." But—"For whatever may be the outcome of the case of Anastasia, there can be no doubt the Romanovs have played their final part in history."

So there.

III

Franziska remained alone with her fears when she returned to Manhattan. She had only herself and her parrots, with which she spent hours, closeted in her room.

Shopping provided a relief of sorts—a spree that fulfilled the dreams of a frustrated window shopper and reassured her with its tangible results. Franziska went wild, according to a letter written by Miss Jennings in March:

"You know there is no doubt that she is perfectly sure she is going to get her money, and she said the other day that you [Fallows] had told her that probably everything would be all right in a year. I told her that she needed six dresses the other day, so she decided to go out—she was in a very good humor—to these various stores—Altman's, Kurtzman's, and so on, with Josephine … Josephine reports that she paid— or ordered—a wrap that will cost $450. Josephine protested at intervals that the things she bought were very expensive, and she had gone extensively into the purchase of lingerie … We will accept what is being done now. There is nothing more for me to say, but when Josephine would make these protests, she would say 'Yes, they are expensive, but I expect to pay back Miss Jennings when I get my money' … "

The new clothes only helped for a little while. Unable to talk about what was really troubling her, Franziska said that she hated her room, complained about the servants, and was indignant when Miss Jennings sent the cook to inquire what Franziska might want to eat. "Nobody sends the cook to her guest's room!" she cried in regal consternation. It was probably an act of desperation on the part of her hostess, anyway. Miss Jennings knew the proper form, but etiquette fell silent when it came to dealing with a guest like Franziska.

Despite much pleading and cajoling, Franziska would not leave her room in order to accompany Miss Jennings to Sunnie Holme in the spring. Miss Jennings had her own bags packed and left. They would be divided from then on, Annie in Connecticut and Franziska in New

York, communicating through letters and intermediaries like Wilton Lloyd-Smith.

The split was perhaps inevitable. Miss Jennings was a woman used to being in control of her surroundings. Back in Fairfield she was a force to be reckoned with. She wasn't above pushing her weight around a bit, either: "She usually carried a fan and when a gathering or meeting bored her she would indicate her attitude by tapping her fan on the seat in front of her … Her remarks on many occasions swayed the decision of the meeting." It seems unlikely that anyone had ever spoken to Miss Jennings as Franziska had; the strain of this unpleasant novelty was beginning to tell.

Her brothers, Walter and Oliver, believed Franziska was abusing their sister's hospitality; they complained to Xenia Leeds, but Xenia preferred not to involve herself again with her "cousin." Franziska angrily rejected any suggestion that she might benefit from psychiatric treatment.

In New York a writer read Gleb's article in the *North American Review* and was fascinated by the story of the mysterious "Anastasia." Jill Cossley-Batt's involvement with the case has earned her calumny over the years. She has been described as an adventuress and an impostor who did Franziska and her cause much harm in the few months she was active in it. In fact, Jill was a respected, although minor author. *The Last of the California Rangers*, published in 1928 by Funk and Wagnalls, quickly went into a second printing. It was a well-researched, entertaining biography of Captain William James Howard, a colorful character and prominent California lawman. In her acknowledgements Jill thanked various archives but stressed that the story came mainly from "materials furnished by [Howard] himself, chiefly through spoken narrative."

With one successful book behind her, she was looking for another interesting subject to write about. Relying on "spoken narrative" would be just the thing for a book about "Anastasia." Jill claimed to have a degree in chemistry and to have been decorated for bravery during the war. She also claimed to be the Dowager Countess of Huntingdon, a friend of Queen Mary and George V, and a member of the extended Battenberg family. None of these claims was true, and it is surprising she made them. It seems likely she gauged her audience and saw that inventing a title was a sure way to get their attention. She would not deny fudging her background when the truth was discovered.

Jill was accompanied by her manager and boyfriend, Irvin Baird. Since Irvin became actively involved in the project, it seems probable that he had prepared by reading the *North American Review* article too. Perhaps Gleb's account inspired him to cast himself in the role of a son of a court physician. In this case, however, the court physician was said to be an actual Scottish duke as well.

Jill and Irvin were received gratefully by the Jennings. The attempt to help Franziska write a book by dictating it to a secretary had come to nothing. Here was an author who was used to writing a story based on what someone told her. Working on her memoirs would give Franziska something to do, and might bring a little peace to the family since she was beginning to complain about the failure of her second attempt. Perhaps a third try would do the trick. Oliver Jennings was enthusiastic about Jill. "She apparently has had an extremely interesting past," was how he explained her allure.

Jill and Irvin got Franziska's attention by telling her that she could get a $100,000 advance for her memoirs. This was a fantastic figure, an amount only someone naive about publishing would believe. Franziska was increasingly aware of money—the quaint habit of "forgetting" her change in stores was not repeated in Manhattan—but had little experience in the field. If a real author said so, why not? Oliver Jennings had been telling her all along that there was a fortune in her story. From April to June, Jill and Irvin spent a lot of time in the Fifth Avenue apartment, chatting and plotting. Franziska handed over documents and dictated a new round of statements.

They were drinkers, Franziska said later, who went through her things, but she seems to have been remarkably tolerant of them at the time. Although she would go on to scoff at their social pretensions, the events which followed plainly suggest that Franziska had been taken in by them. Why not? She had never met an English "countess" before. "I would have liked the freedom to find some friends of my own age and tastes," she would say. "The people whom I was brought in contact with at Miss Jennings' were not interested in the any of the things I was interested in, nor I in their interests ... I was not for them a woman. I was a spectacle."

It appears likely that Franziska thought Jill and Irvin were youthful, amusing, aristocratic, natural. She was especially taken with Irvin, debonair yet a hard negotiator, with a certain disdain of the Jennings and their like. He and Franziska spent a lot of time in her room, lost in conversation. "You realize I spent hours talking to that awful woman," he would complain. This bitterness came later, though. The beginning of their friendship was a cozy, conspiratorial time, full of loose talk and wild ideas. Jill and Irvin seem to have had plans that went beyond writing a book. Having formed a relationship with the Jennings, they went on to undermine them with "Anastasia," fueling her fears of imprisonment and poverty before offering her a way out.

During these intimate hours, discussion turned to a possible escape for Franziska. Jill and Irvin said that the Grandanor contract was illegal and that Miss Jennings had no standing in the matter at all. It was suggested that Franziska could cross the border into Canada. Once there, the Prince of Wales would get her a passport. Jill, who claimed to own several houses in Britain, would look after her once she arrived, and see to her instant recognition by Anastasia's British relatives.

It was like the early days with Gleb at Seeon; the insults directed at Franziska's hosts, the escape plan, the long, dreamy hours locked up in her room with an attractive man. It is hard to tell what Irvin and Jill meant by it, or what they intended to do with her if they succeeded in prying her away from the Jennings. Perhaps Franziska even came to believe that she could start over somewhere else with new papers, or that her recognition by Anastasia's cousins could somehow be arranged. She'd always dreamed of living in England, and it must have been fun to gossip with Jill, who said she knew all the British royals.

England and away, the Prince of Wales and Queen Mary, revenge against the Jennings and Grandanor. The new fantasy would calm Franziska's fears for the time being. The thing that mattered most was the $100,000. Franziska even signed a contract with Jill, a step she never took lightly.

Strangely, at some point the Jennings paid Irvin to try and obtain either a Canadian or a Newfoundland passport for Franziska. Newfoundland was still a Dominion and not yet a part of Canada. Irvin had said he knew important people in both places. Did the Jennings, like Xenia before them, want to ship Franziska back to Europe? Or were they merely concerned about the next extension of her visa, which was coming up soon? Certainly the tension between the Jennings and Franziska continued to grow unabated.

"I wish I had never seen Miss Jennings in my life," Franziska dictated to Jill, "for she has done me too much harm and I have almost paid with my life for that moment of weakness when I said I would go with her."

But on May 30, Franziska saw it differently, perhaps because they were anticipating money from the Jennings: "[Miss Jennings] has exemplified to me the most wonderful hospitality. I can never repay her ..."

A few days later it all fell apart. Jill told her that there would be no $100,000 advance; publishers felt that too much had been written about "Anastasia" lately. No escape to England either. It must have been a stunning moment.

"I have nothing more to say," Franziska said in shock.

Irvin, who had come to detest Franziska, told her to "go to hell."

He promptly billed the Jennings for "services," which evidently included compensation for all the time he'd spent talking to Franziska. The Jennings immediately sacked Jill and Irvin. Lloyd-Smith had a showdown with them while a hidden stenographer took notes. It is an enigmatic conversation, full of both shared knowledge and mistrust. Irvin explained how the break with "Anastasia" had come about: "When we could not do that [get an advance], she said, 'Well that is all. I have nothing more to say'. So I thought we were going to get it and thought I'd say it first."

Lloyd-Smith agreed that Franziska was difficult, but said that he'd heard that "Anastasia's" story could still make money, while perhaps hinting that she had reasons for wanting the cash. "The Bachmanns threatened to write unless she gave them money."

Franziska had made an unsuccessful attempt to get her and Irvin on the phone, Jill noted, adding that a lecture Miss Jennings had helped arrange for her was now cancelled.

Lloyd-Smith told them that they shouldn't have lost their tempers, or misrepresented themselves, and that they had lost the friendship of the Jennings by billing them for services.

"It was only a thousand dollars," Irvin protested.

"Baird did that," Jill said.

It all ended on a peculiar note. Irvin said, "We have ways of making them pay," and then everyone shook hands.

Eventually the Jennings would pay off Jill and Irvin. The chastened Jill and Irvin did not bow out of Franziska's life as has been written elsewhere, but remained in contact with her for several years after the showdown.

Franziska's adherents would be somewhat defensive about the longevity of the relationship; it was certainly odd that "Anastasia" chose to remain friendly with known impostors, although not so strange that Franziska Schanzkowsky should find common ground with them and eventually forgive them for their deceptions.

Franziska had always reacted when she felt in danger, stepping out of the Anastasia role to be herself. She had run away from the Kleists when the strain of being a grand duchess became too much. Harriet's articles and the unmasking had produced emotional outbursts and a spiteful, contentious attitude. The break with Jill and Irvin and the disappointments over the advance and the flight to England resulted in violence.

She began writing threatening letters to Annie Burr Jennings, who remained in her stronghold at Sunnie Holme, letters that further in-flamed the Jennings brothers. Friends of the family were talking. Stories circulated about Franziska's paranoia: she would not ride in Miss Jennings' Rolls-Royce unless the curtains were drawn, and accused the servants of poisoning her.

Talk of committing Franziska to a hospital also began in June, days after Jill and Irvin departed, but the Jennings feared bad publicity and contacted Xenia Leeds, who wrote to Franziska and urged her to seek help. "Do think over my suggestion and try to go [to a hospital]. Please remember I am your friend."

Next came a singular chain of events, one of those rare instances in Franziska's story when the accounts of the participants are more or less in accord. On the night of July 14 Franziska in a fit of rage either stepped on or strangled one of her parrots. She screamed until morning, demanding a replacement. The following morning she went out and bought another bird. She also dropped in at Altman's and discovered that her credit there had been cut off.

This was the end, the final provocation. Back on Fifth Avenue, Franziska screamed, attacked the servants with sticks, ran naked on the roof, made increasingly convincing suicide threats, and threw heavy objects out of windows to attract the attention of the police.

This was not acting.

Wilton Lloyd-Smith had alerted Miss Jennings when Franziska killed her bird. He was also very concerned about the allegations Franziska was making about her: "I am not referring to simple little matters like stealing her money ... I mean the kind of thing that usually would not be printed but which a Hearst paper under the circumstances would be delighted to publish."

Since Franziska's "abusive" behavior toward her patroness had made it clear that she and Miss Jennings could not live under the same roof, she was effectively left in control of the lavishly appointed apartment they had once shared. In the meanwhile, servants were leaving, the apartment was becoming "untidy" and things were being tossed out the window. The idea that Franziska might go to the tabloids with stories about held prisoner on Fifth Avenue must have seemed ironic, but had to be taken seriously nonetheless. She had succeeded in getting media attention before, and often at the expense of others.

Luckily the dilemma had been spread over June and July, warm months Miss Jennings could plausibly spend out of Manhattan. All the same, it was galling to have to drive in and out of the city every time there was a musical evening, dinner party, or Service Club banquet to attend. Miss Jennings was a proud woman, and must have keenly felt the unspoken pity of her friends as well as the fear that Franziska's wild, hateful stories would bloom in the newspapers for everyone to see ("Standard Oil Heiress a Monster, Says Anastasia" perhaps?). Accordingly, Miss Jennings selected the exclusive and discreet Four Winds Sanatorium of Katonah, Westchester County, as the place to send Franziska, at a cost of $475 a week.

The Jennings put off the confrontation again. They weren't used to dealing with a problem like Franziska. Perhaps they hoped she would somehow regain her senses and leave quietly. Couldn't she see how pointless, how embarrassing the situation had become? Another week went by. Franziska made a visit to Altman's, where she voiced loud and incoherent denunciations of Miss Jennings before returning to Fifth Avenue.

That was finally it, as far as the Jennings were concerned. After securing Xenia's approval, Walter Jennings filed a formal application for commitment with Judge Peter Schmuck of the Supreme Court of New York:

"She believes attempts are being made to poison her, she refuses medical assistance, spends much of her time confined in her bedroom talking to two birds. She believes my sister has stolen her property … She is abusive to my sister and has refused all attempts to persuade her to leave my sister's house for a sanatorium. She threatened to shoot the last representative whom my sister sent. My information is from personal observation, conversations with my sister, and reports of a trained nurse and servants who recently have been the only persons she would see."

Three doctors who had never seen Franziska signed the papers. Franziska was adjudged insane, and dangerous to herself and others.

Franziska seems not to have sensed the coming storm. The night of July 24, warm and muggy, was Franziska's last night in Manhattan. She put on a nightgown, locked her doors and went to bed, by her own account. A nurse and two orderlies accompanied by Wilton Lloyd-Smith arrived at the apartment. Admitted by a servant, they knocked on Franziska's bedroom door. When she refused them entrance the orderlies broke down the door with axes. Franziska retreated to her bathroom, but that door went too. No longer defiant, she was bundled into a dressing gown and driven immediately to Four Winds.

IV

Four Winds Sanatorium is now called Four Winds Hospital and treats troubled children and adolescents on its fifty-five acre "campus" near Katonah and at another site near Albany, New York. Both facilities are luxurious, with sprawling gardens, individual cottages, and cheerful recreational rooms in the main buildings.

In 1930, Four Winds was a private san with a capacity to care for forty patients, mostly relatives of those who could afford to pay the steep rates. It was the sort of place Frank Capra gently spoofed in *Arsenic and Old Lace*, where Happy Dale provided a safe haven for deluded gentlewomen and hale young men who thought they were Teddy Roosevelt. Begun in 1902 in the country home of psychiatrist Pierce Bailey, it was situated in foothills of the Catskills near the town of Katonah, a popular summer residence for Manhattanites. By the time Franziska arrived, Four Winds was owned and operated by Dr. Lambert, who personally took charge of her case. Franziska was moved into a four room suite with two private nurses in attendance and watched round the clock for the first eight months of her stay.

Franziska's mental condition is difficult to deduce from the letters which traveled back and forth between Dr. Lambert and Wilton

Lloyd-Smith. At one moment she is writing letters to Europe, the next floridly psychotic. Certainly she needed treatment; this was her fourth admission to a psychiatric facility in fourteen years, and was the result of a breakdown as severe as any she would ever suffer.

Many of Franziska's supporters have suggested that she really only needed a rest after coping with the Jennings and the machinations of Jill and Irvin, but if so, her recovery was markedly slow. Even eight months later she was still not well. On March 31, 1931, Dr. Lambert wrote Lloyd-Smith that "Mrs. Anderson" was in "one of her more comfortable phases at the present time. In the existing mood she is mildly elated, somewhat overactive and talkative, agreeable and cooperative." Franziska spent a lot of time with "art materials," did some hem-stitching, and went to the gymnasium and for walks when the weather permitted. Still, her good moods alternated with withdrawn periods when she became morose and "quite delusional."

What delusions? We do not know. Four Winds, then and now, presents an impassive front to the curious. Unlike Franziska's German doctors, Dr. Lambert did not become one of her partisans. His letters are clear, practical documents, free of references to the "hereditary ingratitude" of princes and the like. No glowing testimonials to her authenticity would result from her stay.

Franziska's accounts of Four Winds are vindictive and unreliable, reflecting the rage she seems to have directed at both Dr. Lambert and his clinic. Dr. Lambert, she said, took away a medallion, "my last souvenir of my mother," and wrung the neck of one of her parrots, threatening to kill the other unless she signed the application for her visa renewal. She complied, "therefore delivering myself completely into my enemies' hands."

The parrots had accompanied her to Four Winds along with all her other belongings: five hundred dollars in cash, "many pieces of valuable jewelry including two bracelets, two rings, jeweled boxes, [a] neck pendant, many pins and brooches, a silver tea set, silver toilet articles, [a] silver seal with Russian imperial monogram from a design made in

Tobolsk upon which her mother had written the date 1917, silver mesh bags and several other articles."

These objects were all locked in a safe to which she had the only key, along with a camera, electrical cooking utensils, a wardrobe costing "several thousand dollars," fur coats and wraps, lingerie, linen, luggage and trunks, and photographs of herself in "various poses."

These were the artifacts Franziska claimed Miss Jennings was holding hostage at Sunnie Holme, but obviously the Jennings wanted to be rid not only of Franziska herself but also of everything she owned. Miss Jennings for her part never spoke of Franziska again and directed her staff not to discuss the "grand duchess" with anyone.

Later Franziska would tell wild stories about her stay at Four Winds:

"After the parrot incident, I was shut up in a narrow, ill-lit cell, the door of which was left open day and night and continually watched, making it very hard to sleep even at night. So this was the friendly comfortable room in the 'home' Miss Jennings had boasted [of] so highly. The country around [it] was bleak, with rocks, stones, snakes, and a bit of shrub … Of course I heard neither from Miss Jennings nor Lloyd-Smith, nor from Xenia. Only the doctor [Lambert] turned up every fortnight, finding every time some new piece of malice … What I experienced thereafter in the hospital was so appalling that even today I still feel incapable of entrusting my memories to paper. I was completely broken by the ceaseless suffering both physical and mental. Only the thought that I should please my tormentors by dying gave me a strange strength to hold on to life."

V

It was all terribly embarrassing for the Jennings. The murmuring began right after Franziska was committed, with an article in the *New York Sunday Times* on August 2 suggesting that "Miss Jennings … planned to adopt … the enigma with the deep blue Slavic eyes and leave her the Jennings millions," although Franziska had "insulted the hundred per cent American servitors of her hostess, causing them to depart in droves." This was old news, but old news from someone with inside information, perhaps one of the disgruntled "hundred per cent American servitors."

By mid-August reports that "Anastasia" was dead were the marvel of the day in towns and cities all over Europe and America. The failure to apply for an extension of her visa, combined with the secrecy of the Jennings, had led to a final burst of mostly unpleasant publicity. Fallows had been kept ignorant of Franziska's recent troubles, and the stories in the European press seem to have come as a shock, prompting an urgent cable to Wilton Lloyd-Smith. "If Grandanor dead, I'm a rhinoceros," Lloyd-Smith wired back, not mentioning her hospitalization and implying that he did not know her precise whereabouts either.

All this was confusing enough. On August 19 the *Herald Tribune* further reported that far from being dead, "Anastasia" was being sought by U.S. immigration authorities.

Six days later papers across America carried petitions which permitted readers to express their wish that "Anastasia" be allowed to remain in the United States. A thick packet of clippings is preserved in Fallows' archives: "Mrs. Anastasia Tschaikovsky, who claims to be the daughter of the late Czar of Russia, has applied for an extension of Permit under which she resides in this country." Could the public help?

Less publicized were the August 20 statements of ex-Secretary of State Robert Lansing that Mme. Tschaikovsky could stay as long as she desired because she had been admitted under a League of Nations passport, and was not likely to be deported since it was policy to protect White Russians. Poor Franziska; all the tensions about her immigration status at the time of the signing of the Grandanor papers had been in vain. She could have refused to sign and still remained in the United States as a guest of Miss Jennings. Grandanor might never have been formed, and terrible risks never run. She had three or four attorneys at her disposal, yet no one ever told her that she'd had options when she still could have exercised them. It's no wonder she had become wildly distrustful of lawyers, increasingly eager to manipulate them and to keep them at arm's length.

There is much to suggest that one of Franziska's allies was behind the sudden flurry of press activity, tipping off journalists and perhaps initiating the newspaper petition. Since the Immigration and Naturalization Service wasn't interested in Franziska, they seem unlikely to have leaked news of her "disappearance" to reporters. Judging from their letters, the Jennings dreaded further publicity, and were equally unlikely to draw attention to her whereabouts. Gleb Botkin would have been capable of the deed, but was also very circumspect about Four Winds, unwilling to admit that his "grand duchess" was currently a patient in a mental hospital. The most likely suspect is a Boston socialite and artist, Miss Adeline Moffat, who had previously organized a "Committee for the Recognition of Her Imperial Highness Grand Duchess Anastasia of Russia," and tried to get in touch with Franziska at Four Winds. Miss Moffat would eventually succeed in her ambitions, becoming one of Franziska's most sycophantic supporters.

Franziska did make an attempt to contact European friends. On September 8, she wrote an innocuous letter to Count Gerhard von Schulenberg, saying she wanted to stay where she was as long as she could stand the cold weather, considering her crippled arm. It was obviously an attempt to let someone know where she was and what had happened to her.

Dr. Lambert confiscated the letter and wrote to Lloyd-Smith at the end of the month to warn him that Franziska had contact with the outside and to ask if the letter should be sent. Miss Jennings was, after all, paying the bills.

VI

Fallows remained in Europe, making contacts and earnestly following up on dinner party conversations. The rush of events seems to have caught him on the wrong foot. On July 16 he learned that the Jennings would not pay his expenses after August 1, although they would continue to make deposits until January 1, 1931.

It would take awhile for Fallows to realize that the Jennings were really pulling out. He wouldn't learn of Franziska's committal until November but was aware of some of the gossip surrounding her "disappearance." Where was she? What exactly had happened to make the Jennings withdraw? No one would tell him, even though he cabled frequently—eight times, he said, and received only negative or evasive replies. He should have sailed at once for New York, pressed for explanations, and demanded to see Franziska.

He stayed on in Germany instead, where he couldn't practice law or even speak the language. His colleague, Gilbert Kennedy, was continuing the search for assets in England, but was not very hopeful. The logical thing for Fallows would have been to hand the matter over to responsible local attorneys and return to Manhattan, where his law practice awaited him.

Not even pressing financial problems deterred him from what was becoming an obsessive quest. He would continue to try to raise money from new subscribers, even though the economic climate had been changed by the crash of 1929, and potential investors were likely to be more interested in their own holdings than in "Anastasia's."

Soon he would begin consuming his own assets in the struggle to keep looking. The process was reminiscent of that of other treasure hunters—holders of maps to lost gold mines or hidden pirate wealth who become addicted to the search itself, with its excitement, near misses, and interesting contacts.

VII

Lloyd-Smith sent a long cable on November 12, explaining the Jill and Irvin affair and at long last admitting that Franziska had been committed on July 24. "Nothing has as yet leaked out in the papers. I suppose it will eventually," he sighed.

Fallows protested indignantly on November 24: "I have never lived through five months of more anxiety and worry, because of this persistent silence in spite of repeated cables from myself begging for information ... The way Mr. Lloyd-Smith and his helpers took to capture the Grand Duchess by breaking down the door of her room ... does not seem humane, to say the least. That alone would have been enough to derange temporarily any sensitive, highly-strung, ill woman."

The idea that Franziska might in fact be insane was troubling. How would this affect Grandanor? He wrote at once to Gleb for an opinion. Gleb seems to have known what had happened to Franziska, although he didn't try to see her, saying later that the Jennings had assured him that they would look after Franziska for the rest of her life. His response was not encouraging: "In the colloquial sense of the word one can say that the Grand Duchess is a 'crazy person', and did crazy things, but she certainly was in no way insane in the medical sense."

How did he know? Gleb would remain sensitive about Franziska's stay at Four Winds.

Fallows tried to find Jill and Irvin, seeking them at her publisher's office. Jill was apparently still in New York, and was keeping in touch with Funk and Wagnalls. She and Irvin had somehow gotten in to see Franziska at Four Winds.

"Yes," Irvin taunted Fallows in response to his letter, "we have had the good fortune to renew the acquaintance of Her Imperial Highness in New York, of which you have no doubt heard."

VIII

As always, we must ask: what was Franziska thinking? She keeps getting lost in the narrative. What is known is that she recovered some degree of normality as 1931 wore on.

No longer under guard, she made cinema and shopping excursions to Katonah. She was permitted to see Jill and Irvin, a situation which must have reflected her own, rather than the Jennings' wishes. Had Lloyd-Smith, his motives never very clear when it came to Jill and Irvin, failed to inform Dr. Lambert of their role in Franziska's breakdown and their threats to make the Jennings "pay"? Lloyd-Smith himself was left off the visitor list as Dr. Lambert had deemed it unhealthy for Franziska to be involved in the "controversial aspects of her case." On Franziska's part it seems that she still hated the Jennings and was growing anxious to return to Germany.

What had started with such high drama, acclaim and promise had ended horribly. On the face of it, what could have been a better fit than a faux grand duchess in a faux castle? The things that had made "Anastasia" seem so real—the genuine emotions under the poses—had worked against her in the end.

It had been a scant three years since she'd seen Doris and Felix at Seeon. The past was not that far away yet. The white dresses and shoes she craved had not brought peace or happiness or security. The fantasy made real by these luxuries was ephemeral after all, and never again would Franziska flaunt fur wraps or pose for elegant portraits.

IX

Franziska was not through with the Jennings just yet. A curious document resides Fallows' archives, one which proposes a settlement between Franziska and the Jennings, and implies that she will sue them if they cannot come to terms. Franziska was to be immediately released from Four Winds and the commitment decree which put her there revoked. Beyond this, Franziska was to collect $100,000, less advances made since March 1, 1930. She was also to be supported by them until her pursuit of assets and various law suits had been concluded—events which were presumably years in the future. It was an audacious demand, only a shade away from blackmail. There is no record of a response from its intended victims, but there can be little doubt that thrusts like this made the Jennings ever more eager to free themselves of "our Lady," as Wilton Lloyd-Smith had come to call her.

X

As Franziska got better, her time in the States began to run out. The Jennings were becoming annoyed at the expense of her care at Four Winds. The bill wound up costing Annie something like twenty-five thousand dollars; no mean figure during the Depression. Fallows' demands were another source of strain. Their wish to finally be rid of Franziska and her cause was buttressed by the verdicts of two visitors they sent to Four Winds to inspect the "grand duchess."

Baron George Taube dutifully turned up, with Prince Basil Woitinsky in tow. They had both served on the *Standart* for two and four years respectively, and had last seen Anastasia when she was thirteen years old. When they arrived Franziska said she had never seen them before and that she had no recollection of the incidents they mentioned. This was unusually frank, but it didn't help. Taube and Woitinsky said that they had never seen her before either. Their opinion, Lloyd-Smith wrote Fallows, would have a bad effect on the Jennings. A conversation between Lloyd-Smith and Xenia Leeds confirmed these fears. Walter Jennings seemed to have derived a certain grim satisfaction from the negative verdicts of the *Standart* officers and went out of his way to make Xenia Leeds aware of it. "He got quite pompous," she complained, going on to say she had heard that "the old lady does not agree with her brothers."

"I don't know," Lloyd-Smith claimed, suddenly evasive.

By June Franziska had improved to the point where her two special duty nurses were no longer necessary. She had also been moved to smaller quarters, at a reduced rate of three hundred dollars per week. It was all part of a pattern; the downgrading of Franziska's accommodations, the loss of her private attendants, the unwelcome visitors, and Dr. Lambert's businesslike manner, so different from the flattering deference of doctors like Rudnev and Saathof.

It was time to go home. Fallows had discovered that the Berlin police were no longer interested in her; the coast was clear for a return to the familiar, homey atmosphere of a German san. She had little choice, in any case. The Jennings would not pay for Four Winds much longer and there was nowhere else in the States to go. Xenia, now divorced, did not want her back.

But how to manage the return trip? No one was eager to publicize her present circumstances. Where would she go in Germany? They couldn't ship her there without a destination of some kind. At the end of July, an assistant of a Dr. Sprague, and an American lawyer named Nebolsine visited the Kurenstalt Ilten, near Hannover, Germany, to make arrangements for Franziska's transfer there. By August 17 funds for a six months' stay had been deposited in a bank in Hannover.

All that remained were the legalities. Here Franziska made a stipulation: she wanted the papers in the name of Anna Anderson, as she wished to be "unknown" during the crossing—strange, in light of the fact that "Anna Anderson" had been widely written about. But was this name known in Europe? Franziska may have thought not.

On August 18, a day that Franziska spent at Four Winds, a blonde woman presented herself at the German Consulate in New York. The Consulate was then in the charge of Otto Kiep, a young career diplomat. The mystery woman duly swore that she was Anna Anderson and signed the visa application with an "X," claiming to be illiterate. In return she was issued a visa for a six month stay in Germany. Curiously,

Mr. Foley, Rachmaninoff's agent, was somehow involved in the subterfuge. His presence there suggests that Rachmaninoff was in his typically oblique manner doing someone—perhaps Franziska—a favor.

Franziska would later say that an impostor had taken her place and
accused the Jennings of kidnapping her, but the idea for the Anna Anderson papers seems to have originated with her. The Consulate knew
Anna Anderson and Madame Tschaikovsky were one and the same,
and in any case, issued a travel visa rather than a passport.

Franziska left for Germany the following day, on the SS *Deutsch-
land.*

Chapter Fourteen

I

Franziska, accompanied by a Finnish nurse, arrived at Cuxhaven on August 28, 1931, and immediately boarded a train for Hannover, seventy-five miles away.

Thirty-five years old. A recently mad woman wearing American clothes, gazing out of the train window at the flat summer fields of northern Germany. Windmills, timbered farmhouses, pigs and dungheaps, women hoeing cabbages, potatoes. Home again, *Heimat*, where once she had worked in the fields. So long ago now, another life.

How much of Franziska Schanzkowsky remained in 1931? Was the remembered past a retreat into solace or a dark cave no longer entered? Did she dream of her fiance, her family? Were the dreams nightmares or a longing glance over the shoulder along the path leading back to Pomerania? She could no longer turn around and go back— that possibility was long past now, but the lingering memories perhaps were tempting: her own inner emigration in the land where meticulous obedience to order sought refuge in the realm of poetry and myth. She did not know yet that her best years lay ahead, that the Anthroposophical retreat into spiritualism and legend would surround and protect her, lift her up and never tire of her tricks and dramas the way the Americans had.

She is a strange metaphor, this small woman looking out of a train window, for the larger retreat into the secret Germany that would oppose Hitler. Germany would change soon. Hitler would come to power in 1933, but in the turbulent period ahead the idea of Anastasia would provide an emotional haven for her supporters. She remains elusive. All these pages written about her now!

The story swerves, inevitably, to the believers and supporters who take over the tale as they witness the cantankerous, irritating, lofty, and rude behavior of "Anastasia."

Is this behavior the result of Franziska acting as Anastasia? Or was Franziska being herself? We do not know. It is her inner life which she revealed to no one, that creates the real mystery of this story: questions about identity and being and the belief of others who see only the magician's results, not the sleight of hand. And the dangers in the hall threatening the performance: the Grand Duke of Hesse, the Bachmanns, Gilliard, Grandanor. Dangers Franziska knew all too well. The possibility of a prison cell, a lunatic's padded room, were images that must have pervaded her dreams and appeared at the moment of awakening before she lived the day as "Anastasia."

As somebody whose actions and peccadillos, like taking her "store teeth" out at a formal dinner, whether intended for effect by an accomplished actress or real, are the concrete details a novelist would use to suspend disbelief.

Aber sie hat sich doch wohl eingelebt, her niece Waltraud mused.

She became accustomed to her life—a loose translation. But the word *eingelebet* is difficult to translate. Literally, it means lived into, became used to.

It is a word used often for immigrants. You come to a new land where even the sky seems different. Smiles instead of handshakes, rice instead of potatoes, rocky shores instead of wooded glades. A new language. Perhaps Franziska's life can be seen as a move to a new country, the bizarre and surreal turning to everyday, the way immigrants build houses and tend flowers and shudder about old battles.

Germany was her own country but it was a perfect haven for "Anastasia" too. Castles, stories of old kings and pagan gods and the longing for a Messiah who would resurrect the myths and connect them to the present. Could her story have lived as long elsewhere?

She would end up in the Black Forest, the most picturesque part of Germany, with deep paths through the trees where boars still roamed but where you would find a cozy inn at the end of the path. And Franziska, like the witch of fairy tale, living in a cottage in the dark woods.

II

Reality: Ilten, the clinic in suburban Hannover, must have been a letdown after Four Winds. Franziska was there as a private patient, with her fees guaranteed, but Ilten was a public mental hospital, the local loony bin. Act up and you'll go to Ilten, locals said, exactly as Berliners talked about Dalldorf.

The Finnish nurse hadn't brought any medical records, apparently, saying only to Nurse Reisenfeldt, who had met the boat at Cuxhaven, that her charge was insane and dangerous. The nurse was gone early the next morning.

Franziska wasted no time in rummaging in her luggage for her "real" identity papers in the name of Anastasia von Tschaikovsky. Yes, she was Somebody: "The expression on the faces of these doctors when they learned who I was, I will never forget," she reported gleefully.

And Somebody had complaints.

The Finnish woman had kept her imprisoned in her cabin, without even a toothbrush or washcloth. And the States! They had tried to poison her and kept her a prisoner. The doctor at Four Winds had strangled her bird over the business with her papers.

Dr. Hans Willige and his colleagues were used to patients with paranoid delusions but Franziska could fool doctors when she wasn't in the middle of a breakdown. Dressed in her New York finery, groomed and manicured, sitting up straight, she wasn't a poor, distraught creature, but a self-confident woman of mystery.

Willige quickly ruled out imposture: "It would require a surpassing intelligence, an extraordinary degree of self-control, and an ever-alert discipline—all qualities Frau Tschaikovsky in no way possesses."

He also felt Franziska was not insane. "The lack of symptoms of insanity was proved so conclusively during the very first examination that we were already able to tell Frau Tschaikovsky on the second day that she was not insane and not in need of any treatment in an institution."

And yet "hers is, however, a personality of unique character, consisting to a high degree of strong willfulness, a highly egocentric outlook and an interior haughtiness ... [he could not] entirely abandon the diagnosis of a psychopathic condition ... "

Willige went on to say that the other doctors on staff agreed with him and the diagnosis was thus not to be questioned—assuredly a relief for Franziska, so recently treated for violent delusions at Four Winds.

He quickly had Franziska moved to a private apartment. She could even have left Ilten, but Annie Jennings had paid her fees for six months and there was nowhere else to go. The Duke of Leuchtenberg had died of cancer, Zahle had been instructed to officially drop the case, and she was still angry with Harriet, with whom she'd had no direct contact for four years. Tatiana Botkin had a young family to care for and little money, so wasn't able to look after her. Franziska refused to see Fallows, President of Grandanor, who was using the investors' money to support his investigations in Europe while the raison d'etre of the corporation lived in a public mental hospital.

But life at Ilten was not bad. She had comfortable quarters, was free to come and go, and occupied herself sewing and learning to type. The Depression had affected Germany as well, putting many people out of work. Their cares were not Franziska's, who did not have to concern herself with finding employment, food, or shelter from the violence on the streets.

And when she tired of Ilten, nearby Hannover, the seat of the Dukes of Cumberland-Brunswick, was a pleasant, historic city to explore. It would be her home for a time in the years to come.

But she quickly sent an apologetic note to Xenia Leeds, wishing they could remain friends. Perhaps she regretted her behavior at Kenwood, and saw what a mistake she had made in alienating her "cousin." Xenia did not reply.

III

Fallows didn't worry about the political situation either. His world remained the enigma of "Anastasia," a mystery that even seems to have eclipsed the more practical business of Grandanor.

While Franziska was settling in at Ilten, Fallows was in England, writing about rumors of rumors, and promising leads that turned up in dinner party conversations. A high official in the government was alleged to have said that the Prussian government had recently acquired documents that "now proved without doubt that [Franziska] is the Grand Duchess. But we shall not publish this for grave reasons."

Everything was so tantalizingly mysterious, hinting of intrigue. And, as always, the equally mysterious reasons why the truth could not be revealed. Actually it all seems to have been a rehash of the old Kruekenberg story about gypsies and lost princesses in Romania, but Fallows would spend an inordinate amount of time trying to track it down.

Even if Fallows continued to be persona non grata at Ilten, Franziska did not mind sending him typewritten—no more handwriting analysis for her—complaints about the Jennings family, whom she wanted arrested, and about the papers in the name of Anna Anderson, which she said had been obtained illegally, although she had suggested the name herself. The affair would become a lifelong grievance for her, and Fallows would expend much energy trying to turn it to their mutual advantage.

IV

Franziska's stay at Ilten soon leaked out, with articles about her appearing in the *Hannover Anzeiger*, owned by Paul and Gertrude Madsack, who would become friends and supporters, even renting an apartment for her during the war. The Madsacks visited Ilten and soon introduced Franziska to Hannoverian nobility.

The most significant visitor was Prince Frederick of Saxe-Altenburg, who would become one of Franziska's most prominent defenders. The son of Grand Duke Ernst of Saxe-Altenburg and Grand Duchess Adelheid, *nee* Schaumberg-Lippe, Frederick was born in 1905. His family was connected to many aristocratic German houses. His aunt Elizabeth married into the Romanov family and his sister, Charlotte, married Princess Irene's son, Sigismund of Prussia.

Frederick, a younger son, was a bit of a dilettante. A slight man with an impish voice, he liked to travel and dabbled in archaeology, spiritualism, and history, especially arcane mysteries of the past. He would go on to write *L'Enigme de Madame Royale*, an account of a woman who claimed to be the descendant of the "Lost Dauphin," the son of Louis XVI and Marie Antoinette, wrongly supposed to have escaped his family's imprisonment during the French Revolution. The conventional account of Frederick's entrance into Franziska's life has him arriving with a set of secret questions formulated by Prince Sigismund; only the true grand duchess could have known the answers. "Anastasia" pondered them for some time before answering them all correctly.

At the time, however, Prince Frederick said he had based his recognition of Franziska on the "psychological study" he had conducted on her "relatives." Perhaps the magic questions did not even exist. Prince Frederick had believed in "Anastasia" in 1929 and attended seances about her at the von Moltke home. Sigismund himself was a devout Anthroposophist who would become controversial among

Franziska's followers for his belief in Marga Boodts, the infamous Olga claimant of Lake Como.

In reality, then, Frederick was already convinced and committed when he appeared at Ilten in October 1931. Over the years his royal relatives would support Franziska and put her up in their castles. Almost all the German royals who became Franziska's supporters can be traced back to the Saxe-Altenburg family. Hermine of Reuss, the second wife of the ex-kaiser, also saw Franziska shortly after Frederick's visit and reported favorably back to her husband. She had her Saxe-Altenburg connections too, through Frederick's aunt Marie who had married into the Reuss family.

The friendship of Prince Frederick was useful. Protection by royalty would give Franziska an aura of distinction and legitimacy. She would become immersed in the royal world of old Germany, learn its secrets and ways, the minor points of family history that allowed her to speak with confidence about her "relatives."

This world suited her better than Manhattan high society. Unlike the Americans, her royal German friends would never dream of suggesting she do anything to support herself.

V

Adeline Moffat still hadn't met Franziska, but hoped to do so soon. She addressed a letter to Her Imperial Highness: "I hope soon to have the honor and privilege of receiving the gracious permission of Your Imperial Highness to present myself for instructions and conference."

Like so many of the other participants, Adeline wanted to write a book. Franziska's reply must have been favorable because Adeline was in Hannover by December, taking dictation. The accusations fell left and right for a time: Harriet the criminally negligent nursemaid; Xenia Leeds, the would-be poisoner; Annie Burr Jennings, the drunkard who served her guests on "chipped and cracked dishes from the ten cent store!"

Franziska delighted in playing Adeline and Fallows against each other, filling Adeline with false accounts of his wild spending and imminent disbarment until the harassed attorney threatened his own client with a libel suit. For his part he saw Adeline as an interloper, a flatterer.

Adeline toiled away on the book, slowly and secretively typing it herself to prevent "leakage," "regrouping paragraphs" as her difficult mistress suggested. Her only goals were to raise money for her "grand duchess" and to tell the world the truth about her: "I think of you always, before I go to sleep at night, the first thing in the morning, how best to help you, how best to comfort you. I think of your splendid courage, your kindness, your charm, your youth which should be bringing you joy, then I think of how you are beset, of what terrible unyouthful knowledge and deceit, dishonesty and disloyalty, greed and cruelty has been forced upon you but which has not been able to dim your spirit or smirch you with any of the loathsomeness, the ugliness, the meanness of it all ... You must not be suspicious of me. I am your friend, not a very attractive one perhaps, but very loyal. No one can have too many of these."

VI

On March 6 Fallows was on a train to Hannover, writing a long and rapturous circular letter to investors and supporters to tell them Franziska had agreed to see him. After two years! It's because of answered prayer, this rapprochement. Faith and prayer have helped him throughout life just as psychic ability and prayer have aided him in locating missing jewelry and winning at cards. "God never works through a discouraged man ... " There was nothing he could do but pray and now God had answered. He wrote to her at Ilten and got a reply that she would "co-operate fully."

Perhaps Franziska was worried that her financial support was evaporating. Annie Jennings' six months allowance officially ended in

February, but here she was, still at Ilten with nowhere else to go—yet. There was also the matter of the "forged passport." Here Fallows might be useful. It was true he could not practice law in Germany, but he could act against the Jennings in the States.

VII

Franziska never considered the Uriah Heep-ish Adeline as a source of immediate money, and instead wrote Fallows asking for money and bragging about the "contacts" she had made. Only Fallows' reply remains: "I keenly appreciate the importance of those contacts you have made. If I could borrow the cash, I would, but as you can infer from my 1930 letter, I have already exhausted my credit."

But there were other ways to get money. Fallows began to make sinister rumblings about Franziska's removal to Germany, and about lawyers who referred to her as an "insane lady." He was fast becoming a specialist in slander and libel law. After about a month of this, word came that a representative of the Jennings would visit Franziska at Ilten and possibly authorize the spending of another thousand dollars. Franziska's initial idea, which seems to have been to cause trouble for Annie and to draw attention to herself was paying off.

Making noise worked.

They did not get much more money out of the Jennings, and certainly not years of support. Miss Jennings paid Franziska's fees at Ilten for a few more months and no lawsuit ever materialized against her family or its agents.

"I have had my own problems with her," Fallows wrote Gleb. He suggested that Gleb preserve copies of Franziska's letters, given her "changeable and suspicious nature."

VIII

They all wanted to write a book. Franziska seems to have encouraged all of them at one time or another, dictating to one while sending letters telling another to desist immediately. She was plainly bored at Ilten and the game of setting them off against each other may have seemed an entertaining way of keeping everyone focused on her. Unlike an assets search, a biography required her constant cooperation; someone hoping to write one could not afford to ignore her.

As Adeline soldiered on, Jill and Irvin were preparing to show a manuscript based on their collection of documents and dictations. Fallows had plans of his own which rose and fell according to the state of his relationship with Franziska. He fired off threatening letters to the other prospective authors. Publishers were contacted. Sometimes he seemed to want to write a straightforward account of "Anastasia," sometimes an expose of the sins of the Jennings clan, and at other times a more mystical exploration of Kaspar Hauser and his occult connections to "Anastasia." He even worried that Curtis J. Mar would enter the race with his own set of dictations and warned his fellow board member off with a sharp letter.

Unknown to Franziska, Jill and Irvin were concocting a fantastic narrative of a journey they claimed to have made in search of a secretive tribe of "lost Chaldeans." Breathless stories about their imaginary British American Himalayan Expedition would crop up in regional newspapers for the next couple of years, culminating in the 1933 publication of *Elixir of Life*, based on something called the Batt-Baird Vitality System which they had supposedly discovered in Tibet. James Hilton's *Lost Horizon* with its hidden valley of Shangri-La was a popular sensation, but the Vitality System never caught on. Perhaps the back story was too wild. Jill and Irvin were clever and energetic but they didn't know when to stop embellishing, when to stop talking. Franziska could have taught them a lot about restraint and plausibility. As it was, their parting with her seems to have been gradual and unusually amicable.

Franziska stopped communicating with Adeline eventually, but always seemed to favor Jill and Irvin over Fallows, much to his dismay. In the end none of the books would see the light of day, which suited Franziska very well. It was Gleb who eventually won with The *Woman Who Rose Again*, but that would not be until 1937. No other book about Franziska would appear for almost twenty years.

IX

Franziska started her journey through old Germany in September 1932 when Annie Burr Jennings' funding ran out. Accompanied by the same Dr. Voller who had drawn up the protocols at Wasserburg, she went to Bad Liebenstein, a small spa town in the Thuringian forest near Eisenach. Franziska apparently wanted Voller to be her lawyer now, just as she would try to hire other lawyers in the coming years, but she was bound to Fallows and there was very little she could do about it.

After the restful spa, she moved in with the von Gerlach family, and true to form, soon argued with them. Perhaps her bad temper resulted from an article in the British tabloid *News of the World*: "Impostor Unmasked! 'Princess' Confesses she is a Fraud!" In this scenario Franziska was supposed to be a Romanian actress who had confessed all to a representative of the Romanovs before agreeing to disappear into a convent.

Perhaps Franziska was simply annoyed. Her hosts disapproved of her spending three hundred marks on frivolities and had noticed her practising her handwriting. She worked a lot on her "Anastasia" signature, never quite getting the "A" right.

"She shows a pathological mistrust of everyone," a new acquaintance wrote to Serge Botkin's wife.

The break came when Franziska discovered that a meeting with a "Princess M" was not a chance encounter, but a carefully arranged confrontation. She "left everyone who had helped her in the lurch." Off for Berlin and Harriet, whom she had just told the Gerlachs was responsible for her maimed arm.

The rapprochement with Harriet was not as surprising as it might seem. Prince Frederick, so closely allied with Harriet and the Anthroposophists in Berlin, had been trying to reconcile the two women for some time. Harriet moved Franziska into a pensionne and took her along to art galleries and musical evenings, the artistic haunts of her Anthroposophical friends. Dr. Rudnev gladly renewed the acquaintance of his former patient. The Zahles sometimes quietly allowed Franziska to stay at the Danish Embassy.

This was the real homecoming for Franziska, a gathering-in by all the people who held seances about her and remained fascinated by the mystery. It was also the last year of relative freedom in Berlin. The talk was of strikes and dictatorships to come; banks failed, the stock market temporarily closed, and many were forced to seek shelter in tent cities. Only professional clairvoyants seemed to prosper. A reluctant Hindenburg was elected in March, but the upstart former lance-corporal Hitler had doubled his vote and another election was on the way. In Berlin Communist Ernst Thaelmann received twenty-nine percent of the vote to Hitler's twenty-three.

Steiner had worried about Hitler and the rise of fascism and military might in Germany. "If the German individual manages to truly grasp the spirit, he is a blessing for the world: if he does not, he is the world's scourge." The task of the Germans, then, was to cultivate the spiritual life, "that spiritual power of the future, from which the Slav culture of brotherliness is to arise."

Around this time, Franziska met Steiner's widow, the Russian-born Marie Steiner-von Sievers. Marie Steiner was a friend to Franziska until her death in 1948, giving her a ring and advising her to read only Anthroposophical books.

Another new friend was Eliza von Moltke's daughter, the psychically inclined Astrid, Countess Bethusy-Huc, who had figured prominently in the messages relayed by Steiner from Eliza's dead husband. General von Moltke had met Nicholas II several times and was present at his coronation. Now Astrid met "Nicholas' daughter" and often hosted Franziska at her estate in Silesia, not far from Kreisau where her von Moltke cousin would plot against Hitler.

X

Summer in Franziska's own Pomerania. Not a hut this time or someone else's fields where Franziska and her siblings stacked hay and dug potatoes, but the estate of Count and Countess von Kleist-Retzow, grandparents of Princess Helga von Bismarck.

Early morning, but the sun is already warm. It's been a dry year, hard on the gardeners who must watch the water level in the reservoirs. Still, it's nice to water the flowers before the heat of the day, Franziska thinks. She especially likes the flowering shrub, in bloom now. Rose bush, *weigela*, a tulip tree? We do not know, but there is Franziska, a sunhat shading her face, pouring water from the big tin can. Using her good arm, the other pressed against her side.

Perhaps she has become Harriet's child of nature again, or maybe the Pomeranian air, the sky, has awoken something—not the memory of toiling bent over in the fields, with her skirt hitched up, but the smell of the earth. *Boden.* Or—an Anthroposophist's interest in making things grow? Her friend Baroness von Miltitz would later say Franziska had "the lifestrength, the Russian ether life and ties to the earth …"

It is hard to reconcile with the Manhattan Franziska. And there is something strange about this Pomeranian picture: while Franziska waters, the gardeners watch and shake their heads. So much water for the shrub and flowers! She has emptied the water reservoir several times, she has been warned the water is needed for other things, and still she waters, this strange Mrs. Anderson, this fine ladyship, about whom the servants whisper. They say she's really a peasant from their own *Pommernland*, but wouldn't a peasant understand about wells being low in the heat of the summer?

But only a peasant, one of them, would react so harshly. There she is, face darkening, eyes flaring, the empty watering can in her hand when she sees the reservoir has been turned off. They chuckle and poke one another, pull at caps and puff at pipes—there she goes, her ladyship! as she flies into the house.

Her shrill voice carries into the garden. She wants the person responsible fired, at once! This is an indignity, she has never been so insulted!

They can barely make out the countess' quiet, soothing voice. Poor countess. She has been worried about the water too, and when they see her, later that morning, she shakes her head. After the big meal at one, word from the house is that Frau Anderson did not come to the table, no *Rinderbratten* with new carrots for her. She had locked herself up in her room. The countess knocked and knocked and pleaded. At three she sent up coffee and cake, but no answer from her ladyship.

Trays of coffee, of potatoes and tiny sweet carrots, of milk soup: all spurned. What did she do in there? The curtains remained closed, but once her odd face with twisted lips—teeth out again—and angry eyes peered out of the slit.

Yes, one of them. For certain one of them, and whom of them wouldn't be tempted to lord it over the high and mighty if given the chance? No more field work for her ladyship, although they could see her, picture it, the bent back and squatting feet as she lifted potatoes. No better than any of them.

No one fired of course, but the countess pale and worried, the count shrugging ... three days, and then, at daybreak, she was gone, disappeared and good riddance to her, the demented creature, but the countess wired Berlin and there were raised voices in the study.

A few weeks later, Franziska turned up in Altenburg and asked Prince Frederick for "protection": "Her feet were bleeding, her white dress was in tatters, but she remained nevertheless a very great lady."

What does this mean? The stubborn, angry behavior, the secret departure, and the arrival at Prince Frederick's palace of a tattered and bleeding "grand duchess"? A wretched creature appearing at the old Schloss in the old city, noted for its museums and parks, for the factory manufacturing playing cards. The family had given their huge palace to the state after the war, but lived in a wing and retained a smaller palace on the outskirts. And Franziska trudging, on dirty, bleeding feet, Kaspar Hauser-like, through the streets...

Did she really care so much about that shrub and the flowers? Or was it the fact that servants dared to show her up and that her aristocratic hostess had stuck up for these same servants? Had Franziska's opinion of herself risen so high? Was it just her temper out of control again? Or was it the proximity to her old home in Pomerania that made it all unbearable?

Certainly the von Kleists-Retzows were not the only aristocratic hosts she spurned in these years before the war. People were good, they housed and pampered her, she had servants to wait on her and while she did not collect the extravagant gifts that had been bestowed on her in America, the standards were different: more subtle, less showy.

Everything was fine, Franziska was polite and properly grateful, and then—something didn't please her, a wrong word was spoken, and zip, away.

She has this dark side, Prince Frederick warned Baroness von Miltitz.

The Anthroposophists felt Franziska's darkness came from demons struggling within her; she herself cried, "Why do the demons have to be in me?," perhaps recognizing, in fact, that despite the ease of her life her fears and rages were, indeed, demons.

And just as mysterious, the question of what Franziska did when she disappeared from time to time. As far as we know, she never ran back to old friends or relatives, and it is unlikely that she existed for weeks, as she once said, on berries and mushrooms in the Teutoburger Wald.

On a similar occasion she had slipped away to enjoy a bus tour of the pretty castles along the Rhine as her friends agonized, certain she was starving herself to death behind the locked door of her Hannover apartment. It is refreshing to think that she might have holed up in a country inn where she did not have to be "Anastasia"—a few weeks of normality, a respite and retreat. She could say anything to the people she met. Invent another story: a war widow, on her way to visit her family. Or a farmer's wife, traveling to meet her husband.

XI

Still there was Grandanor. What did Franziska's growing mystical veneer have to do with that much resented enterprise? Fallows should have wondered about this as he spent his own money and time in the growing chaos of Germany. Even the Hesses did not seem to care about Franziska any longer, although they would appear again when her case came to the courts.

Hitler became chancellor in 1933 following the Reichstag fire. A torchlit parade through Berlin heralded the victory. A shift had been occurring for some time among Franziska's supporters. The hard right element—the Orden organizers and Hitler enthusiasts—had fallen away, distracted by the rich opportunities of the new political climate. Others had come to realize what Hitler really stood for and had quietly redefined themselves. The Anthroposophical Society itself would be outlawed in 1935, although members discreetly kept in touch and the Goetheanum continued to function in neutral Switzerland. Baroness Miltitz herself spoke after the war of being in the hands of the Gestapo.

Franziska seemed unaffected by the new regime, although a daughter of the tsar might enjoy special status under the Nazis. She later spoke of meeting Hitler and being impressed by him. Franziska has been said to have been intensely anti-Semitic, either mirroring the prejudices she thought Anastasia would hold or because of her own feelings, typical of the rural Poland of her youth. On the other hand, Harriet Rathleff was Jewish and a neighbor who knew Franziska later said she was not anti-Semitic at all.

Fallows also seemed to be unaffected by the new order. Still, he wasn't happy. Enquiries at banks yielded no results. He started action in a libel suit against the *News of the World*, but the case would drag on for years. The Mendelssohn Bank in Berlin still held some money, and Fallows became active there. But new witnesses were not coming forward. He didn't pursue the phantom child and seems to have disregarded the "Shantkovski myth." Franziska often refused to see him and there was a period when she even concealed her address from him.

"I am nearly broken in spirit as I entirely am in purse," Fallows wrote Gleb on January 1, 1933. "It begins to look as if I had been a big fool to persist so long in an unappreciated effort to win the girl's name and fortune."

The same year, on September 8, the Central District Court in Berlin ruled that all of the members of the immediate family of the former tsar were dead. This was in response to a petition drawn up by Countess Brassova, the morganatic wife of Nicholas' brother, Michael, who became the main heir following the death of their son in a car accident. The ruling cleared the way for surviving Romanovs to recover Nicholas' remaining property in Germany. At the end of the year the countess applied for a Certificate of Inheritance, which was granted on January 4, 1934. Brassova, the Grand Duchess Olga, Alexandra's surviving sisters, and Ernest of Cumberland were all entitled to the money in the Mendelssohn Bank, but the money was not dispersed at the time and Franziska's lawyers would attempt to have the Certificate of Inheritance revoked.

XII

Harriet died suddenly in 1934 of either a burst appendix or cancer—accounts differ. Another Jewish artist dead ... neither Harriet's conversion to Catholicism nor her adherence to Steiner's doctrines would have saved her from the restrictions of the Nuremberg Laws which were proclaimed the following year. Grievances forgotten, Franziska would have fond memories of the woman who had looked after her. In old age, Harriet's book of short stories would be one of her most precious possessions.

For a while, Franziska remained in Berlin before starting on her "wanderings" to the castles and manor houses where she was welcome. Another woman enters the frame; Anna Samweber, an early disciple of Steiner's and a close friend of his widow, Marie. She had been a teacher in tsarist Russia and had met the tsarina and the children in 1914 at the German School in Odessa. Samweber's students had entertained their visitors with songs and she had said the words of welcome. Memories of another time ... Samweber secretly took a picture. "I always kept it with me ... Later on, the picture was to become of special interest."

The "special interest" was "Anastasia." Samweber says she first read about "a Polish farm worker ... [passing] herself off as Anastasia." Samweber learned about the Saxe-Altenburg family interest in the case and was able to meet her. Franziska was staying with the Zahles at the Danish Embassy when Samweber invited "Anastasia" to her apartment on Christmas Eve. Franziska herself brought up the visit to Odessa—the utterly guileless Samweber had likely mentioned it to someone who told Franziska—and Samweber admitted she had been the teacher.

"This for me was irrefutable proof that she was Anastasia."

Samweber believed the Grand Duke Cyril was against Franziska because of the money in the Bank of England. And something new:

"Since Anastasia spoke only the Russian of the ordinary people, this was seen as a reason to eliminate her."

One day, Franziska and her new friend were walking around Berlin when Franziska spied a poster advertising the film *Rasputin and the Empress*, screamed "The Holy Man!" and fainted. They tried to revive her but she didn't regain consciousness for two hours.

The laughter behind the closed eyes, the immobile face … lying on the pavement, a crowd gathering, Samweber fluttering, crying for water, for a doctor …

XIII

From Bavaria to Silesia, from Pomerania to Westphalia, from Wurttemberg to Thuringia: Franziska wandered, staying in castles and on estates. The Grand Duke of Saxe-Weimar-Eisenach (Franziska would even become godmother to his son, Michael), Prince Philip of Hesse-Phillipstahl (nephew of Prince Frederick), Mrs. von Stahlberg (the aunt of Princess von Bismarck), Countess Astrid Bethusy-Huc, Baroness Monica von Miltitz—they all welcomed her. And others, whose names have not entered the record.

Along with castles, there was always the Danish Embassy in Berlin and in Hannover, the lavish Madsack apartment at Wilhelmstrasse 6. Perhaps this suited her best of all, wandering from estate to city splendor as she had once gone from apartment to coffeehouse to rented room, with the vital difference that comfort and concern could be expected at each stop along the route.

She fell ill at the Madsacks' in October 1935. A nervous breakdown or a recurrence of the abscesses and fissures that continued to plague her? The facts are unclear, but it was probably the latter because Fallows, in London at the time, worried no death mask would be made:

"Are you still in touch with Dr. Madsack, so that in case of her death these casts could be taken—in case I do not reach her in time? I dislike to write directly to the Madsacks about this just now—it seems rather unfeeling. But this is not intended as she went incorporating herself as Grandanor Corporation gave me specific directions as to what to do with her property in case of her death … "

Grandanor, not Franziska. It wouldn't really matter if she died or not. As it happened, Franziska survived. The libel suit with the *News of the World* seemed the best bet for funds, but the case was slow in starting. J.J. Edwards would act on Franziska's behalf in Great Britain; documents had to be prepared and Franziska's cooperation sought. Fallows wrote J.J. Edwards they would sue for $100,000 and settle for $25,000.

Fallows kept on. He wrote to Hitler in October 1935, asking for assistance in the "Anastasia cause," specifically the name of an alleged witness to the escape of Anastasia at Ekaterinburg. Hitler even replied. The German Vice Consul, Herr von Nostitz, telephoned six months later and said that the witness was an Alex Rambau of Hamburg.

Gleb Botkin's book about Franziska was published in the fall by Fleming Revell with Franziska's endorsement. Hitler received a copy of Gleb's book, presumably a promo from Fleming Revell. Fallows reminded Hitler of this freebie when he wrote again on January 20, 1938, asking for the file of the Prussian Ministry regarding the Anastasia's rescue.

Franziska back in Europe, 1930s

Chapter Fifteen

I

Garba, the Madsack chauffeur, would later tell an interesting story about a trip Mrs. Madsack and Franziska made to Bavaria in 1938. The ladies got into Gertrude's big touring car and had themselves driven straight to Berchtesgaden, site of Hitler's alpine retreat, the Berghof. All this must have been Gertrude's idea, although Franziska may have been initially carried along by her sheer enthusiasm. Frau Madsack was a bossy, take charge sort of woman. Her husband's newspapers had done well in their negotiations with the government; she was confident, capable of launching a "we'll go to the top and clear this up directly" offensive. It was not a plan that was ever likely to succeed. The Berghof was more like a fortress than a holiday villa and impromptu visits were sternly discouraged.

Gertrude and Franziska must have caused a stir, though, showing up in their fine car, and were not merely turned away at the gate. Instead of seeing the Fuehrer, they were given a senior Gestapo officer to talk to. All that could come of this meeting was renewed activity on Franziska's case, something Gertrude may have naively insisted was their own wish in the matter. A protocol was duly written up, and official interest was not long in manifesting itself. The files the Berlin police had accumulated on Franziska were sent to their counterparts in Hannover for prompt action.

Police officers turned up at the Madsack house and took photographs of Franziska and made copies of her registration papers. "Certain officials higher up" had ordered them to clear up this "Famous Criminal Case" by determining whether Franziska was "the person she claimed to be or an impostor." They planned to show the new photographs to the Schanzkowsky family in Hygendorf.

Franziska had been sick again in 1937, but had recovered and wrote Fallows that the "black angel" hadn't come for her yet. Now, when she was beginning to enjoy the best health she'd experienced "since I was at home," black angels of another kind turned up at her door.

There was a bit of hope. Hannover Police Commissioner Lindner reassured Gertrude that the Schanzkowsky sisters said that they hadn't identified the photo as that of their sister, missing for eighteen years now. But Lindner wanted to be sure and proposed a face-to-face confrontation in Hygendorf; he would go to Pomerania with Franziska and Gertrude in the Madsack car.

Franziska refused to go. Going to Hygendorf was "beneath her imperial dignity." She hadn't been back for almost twenty years, but her frantic refusal to return to the family home, to see her siblings in these familiar surroundings, speaks for itself. It was one thing to see Felix in a Bavarian inn, quite another to see Felix, Walter, Gertrud, and Mariechen in their old cottage in the village where she had paraded around in high heels and fussy, homemade dresses. It would have been an overwhelming experience that could have broken her and revealed her as she really was. Gertrud and Mariechen had loyally denied recognizing the photo, but who knew how they would react if their Franziska returned home?

Who knew how she herself would react? Her emotions had been hidden for years; she had not had an honest or natural conversation with anyone since she talked to Felix in the shadow of Castle Seeon. Obviously she didn't know if she could keep up the pretense in the Hygendorf she remembered, perhaps dreamed about still—all could be gone in a minute of truthfulness. The result would be an asylum or worse ...

While she fretted, the legal drama continued. The Mendelssohn Bank wrote to Franziska in February, addressing her politely as "Imperial Highness," and informed her that the tsar's account, shrunken through inflation to 157,000 marks, would soon be dispersed to his official heirs. At the same time, there was the ongoing libel suit in England and a claim Edwards wanted to pursue concerning Romanov property in England. Fallows was able to get Franziska to sign a letter to Edwards—"Please act for me"—in which she mentioned the tsar's

English hunting lodge and his "Finnish village," which likely referred to the village of Halilia. The Grand Duchess Xenia had been compensated for this property in 1934; Franziska said the money was hers.

Franziska also signed an affidavit for the libel suit against the *News of the World*, but balked at the rest. She lived alone now, in an apartment the Madsacks had rented for her on Trojanstrasse. Gertrude was another surrogate mother, one who didn't hesitate to speak her mind to "Anastasia" while at the same time dispensing limitless patience and care. She was perhaps the only person who could make Franziska put in her dentures and dispense with the wad of paper napkins she still used to conceal her mouth.

Franziska now suffered what Fallows called a "nervous hysterical collapse." She maintained her absolute refusal to go to Hygendorf, but also knew the police could force her and in desperation made a counter-offer. The Schanzkowskys could come to Hannover. And even then she would not meet them, or assist in any further investigations, unless Gleb Botkin came to Germany to advise her.

Waiting for him could set the confrontation back for weeks, even months. He was a person to rely on, a person who had never hesitated to come to the aid of his "grand duchess," even as he made his loathing of Franziska Schanzkowsky plain, defaming her in his new book as a "demented Polish peasant" with "black and decayed" teeth.

The ongoing Mendelssohn Bank affair meant that Fallows had drawn up a bond he wanted Franziska to sign: "I know of nothing which would contradict the truthfulness of my deposition [that she was Anastasia] and to make application to the proper Court in Germany for a Certificate of Inheritance."

It is typical of Fallows that he carried on, pressing her to sign a fresh set of incriminating documents at just the moment when she was in the greatest danger of being exposed as an impostor. He found it rough going, never dreaming why Franziska might refuse to go to Hygendorf, let alone hesitate to sign a simple declaration. Here was something new: "Our client is too ill even to sign her name ... Her breakdown is aggravated apparently by her hereditary taint of the 'Hesse disease'."

As the long, nervous spring wore on Fallows wrote a spiritual letter to Franziska. Maybe that would do the trick: "Today is Ascension Day, commemorating the return of Jesus to His Father in Heaven ... As the last of the Romanovs you have the responsibility of developing a character, according to the standards of God, commensurate with that obligation. The Holy Spirit is waiting to help you do this."

Two days later he was back on the Hessian thing. "Only recently have I learned that the so-called 'Hessian disease' or haemophilia, afflicts males only before maturity, but daughters only after maturity," he wrote Tatiana Botkin two days later. "Its symptoms are excessive fear and suspicion. This undoubtedly is aggravating her shattered nervous constitution. She has had similar attacks before and after a time has gotten over them."

The use of a form of the verb "aggravate" in two different letters says something about the mood in the besieged Madsack apartment.

II

Imagine you have not seen your family for years, not even in photographs. Wars, oceans, and lost addresses have separated you, but you know as you wait in the airport terminal that you will recognize your sibling. Fatter, slimmer, greyer, modishly dressed. Glasses, perhaps? None of this matters. You have retained a sense of their visage, of their being, and as the plane comes in or the customs barrier is cleared—why! There they are! Different, but recognizable and curiously the same. You go forward (carrying flowers?) and melt into the family embrace of a thousand memories—the smell of the summer garden, your father in his chair on a winter evening ... all the legends and family lore impenetrable to outsiders.

But imagine the reunion if you had to deny your family, if after long years of separation, you had to pretend you didn't know them at all, to maintain a disinterested expression, fully aware that here in front of you are family who know you: yes, here is our sister. Here she is, our Franziska.

The Schanzkowskys had already made up their minds not to recognize their sister. They would present a united front, going along with what Felix had agreed to back at Wasserburg and what Mariechen and Gertrud had restated in a recent letter to the police. The family vow of silence, as Waltraud put it.

Felix came from Ammendorf; Walter, Gertrud, and Mariechen from Pomerania. Felix would serve in the German Army and be released from a prisoner of war camp in 1948, eventually settling near Mereseburg. Walter would remain in Poland, although his son, Siegfried, lives in Germany. Gertrud would end up in southern Germany with her grandson, Karl Maucher. And Mariechen, pretty Mariechen with light hair and blue eyes, would die of tuberculosis, and leave behind young children. One of them, as an adult, would recognize Waltraud on the street in Hamburg because she resembled her father so closely.

What did they think as they traveled to Hannover? They arrived on a Wednesday for a meeting scheduled for Saturday, so they must have had a few days to take in the sights, make statements, and perhaps talk to people who knew their sister. Where did they stay? Someone—one of the lawyers, perhaps—was obviously paying their expenses. Hannover was a strange city to them, but they were hardly the yokels Franziska's supporters said they were. Butow was only a few miles away from Hygendorf; surely they must have been to Danzig. Gertrud had lived in Berlin and Felix had handled himself well at Wasserburg before going to Berlin to make his own enquiries.

Did they worry that Franziska and her schemes might get them in trouble? Especially in these times? It is easy to imagine Walter, with his chronic suspicion of outsiders and disdain for Franziska's pretensions, saying so, and loudly too.

Had Franziska been in contact with them covertly, perhaps with one of her typewritten letters? Waltraud tends to doubt it. Even without letters there was still a family unity Franziska could count on. They had helped her after she was declared legally insane. Tolerant if not indulgent, they had made fun of her airs and fancies but had done what they could to see she got a fresh start in life.

While the Schanzkowsky family traveled to Hannover, Franziska was renewing her friendship with Gleb Botkin, who had arrived days before the confrontation. Dinner at the Madsacks', a visit to Hannover's pretty Maschsee, a man-made lake surrounded by gardens and an amusement park. They rode the ferris wheel, Gleb and Franziska. Franziska hanging on his arm, looking into his eyes? He was the only friend from her Manhattan days who had stayed true to her. She liked his book, which left no doubt about his belief that she was Her Imperial Highness the Grand Duchess Anastasia Nicholaevna of Russia, left out unappetizing facts about Four Winds and Grandanor, and took potshots at all her former friends as well. Did she wonder if her family had heard about *The Woman Who Rose Again*? Did they know about Fifth Avenue, the German princes who invited her into their castles, all the important people in Berlin, and the big American lawyer working on her case?

Franziska finally had competent German lawyers working for her. She was being represented by a distinguished firm founded by a pair of childhood friends from Lubeck, Paul Leverkuehn and Kurt Vermehren. It was a liberal firm, one which provided a safe haven for dissident gentry like Adam von Trott zu Solz. Leverkuehn would devote a great deal of time to Franziska's case, even though it was unclear how he, Vermehren or their new junior partner Helmuth von Moltke would ever get paid.

But how fitting that she would choose Gleb to be with her at the moment of confrontation. Mrs. Madsack would be there, as would Leverkuehn and Helmuth von Moltke, but for personal support she had chosen neither Prince Frederick nor Anna Samweber nor Astrid Bethusy-Huc, but Gleb Botkin. Was it all those summer hours spent together at Garden City? Did she feel less of a fraud with Gleb there? Or more a fraud, which made it all strangely more bearable, a sustainable joke, a small piece of drama? She trusted him enough to allow him to see her family, even Gertrud, whom she was said to closely resemble.

She knew that Gleb would have a low opinion of them and perhaps that made the prospect of seeing them easier. Look how far she had come since those days when she and Gertrud left Pomerania for Berlin. Poor country girls, with their packages of sandwiches and cardboard suitcases. Here she was, "Anastasia," with a handsome man, a mysterious New York Russian, by her side.

July 9, 1938, in Hannover, sunny and warm.

Franziska wore a new suit. Light wool.

At the police station Franziska had to sit in a waiting room with her family as her siblings were questioned one by one. Imagine that: the stiff faces, the averted eyes, everyone afraid to breathe. Gleb was there, watching. He was surprised to see that Gertrud looked like Franziska, but this was only the "kind of resemblance which a horse or a bird can have to a human being;" as an animal might, a beast in a field. Perhaps the Schanzkowskys were watching him too, this Russian toff who lacked the sense to see through Franziska's ruses. Fallows, unable to practice law in Germany, was not allowed to be present.

Gertrud, Felix, Walter, and Mariechen had signed statements denying that Frau Tschaikovsky was their sister. Franziska was preparing to leave when suddenly all bets were off. Gertrud, always the unpredictable one, had had enough. Moved by memory and emotion, she began screaming, "She is my sister, she is my sister!" The others tried to calm her but she kept on: "She is my sister! She is my sister!"

The police ordered Franziska and Gertrud to remove their shoes and stand back to back.

Gertrud and Franziska: the two sisters who had argued in Berlin and fallen out. But they had been close too, and Mrs. Madsack later recalled Gertrud reminding Franziska of this as she grabbed her shoulder and cried again, "You're my sister! You're my sister!"

This may have been one of the worst moments of Franziska's life—the bodily contact, Gertrud's face inches away. And still Franziska kept at it. They were taking photos. She contorted her face, as she had at Dalldorf. Their kinship was plain to see. Later, the lawyer for the opposition would simply say that he could see the resemblance with his own eyes.

Du bisst meine Schwester!

You are my sister.

Felix, Mariechen and Walter kept protesting, Felix saying that Franziska did not even look like the woman he'd seen in Wasserburg, but Gertrud continued her refrain and did not let go of her sister's arm until Police Officer Parr intervened.

Years later, an opposing lawyer would write Gertrud " ... following your confrontation in 1938, you weren't the only one to recognize her for your sister Franziska ... Your brothers and sisters also recognized her but absented themselves from saying so as not to put obstacles in the career of their sister ... "

The confrontation had become disorderly, noisy. The police sought to contain it, and allowed Franziska to leave, which was doubtless a mistake. Who knows what might have been said if Gertrud had been allowed to continue working on Franziska, or if Walter or one of the others had begun to turn as well. As it was Franziska climbed into the big Madsack automobile and Garba sped her away.

Dinner at the Madsacks'. Franziska, relieved and giddy, gave Leverkuehn papers and documents she'd refused him before and "worked with him until late in night ... A cordial goodnight."

Alone in her apartment at last, with time and privacy to think about what had happened, Franziska fell apart. It was reality, the secret out in the open. She had already known the kinds of things her friends said about Franziska Schanzkowsky. The Schanzkowskys must have been discussed too, their quirks, appearance, and manners laughed at, especially by Gleb, who had earlier demeaned them as people "who ... appeared willing, for a price, to testify to almost anything." Gertrud would have been the particular butt of their derision: this simple, "insane" woman who had the audacity to mistake Her Imperial Highness for her own sister.

She was supposed to meet the former Russian officer Arapov the next day at noon, but of course she didn't turn up. How could she immediately slip back into that precarious, crazy role? One of the Madsacks went to Franziska's apartment and found her "angry and ugly" about the "Schanzkowsky mess." No one heard from her for days. Garba pushed a letter under her door which went unanswered. Gleb came and pounded on her door but did no better. Franziska threatened to call the police.

The old vitriol appeared, slung this time at Gertrude Madsack. She wrote nasty notes to her, notes said to have been even more vile than the ones she had once addressed to Annie Burr Jennings. Notes so awful that Fallows turned around and threatened to sue her for libel if she sent any more. The Madsacks swore they were through with "Anastasia."

Fallows engaged in a bit of arm-twisting; he and Franziska still needed the Madsacks, especially Gertrude: "Could you ever forgive yourself or would your friends or the world understand, if you now abandon her and leave her in a flat you rented for her, mentally and physically sick and perhaps dying? Every day without food or care she surely is growing weaker, and the danger of death is becoming more imminent and horrible to contemplate."

In reality Franziska had snuck out of the apartment and joined a jolly bus trip along the Rhine. All was forgiven, though. No one questioned why "Anastasia" would be so upset by meeting strangers, especially as the confrontation had ultimately proved nothing against her. Nor did anyone wonder about Franziska's behavior at the meeting, which despite all her efforts, was disturbing. There are indications that she hadn't been as controlled as later biographers would claim, that seeing her family had visibly unnerved her.

In an undated memo to Fallows from this period, Helene Noeggerath said Helmuth von Moltke had already told the British lawyers Edwards and McCaskie that Franziska could not go into the witness box until she experienced a "lucid interval" again. Helene went on to say that Franziska would not make a good witness: "Leverkuehn had seen [that] at the Schanzkowsky confrontation."

Franziska would never have withstood a confrontation in Hygendorf.

III

Franziska continued to live in the apartment the Madsacks were subsidizing for her. Later that summer she made another attempt to reconcile with Xenia, now remarried and living in Syosset, New York: "Could you not forget what happened between us for I have been very ill after many operations but am now better and thinking carefully about everything. I would be happy if we could be friends again."

This plea would also go unanswered.

Other things had been going on. It was a time of threats made real, of a burgeoning SS, of concentration camps and mobilization plans, of purges in both the foreign service and the military. Hitler, already addicted to grandiose fantasies of his eventual departure from power, speculated about the possibility of presiding over the coronation of a properly National Socialist kaiser before retiring to his hometown with his faithful mistress, Eva Braun. A state visit to Italy and the rude behavior of the court of Victor Emmanuel III had ended all that. On the way back, Hitler morosely noted that they ought to thank the Social Democrats for overthrowing the German princes in 1918. There was no more talk of a monarchical restoration and the princes were further downgraded in importance.

Snags had developed in the *News of the World* lawsuit. Superficially, it seemed the strongest of Franziska's legal actions. She certainly wasn't a Romanian actress, and hadn't confessed anything to anybody. The tabloid had declined to settle, however, and her only prospect of getting them to pay lay in taking the matter to court. The trial would have to be held in England, site of the offense. A British law firm had already advised Fallows against proceeding, reasoning that the risk of an adverse ruling was simply too great and pointing out that Franziska would be obligated to get in the witness box and face stiff questioning about her finances, among other things.

When asked if it had been unwise to level with Franziska's English attorneys about her limitations as a witness, Leverkuehn replied that "he could not do otherwise, he simply had to play for time because if the case would come to trial presently everything would be lost."

Greater events were beginning to affect Franziska and her friends and acquaintances. Her aristocratic supporters began thinking about getting rid of Hitler. Helmuth von Moltke, Adam von Trott zu Solz, Otto Kiep, and Kurt Vermehren's son Erich were among them. The law offices of Leverkuehn and Vermehren became known as place where a variety of dissidents could meet, and find work or legal assistance. It was a loose confederation of well-bred, well educated men, as alternately casual and selective as any secret fraternity: officers who would swear an oath on the romantic poet Stefan George (and keep it), men who died for religious principles, lawyers who took up lost and romantic causes.

IV

Undefended by what it thought had been its allies, Czechoslovakia fell to Germany, March 14, 1939. Hitler, having made a pact with the Soviets, was prepared to go farther. On September 1, 1939, Poland was invaded and portioned out between the Russians and the Germans. War had returned to villages like Hygendorf. Jews, officers, intellectuals, and the native nobility began to disappear into camps and mass graves in remote forests. When Felix married, he had to prove the Schanzkowskys were an Aryan family, not Jews or potential slave laborers.

It seems probable that Franziska was initially sheltered from the worst of the new Germany. Her friends in Hannover would have seen to it, and her ties to the estate owners may well have garnered country delicacies no longer seen in the cities. A later biographer would even claim that Franziska's fear of officialdom kept her from applying for a ration card, although that seems unlikely since she waded through the red tape needed to keep her apartment in Hannover.

It can't have all been bad, from Franziska's point of view. The legal dilemmas which had haunted her for so many years had begun retreating as soon as the first German soldier set foot in Poland. The state of war existing between Germany and Great Britain made it impossible for a German national to sue a British citizen or, more to the point, newspaper. The perilous documents which had brought on the attack of the "Hessian Disease" months before were now dead letters. The tussle over the Mendelssohn bank account and the Certificates of Inheritance was on the back burner too.

V

The futility of further action may have finally suggested itself to Fallows as well. He was ill, and in Waldeck, where Helene Noeggerath had guaranteed payment for his treatment. Earlier, he had assigned her a share of the anticipated Grandanor profits equal to that promised to Franziska's German lawyers. Now it began to look like time to leave. His illness, unspecified in his archives, was serious and Germany was at war. He was a citizen of a neutral nation for the moment, but who knew how long that would last?

Late in the year Fallows sailed home third class on a ship crowded with refugees. He may have felt rather like a refugee himself, fleeing a calamity in Europe to begin again in rented rooms in New York. His obsession had cost him all the usual comforts of life as a successful attorney—his summer house, his town residence, his car, his stocks, bonds, and insurance policies. His wife, Julia, and daughters had remained loyal, if somewhat bewildered by the turn of events.

Largely unnoticed by the other participants in Europe, Fallows died at the end of the month. His wife and daughter Annette would blame

Franziska and her demands and legendary ingratitude for his demise, although it might be that Fallows' own feelings were better represented by a late fragment found in his archives: "I shall persevere in this case as long as I have breath ... "

VI

Once the terrible winter dissipated, Germany began a run at the rest of Europe. Blitzkreig, the lightning advance of armor backed by an equally aggressive air force, conquered Norway and Denmark, Holland, Belgium, Luxembourg, and finally France, which collapsed June 21, 1940.

Prince Wilhelm, the eldest son of Crown Prince Wilhelm and "Aunt Cecilie" had been killed in action and his funeral at Potsdam in early June had attracted upwards of fifty thousand mourners. Hitler, enraged by this evidence of lingering monarchist feeling, responded by forcing most members of ex-ruling houses out of the armed services.

The Germans were finding themselves in the opening stages of a stalemate. The British had managed to rescue much of their expeditionary force at Dunkirk, and although weakened by massive bombing and largely blockaded by sea, were not seeking peace as Hitler had been led to believe they would. As the year went on and American aid began to flow, they would start to bring the war to German civilians. In October the Royal Air Force focused on industrial targets located within heavily populated areas. Hannover was to be one of these. On February 10, 1941, 221 British bombers took off to attack the industrial district of Hannover, chosen for its role in manufacturing key components for the U-Boats which enforced the blockade. This was the largest force sent against a single German city to date, and it was only the beginning.

VII

Who could blame Franziska for resuming her wandering? Her country friends welcomed her. Here the skies were clear of bombers and the staples of life—fresh meat, milk, eggs, vegetables—were still available.

She seems to have spent much of her time at Siebeneichen—Seven Oaks—the Miltitz castle in Saxony. These visits went the way they always did. A good beginning, perhaps some gardening, the baroness personally waiting on Franziska so that "she wouldn't have anything to do with the servants." Franziska played her part, archly dismissing the baron from his own art gallery. She received people in bed, and the snobbery of these visitors can be glimpsed in the duchess who duly assured her hostess that Franziska's greeting to her was "completely aristocratic!"

"She is so obviously aristocratic, so obviously the child of a reigning house, that one must be blind not to see it ... Nothing outward existed to form this impression. She could lie in bed and this aristocratic aura emanated from her," Miltitz herself wrote.

Then, like clockwork, Act Two. The darkness arrived "like thunder." It began with another quarrel with a servant, and led to a sudden departure: "All she wanted was to go away—away from this place where she had been so happy ... "

She turned around once she'd returned to Hannover and found only a packet of wormy oatmeal in her apartment. Incredibly, once she arrived at the station nearest Siebeneichen she turned around yet again, after sitting on a bench and looking at the clock. Back in Hannover she sent Miltitz a card, saying that she was ill. Despite the difficulties of wartime travel, the baroness rushed to Hannover to find Franziska malnourished, but unwilling to go to Siebeneichen. When finally persuaded to return, she was "very weak, undernourished," and spent her time in a bed beside an open window which overlooked the park. They should have closed the black-out curtains, but kept them open as the night passed, "sometimes lit by moonlight over the silent park, sometimes accompanied by wind or sheets of rain."

"Speak to me," Franziska said in the darkness.

Miltitz responded with a lecture about humanity and the Cosmos. "I could feel her drinking in the words ... then she spoke about her dead dear ones ... I repeated the Lord's Prayer."

The internal thunder broke. "She showed her darkness, speaking with another voice and another expression."

Demons again. What did Franziska say? The baroness didn't tell but the next morning when she carried in a breakfast tray, Franziska refused it. This went on for five days, Franziska rejecting all food with "coldness and strength."

On the fifth day, Miltitz found Franziska lying before her bed. Revived, Franziska cried out, "Why do the evil spirits have so much interest in me?"

It was a bravura performance, a strange mixture of cunning and genuine chaos. Franziska's hunger strike and fainting spell convinced the baroness not only of her identity as Anastasia—would an impostor dare to act this way?—but proved that she was even more than that, an angry woman of fate like Electra or Kriemhild of the *Nibelungenlied*.

VIII

That spring the old kaiser died at Doorn, after refusing refuge in both England and Germany. The stalemate in the west stood much as it had, invasion plans still on the drawing boards. Hitler, never good at dealing with frustration, confounded expectations when he simply turned and went the other way, invading his former ally, the Soviet Union, on June 22, 1941. This second front, so promising at first, would have terrible consequences for Germany at large, and for Franziska's friends in the east in particular.

The banning of the Anthroposophical Society caused the Steinerites to draw together for secret meetings which would continue during the war. Eliza von Moltke, for instance, still held gatherings in her Berlin apartment. She had even, as a kind of macabre joke, displayed a stolen sign reading "The enemy may be listening" in her salon. But these cozy and reassuring get-togethers were endangered by a momentous event in 1941.

The whole world soon knew of the secret and unauthorized flight of Rudolf Hess, the Deputy Fuehrer, in May 1941. He had intended to meet with the Duke of Hamilton in hopes of arranging a peace, but was captured and imprisoned as soon as he landed on British soil. This wild gambit—Churchill would liken it to his trusted Foreign Secretary jumping into a stolen Spitfire and parachuting into the grounds of the Berghof—enraged Hitler, who promptly arrested many members of Hess' staff. The official German pronouncement was that Hess "lived in a state of fantasy;" his British captors would soon concur with this assessment.

The surprise—and peril—was that the Security Service had determined that Hess had become a "silent adherent of Rudolf Steiner and the Anthroposophists." Indications were there all along. Hess had been eccentric about food, bringing his own "biodynamic" food in a lunch pail to Hitler's table. It probably seemed funny at the time, the earnest health food enthusiast annoying his middle-class boss with his unappealing diet, but people must have begun adding things up once he was gone. Steiner was the impresario of biodynamic farming. Hess had also supported Steiner's devoutly apolitical Waldorf schools; the Waldorf schools were closed and arrests made.

Franziska thus had another fear. As unworldly as people said she was, no one was impervious when they learned that their friends were suddenly of interest to the political police. Could she maintain her role without their shelter and support? Could she herself be arrested as a Anthroposophical adherent? She had never formally joined the Society, but no one knew if the Gestapo would recognize niceties like that when they were seeking people to punish for Hess' strange adventure.

After the opening of the eastern front she was seen as a Russian—a potential enemy. Although it seems doubtful that the Germans would have arrested "Anastasia" on this basis, it was still a risk. As Franziska Schanzkowsky, she could have been sent to a camp, prison or asylum. She may have been aware of the Nazis' attitude towards the mentally ill; confined to another mental hospital, a timely injection could have ended it all. No wonder, then, that Franziska's friends kept her identity as "Anastasia" a secret during the latter part of the war.

But what did Franziska herself make of all this? In the Sixties she would tease the sensitivities of her friends by revealing an alleged visit with Hitler, a wild tale that seems breathless in the telling, reverential and awestruck.

A black limousine collected her one day in 1940 or early 1941 in Berlin and delivered her to the Reichstag Building. "Two tall, handsome guards" led her down the hallway to "a set of massive double doors." And behind the doors—perched on a corner of the desk!—Adolf Hitler awaited her. He "rose and bowed" and then they sat facing each other. He told her his government had investigated her case and concluded she was Anastasia. He would "destroy" the British Royal family who had "betrayed her family." Soon he would "invade the Soviet Union and annihilate the Bolshevik government that had murdered her parents ... once this feat was accomplished, he would personally restore the Romanov monarchy."

Was Franziska spinning another story? Whatever the truth was, what she said suggests something about her feelings during the war. Possibly, like so many Germans, she was not immune to the charisma of the Fuehrer. It was not a feeling her friends shared and formed another barrier between them, but Franziska was often like that, willfully contrary. She may well have convinced herself that Hitler was actually not so bad. She was proud of being German—not Polish, and would call herself a *Wend* in years to come, a term that conveyed an intense pride in the early medieval origins of her people, who took possession of the southern shores of the Baltic and Germanized it.

Franziska definitely got one detail wrong. Hitler, stolidly *korrekt* when meeting women, would not have perched on a corner of his desk to receive Her Imperial Highness the Grand Duchess Anastasia. But in the imagination of Franziska Schanzkowsky, Hitler on the desk, like a jaunty garden gnome, was just the right touch. Like the Queen burping in the privacy of your flat or asking for your recipe for scones. As Russian peasants used to say, it was far to the tsar. It was far to the Fuehrer too. In her imagination, Franziska had seen them both.

IX

Franziska's affairs were now being handled by Kurt Vermehren and what remained of his firm. Leverkuehn himself had been absent from March 1940, when he had been appointed Consul to Tabriz. From there he had gone on to Istanbul to serve as the local head of military intelligence, the Abwehr. In September Franziska's petition to revoke the Certificates of Inheritance issued to the surviving Romanovs was denied by the Berlin Central District Court. This decision was immediately appealed, but little happened. The year ended with the failure of the Germans to take Moscow, with Pearl Harbor and a declaration of war on the United States. Franziska's case was formally suspended until the end of hostilities.

X

Kreisau, Helmuth von Moltke's estate in the east, had been one of Franziska's stopovers. He had acted on her behalf as a lawyer and in a more personal way, as the nephew of Eliza von Moltke and the cousin of Astrid Bethusy-Huc. As time went on, his country house became the meeting ground of the Kreisau Circle, the most intellectual and spiritual of the interlocking circles of plotters. The circle broke down into study groups which carried on systematic conversations about what post-Nazi society ought to be like. Most members rejected violence, to the extent of forbidding discussion of the possible assassination of Hitler. They consecrated themselves to the task of creating a better Germany.

They were intensely religious people, and it is likely that here lay their common ground with the Anthroposophists. They also shared a sense of immediacy, a feeling that the direct contact of an individual with the divine, and the promptings of the individual conscience, were paramount. Alone, they pondered the imminent defeat of demagoguery and the revival of German virtue and honor. The Anthroposophists among them guarded Steiner's words and prayers, heartened by the larger cosmic world. Once the war was over, "Anastasia" would fulfill her destiny and a new rule of brotherhood would supplant the Bolsheviks in the east, to the benefit of all.

XI

Franziska's own movements at this time are difficult to trace. She would notice this herself as an old woman, and be annoyed by it: "[it was] never recorded by nobody. That nobody is interested to hear." So many of the usual markers of Franziska's life are absent; no evidence was being collected, funds sought, or papers filed. Here is the genuine woman describing something awful which has really happened to her:

"All Hannover washed away ... All was smashed, but our little house was standing. The large windows all were out, but the house was standing ... it was standing. I had at once doors put in and at once were the windows put in, that was quickly done. And then I had done the mistake to stay there for a few days, I wanted to stay there ... I was terribly sleepy, and had gone to sleep and suddenly the room is lit white. White lit is the room. Snow white is the room lit ... And I [got] out of the bed [and went] to the window, and there hangs a 'Christmas Tree,' directly at the corner hanging. They were called 'Christmas Trees,' these signs which the Americans and the British throw down. They throw four such things ... When they centered something out, where they wanted to throw the bombs in, then they made it with four such trees that they were called 'Christmas Trees.' And such a beast was hanging just at my corner, directly ...

"Then, a woman who had left the electric train, was driving the electric train, wanted to run to her children home quickly too. It catched her, this bomb, on the street, when she was running. Tore her head off, tore her stomach open. She was torn entirely open. And so this was, in the last second, prevented, that I am still as a poor idiot sitting here. Otherwise this would not have been the case."

Franziska's abrupt returns to Hannover were not all precipitated by her hot temper or wounded dignity. Her apartment was subject to strict wartime occupancy regulations in a city already devastated by Allied bombing. If Franziska wasn't going to maintain residence in her apartment, the authorities were prepared to take it away and give it to someone who would. It was an independent base she was determined to keep, even at considerable risk to herself. Perhaps Franziska, like many other women in Hannover, could imagine a day when it would all be over, and she would be left in peace to enjoy the home she had hung onto with such persistence, courage, and wit.

"You have no idea what it was like," says a woman who lived through the bombing. "Anyone who has never experienced it doesn't understand. The sirens came ... you ran and ran into the nearest shelter. At night, we went to the cellar. I always kept a suitcase packed. With photos. Everything might be destroyed, but I needed the memories."

The worst were the potassium bombs that shriveled people to a third of their size, burned to a cinder. "It was so sudden. The bombs could come any time. I never want to experience another war."

In the bomb shelters Franziska was just another German woman, huddled in a fur coat thrown on over a nightgown, her house key on a string around her neck. Perhaps she had come to prefer the bombs and the bomb shelters to the increasingly tense households of her friends. Aristocratic women were disappearing into prisons and camps too. Princess Mafalda of Savoy, the wife of a secondary Hessian prince had been arrested largely as a result of Hitler's animosity towards her father, Victor Emmanuel. She died in Buchenwald in the spring of 1944. Years later Franziska would remember Mafalda's fate: "They had taken the daughter ... and put [her] in a concentration camp where she had under some different name been kept. It's so horrid! I could die!"

XII

Trouble was coming to people she knew, as well. Kurt Vermehren's son Erich had gone to Turkey to join Leverkuhn's staff at the Abwehr. In January 1944 Erich and his wife, the former Countess Plettenberg, had defected to the British, a move which infuriated Hitler and led to the arrest of various associates, Erich's parents among them, and the demotion of Leverkuhn.

The month of June 1944 struck hard. On the 6th the Allied invasion of Europe began, at a time when it was becoming increasingly apparent that inundation by the Soviets to the east was imminent.

Thus it went until Colonel Count Claus von Stauffenberg, a relatively new member of the conspiracy, carried a bomb-laden briefcase into a June 20 staff meeting and very nearly killed Adolf Hitler. The savage wave of reprisals undid the precautions that people like Franziska's friends had organized their lives around.

Stauffenberg was executed July 20, near the Belderstrasse building, not far from the canal where Franziska had tried to drown herself in 1920. His last words belonged to Stefan George: "Long live our secret Germany."

Otto Beck, husband of the countess who had attended the von Moltke seances in Berlin in the Twenties, was shot the day after he bungled a suicide attempt. Adam von Trott zu Solz, Helmuth von Moltke, Otto Kiep, Fritz Dietlef von Schulenberg, and Pastor Dietrich Bonhoeffer, whose father had examined Franziska and found her authentic, lost their lives in the plot. They had all been leaders in their own way, as well as "spiritual cousins," as an Anthroposophist would later say.

All at once Hannover seems to have become too much for Fran-ziska. Prince Frederick turned up and escorted her southeast, to Schloss Winterstein, the country seat of his cousin, Louise of Saxe-Meiningen, an unusual choice in a time when a vast array of Soviet forces was closing in on eastern Germany.

Hitler had long since retreated into his bunker deep beneath Berlin. Although he sometimes spoke of defending the Ruhr, or of hanging onto the Hungarian oilfields or Vienna, he had never liked or trusted the landowners of the east and seems to have been quite willing to abandon them to their fate.

The remnants of Army Group Center combined with a desperate home army to strike up a patchy resistance, but few held much hope for it. The roads were choked with an entire civilization heading west in hopes of crossing the Elbe and surrendering to British or American troops. Pomerania had already fallen and accounts of the barbarity of the Red Army were being carried west rapidly, often by eye witnesses. In some instances the nobility were actively sought out and murdered; there were reliable reports of people being blinded or mutilated or simply hacked to bits. Others described men and women dragged to their deaths behind horses. Rape became hideously commonplace.

Prince Frederick and Franziska's faith in the protection offered by ancient estates must have been strong indeed. He entrusted her to the care of the castle before leaving again, perhaps to return to Altenburg. Franziska became one of a band of aristocratic refugees sheltering there. Thuringia was engulfed in a giant pincer movement as 1 Belo-russian Front and 1 Ukrainian Front raced to encircle Berlin. All over eastern Germany people awaited the end. Survivors reported that talk often turned to speculation about the most efficient methods of sui-cide, or, only slightly more optimistically, how to react when con-fronted with their first Soviet invader. The inhabitants of Schloss Winterstein waited it out.

Soon enough the Russians made an appearance.

Their arrival was the worst possible news for Franziska, the alleged daughter of the tsar. The Soviets were dragging thousands of generals,

Cossacks, and princes back to Russia. The White Russians were seen as people who had backed the wrong side. Many had worked for the Germans; all seem to have been viewed with some suspicion by the Allies.

There would be stories of Franziska's defiance of Russian soldiers, of her threatening one with a knife, for instance, but they all have a distinctly apocryphal flavor to them. It's more likely that Franziska tried to avoid attracting attention to herself, melting into the pool of small, drab, nervous women at the Schloss, most of them elderly, all of them unmistakably poor and defenseless.

Word was out about princesses—Prince Frederick's sister among them—being forced to work the fields once owned by their families. The Soviets may not have been particularly interested in the inhabitants of Schloss Winterstein but were unpredictable. As Baroness von Miltitz wrote later, she learned "how sometimes they seemed to be in the light of angels and in the blinking of an eye were shadowed by the devil."

Somehow an alarm was raised, followed by the arrival of Prince Frederick, who seems to have traveled some distance to take charge of Franziska's affairs. His playing card and opera house principality was coming apart, and there was little to keep him in the east. Not for Franziska the weary wagon ride west to the safety of other zones in the dead of winter. She and her escort seem to have traveled up the road to Eisenach, a city on the Warra River, and thus right at the border of the Russian and British Zones of Occupation.

What occurred next is confusing. One account has Franziska helped across by an "old friend" while at another point she claimed "and that my head is still on my shoulders, I have only to thank the chief-leader of the SS in Eisenach."

What really seems to have happened is that Prince Frederick contacted a friend in the Swedish Red Cross, seeking preferential treatment for the "grand duchess." Franziska crossed the Warra on December 18, 1946, with Red Cross assistance. She would later describe being in a leaky rowboat, and Frederick, exasperated or hysterical, attempting to lighten the load by throwing suitcases of "precious goods" into the river. Franziska rescued, among other things, the photo album of the tsar's family that Tania Botkin had given her so many years before.

Franziska had told so many tales of crossing borders secretly, fleeing the Bolsheviks, and now here she was, slipping over into the British Zone, not far from old haunts in Hannover. She crossed into the French Zone next, winding up in Bad Liebenzell, a spa village in the Black Forest where Rudolf Steiner had founded a clinic which Franziska promptly checked into. It was the end of her run, and only a handful of kilometers from the town where she would spend the next two decades.

Chapter Sixteen

I

The Black Forest is perhaps the most beautiful and romantic corner of Germany. Deep forests where deer and boar roam, sparkling lakes, clear air, picturesque villages, homey inns and meadows and brooks and mountain trails: it is a child's fairy tale land come to life. And in winter, when the snow lies heavily on the trees and the moon shines over the snow, it's everybody's Christmas card. The shady Black Forest highways wind through kilometers of mountainous landscape, past old castles, monasteries and vineyards. You can eat Black Forest cake and ham and sample the famous Kirsch at country inns where the owner's braided little daughter might wait on you. You can hike the trails—all very civilized, with a terraced cafe at the end, and perhaps a workshop selling Black Forest cuckoo clocks and carvings of woodcutters and the Madonna. Chapels and ancient churches dot the countryside. The people are proud of their down-to-earth ways, their folklore, their ties to the land. One can imagine Hansel and Gretl here, the goose girl weeping in the forest . . .

A witch in a hut . . .

Here she is again. It's March 1949 and it looks as if she is being presented with something. Adele von Heydebrandt stands nearby, her beautiful white hair smoothed into an immaculate bun. She wears an old black dress, practical but well-cut. Prince Frederick stands between them, flexing and glancing to the side as if waiting for a ceremony to begin. He is in country squire clothes—baggy trousers and a shetland sweater over shirt and tie. Franziska alone faces the camera and smiles broadly. Her cotton dress is crisply pressed and her hair has been shaped into a flip and combed away from her soft, wrinkled forehead. Her teeth are in and she clutches a loose bouquet of mixed garden flowers. The age in her face is surprising, after a gap in the photographic record. She is suddenly an old woman at 53, small and wizened. It's been a hard slog, these past few years.

It was natural that Prince Frederick would take her to this haven of Anthroposophy. Baroness von Miltitz owned a house in Unterlengenhardt and the village was filled with Steinerites. The farmers had grown used to their otherwordly and often aristocratic neighbors. Suddenly they were all poor, poorer than the landed farmers. Titles, prerogatives, estates and wealth—all gone. Their sons and nephews, like those of other Germans, had fallen for the Fuehrer and Reich. Prince Frederick's own sister Elisabeth had to work in a hospital laundry and the nieces of Adele von Heydebrandt, the elderly Anthroposophist who looked after Rudolf Steiner long ago and who would become Franziska's companion, had had to do field work for the Russians on her brother's estate in Poland.

In Unterlengenhardt, the local Anthroposophists revolved around Franziska, their own secret "grand duchess" with her karmic significance for the world. She was also a connection to the lost world of royal courts and old values; her store of small details, falling effortlessly now from her lips, recalled that old life. Her drama enlivened the dreary days of making do. She gave them something to talk about, an excuse to write letters, reasons to fret and complain and secretly exult over the "royal" monster among them. As time passed there would be other ladies-in-waiting. A photo of some of them shows the solid looking forms of Adele and Baroness Gienanth, with Gertrude Lamerdin perched jauntily on the hood of a car, wearing a headscarf that makes her look a bit like an elderly Squeaky Fromme.

Franziska's "Anastasia" identity remained a tightly kept secret. You never knew. Even Hermine, the kaiser's widow, had disappeared into an internment camp in 1947, never to be seen again. At first locals knew Franziska as Frau Anderson, just another Anthroposophist who had taken refuge in the village. Rationing and shortages were a fact of life, but at least there was fallen timber for fuel and berries and mushrooms for the picking. All the same, she and Mrs. von Heydebrandt yearned to emigrate to Switzerland or the United States. They could get visas for America, Adele wrote a friend, "but we don't have the money." Prince Frederick bought himself an old army barrack ("the hut"), then reluctantly allowed the women to take it over. The photograph of Franziska with the bouquet commemorates their moving day. Prince Frederick removed himself to the basement of Baroness von Miltitz' house.

II

Once inside the Unterlengenhardt hut, Mrs. von Heydebrandt seems to have kept everything in a series of small brown boxes which came to light only recently. This homemade archive was stuffed with every scrap of paper from their lives together there: letters from friends and admirers, grocery lists, poems, receipts from the post office, drafts of letters which issued forth from the hut. Franziska is revealed here—busy, involved, capable, inconsiderate.

"Mrs. Anderson knows how to protect herself," reads one draft. "Mrs. Anderson has already had one person jailed in Hannover."

"I wanted to write," a relative wrote Adele, "but I hesitated to intrude on the unknown atmosphere ... it's a terrible time when one is surrounded by malice. In the Hitler years we swallowed the same thing; I know all about it. But such reminiscing doesn't serve anyone; one is never safe were there is evil; let us not speak about it."

Baroness von Miltitz wrote about Adele's exasperating passivity and that "Never have I felt such evil standing before me as in the times of Anastasia's darkness ... It was something hugely powerful, totally impersonal ... "

Even Prince Frederick mused that one could almost imagine at times that "Anastasia" was a Polish factory worker, such were her bad manners.

Yet everyone wanted to spend time with Franziska in her hut. The correspondent who compared the oppressive atmosphere there to the

"Hitler years" also longed to visit "Dona Anastasia." Another wrote, "My thoughts are always with the hut … How is Mrs. Anderson? Tell her please that I think of her and send greetings … "

III

The first years in the Black Forest were largely happy ones. There was no publicity, fears of unmasking, or documents to sign. Franziska led a fairly public life in Unterlengenhardt. The hut was only about four hundred square feet in all and lacked indoor plumbing but it was safe. The Botkins sent food parcels and she shared the goodies with the farmers. It was significant generosity at a time when coffee and butter were still impossible to get and cigarettes were traded on the black market. Poor as she was, Franziska indulged her love of reading. "Please return the borrowed books to my address at the K-W Institute, as you may not borrow other books until yours are returned," wrote a librarian to Franziska in 1949.

IV

Franziska displayed a portrait of Rudolf Steiner over her bed. She had come to accept the Anthroposophical doctrine of reincarnation, saying that "only the shell" changed; souls remained the same from incarnation to incarnation. A reassuring thought, perhaps, to someone who had so radically changed her "shell" on the earthly plane. She rediscovered a love of animals and stopped eating meat.

"I only became a human being because of Anthroposophists," Franziska told Baroness von Miltitz. Her life in New York, and its fascination with adornment and bank accounts was now repudiated. She had come to hate the cutting down and pruning of trees. She spent many hours "sowing and weeding" in the garden behind the hut, even when ill and feverish from a "thick abscess."

She had once enthused about nature and flowers to please Harriet, but her genuine love of the soil only came later. Gardening, like the hours she spent with her pets, was a private endeavor which had nothing to do with pretending to be Anastasia, and everything to do with her secret life.

"She knew how to make things grow," Miltitz said. "She has what the English call a green thumb, although really she knows little about gardening."

Wishing Franziska a happy New Year and extending greetings on the name day of St. Anastasia the Chain Breaker, a German nobleman wrote in 1947 that "many, many cousins have preached of YOU as the representative of the Holy on the Earth." The word "cousins" is significant, referring as it does to the highly placed circle of interconnected nobility who shared this particular belief. Once travel became possible, she and Adele often stayed in his castle. Did Franziska absorb this part of the faith as well? Later she would say that only her death would free Russia from its "devils."

The day comes nearer, where I leave This world and make another way—
And without sorrowness;
And is fulfilled—not changing much. I am and I stay as I have been
God knows my way—I'm in his Judge[ment],
she wrote in the meanwhile.

V

In 1949 it was decided that it was time for Franziska to make a new will. Grandanor was still around, "controlled by me and Gleb Botkin for my mother," Annette Fallows wrote Carl Vett. She was bitter about her father's unremunerated efforts and intended to stake a claim on any assets that might still turn up. "There is no statute of limitations on Grandanor," she informed Franziska's lawyers. Gleb's ongoing involvement in the corporation may explain the growing animosity between him and the Unterlengenhardt crowd.

There would be a series of wills composed during the Black Forest era. The disposition of "Anastasia's 20,000,000 gold rubles" was a topic of considerable interest to the faithful. They were poor now and found it difficult to remain detached. Who would get what? Who deserved something? How to keep Grandanor from getting most of it? How would her enemies be affected?

For Franziska the wills must have seemed a harmless diversion, immediately sealed up in envelopes which were not to be opened until after her death. She could say what she liked: make her claims, reward her friends, and punish her enemies with impunity.

Franziska, "sick in bed," received Notary Hiller on January 2, 1949. Hiller administered a reading test and determined that she was capable of making a will. The will itself, comprised of four single-spaced typed pages, was handed over in a sealed envelope. In it she affirmed her "Anastasia" identity and spelled out the story of her journey to Romania, the people who recognized her and the motivations of the people who did not. The Story has solidified; the account is much as it will appear for decades to come.

History disposed of, "Anastasia" went on to the inheritance. The largest portions went to her godson, Prince Michael of Saxe-Weimar-Eisenach, to "my cousin" Prince Sigismund of Prussia and to the former kaiser's daughter, Princess Viktoria Louise of Prussia and Braunschweig. Prince Frederick was in for ten percent of everything realized, while Gleb and Tatiana Botkin were to split another ten percent. The lawyers who had worked for her for ten years and "to my knowledge their expenses have only been paid to a small degree" were also down for ten percent. It seems like a very status conscious bequest; the better the title, the bigger the share. Franziska acknowledged that Grandanor stood to receive the bulk of her estate, but said she felt that Fallows (and thus his family) had already been adequately compensated in light of his lack of results. "It will be the concern of my heirs to work to shrink this amount."

Franziska approved this document with a wobbly "Anastasia Tschaikovsky." This shakiness is not apparent in the handwritten artifacts she left behind in those little brown boxes.

VI

Madame Lili Dehn, a close friend of the tsarina, was located by Prince Frederick and quickly concluded that Franziska's small, worn face was indeed Anastasia's. They discussed the night at Tsarskoe Selo after Nicholas abdicated; the women had played cards to pass the long, anxious hours. At the time Dehn had known that "I should follow the Imperial Family wherever Destiny might beckon me."

Dehn's 1922 book, *The Real Tsaritsa* had doubtless been useful to Franziska—it was a treasury of small, particular facts like the names of pets, nursemaids, and favorite perfumes. At Unterlengenhardt Dehn revealed something new, something which was cheering to Franziska's supporters. At the time immediately following the abdication, Dehn claimed that Alexandra had talked about taking refuge in England and had then gone on to say, "At least we shan't have to beg, for we have a fortune deposited in the Bank of England." Dehn herself said that "I cannot remember exactly the amount, but I do remember that it was 'gold and in millions'."

It was all rather curious. The statement about gold in the Bank of England doesn't appear in her book. There she chose to write about the imperial family's immense sacrifices for the war effort, their patriotism, and most emphatically, that they had never at any point considered taking refuge in England.

The temptation to please the "grand duchess" by remembering things differently must have been intense. When Lili said that she felt tied to the destiny of the imperial family, she meant the immediate family of the tsar, not the extended family which had scorned her as an ambitious outsider. She had written of being judged "unworthy," along with Anna Vyrubova: "for although we were wellborn, we were not of the 'sang azure' of certain noble ladies who were desirous of admittance into the charmed circle."

The court of "Anastasia" would raise no such objections. Lili's recognition would become a major piece of evidence in the legal actions to come.

VII

There had always been a lot of other claimants. At this point Franziska had outlasted a crop of early, naive impostors, the sensations-of-the-day Alexeis and Anastasias who were quickly unmasked and disposed of. As events receded a second generation with more staying power began to emerge. There was Eugenia Smith, an Anastasia who was supported by a wealthy Chicago woman for some years before writing a book, passing a lie detector test, and becoming the subject of a major *Life* magazine article in 1963. Her activities as Anastasia eventually overlapped with those of the Alexei impostor Michael Goleniewski, a tempestuous Polish military intelligence officer who defected and then embarrassed his CIA handlers by loudly proclaiming his "true" identity. As improbable as it might seem, a former playmate of the real Alexei was impressed by Goleniewski's "autocratic demeanor and behavior." A bizarre scene would ensue when Smith and Goleniewski were brought together for an emotional "reunion."

An Olga claimant named Marga Boodts haunted Lake Como. She was arrested several times for jewel theft but still managed to attract a circle of believers.

Soon after Lili Dehn's visit, Franziska was introduced to one of the stranger claimants. Suzanna/Alexandra de Graaff-Hemmes was a Dutchwoman from Doorn, the former kaiser's place of exile. Suzanna/Alexandra claimed to be a secret daughter of Nicholas and Alexandra. Her birth was supposed to coincide with a false pregnancy suffered by the tsarina in 1903. It had not been a false pregnancy at all, the story went; a daughter had been born and then spirited out of the palace and adopted by a Dutch family because she was not the longed-for male heir.

Suzanna/Alexandra arrived in Unterlengenhardt in 1950, carrying old Russian money and pieces of pottery. Mrs. von Heydebrandt allowed her inside the barrack for a chat. She and Franziska went on to have a number of visits over the years. "I do accept Mrs. Suzanna Catherine de Graaff-Hemmes as my sister Grand Duchess Alexandra. She is the fifth daughter of the Czar and Czarina, but the world didn't know of her existence," Franziska later told a reporter.

Franziska was untroubled by the information that "Alexandra" had recognized Marga Boodts as Olga. Well, Marga might be Olga, Franziska allowed. This was dangerous, as Franziska's ladies were quick to see. Franziska's story depended on her being the only survivor of the family; she had signed legal depositions to that effect. And what would outsiders think of her acceptance of the improbable tale of the "fifth daughter"?

It must have been like a strange "let's pretend" game when the "Grand Duchess Anastasia" and "Princess Alexandra" drank tea in Franziska's garden. Perhaps meeting another claimant made Franziska feel a little less lonely; perhaps the fact that it created a bit of a stir in the close confines of the hut was the best fun of all.

VIII

Time passed. There was food in the market, and even cosmetics were becoming available again. Franziska had resumed visiting the hairdresser in town to have her graying hair dyed "my old brown color with a reddish tint."

Friends continued to wire small amounts and to send parcels. Both Franziska and Adele received funds from the local government and from the Red Cross. "I hope this parcel will give you joy," read a cheery cover letter.

Adele gingerly tapped out a note to an unnamed relative, alternately threatening and pleading for monthly maintenance:

"You promised me, if I approved of your relationship with a stranger, that you would give me, beginning in April and by May at the latest, 150 marks a month ... I have your letter beside me. So please, remember your promise ... The money for the hospital was paid by Prince Frederick—1,000 marks ... I advise you to be sensible and act accordingly. Send the money immediately in the proper manner. [added in English] This letter I write to you as your friend—do not force me to put this case in other hands."

The letter was preserved as an early draft in what looks like Franziska's handwriting and in a presumably final typewritten version. Its author still enjoyed small luxuries: Yardley soap, English tea, cigarettes, and magazines like *Quick* and *Welt*. Franziska and Mrs. von Heydebrandt had begun to talk about setting up a home for the aged. They corresponded with an acquaintance in Dornach, in hopes of establishing it there, in the center of Anthroposophical culture.

There was talk of lawyers preparing to finally take Franziska's case to court, and of how they all might finally find some security in their old age. A new will appeared, dated February 2, 1953. This time six single-spaced pages went into a sealed envelope. After repeating The Story and offering the standard excuses, Franziska left one-fifth to the Grand Duke Andrei, "who for years worked to clear up my fate." But then—another fifth, to be divided equally between the Grand Duchesses Olga and Xenia. Three-tenths to another enemy, the Grand Duchess Kyra Kyrillovna, wife of Prince Louis Ferdinand of Prussia, who was bitterly opposed to Franziska. The same would go to the Grand Duke Vladimir, also an enemy.

The clincher was that these enemies could only collect their portions if they acknowledged Franziska as Anastasia. If they continued to deny her identity as Anastasia, the money would go to Prince Frederick. It's possible that he was behind this audacious taunt. He had been working on his book about the supposed descendant of the "Lost Dauphin," and the parallels between the cases had made him doubly determined that Franziska should some day be recognized, even if this honor came posthumously.

The will also made arrangements for an "Alexandra Foundation" which would provide a home for the now impoverished followers who had supported Franziska throughout the years, as well as people who were prepared to do spiritual work to free Russia from communism. Franziska was to elect the recipients and the board of directors during her lifetime; plenty of opportunity for score-settling there. "I establish this foundation," she wrote, "in memory of the thoughts of my mother who would have felt that everything done in this direction fulfilled her deepest wishes." Typically, this pronouncement was followed by an angry codicil re-shuffling the board.

IX

Franziska's unobtrusive life in Unterlengenhardt ended in 1954. The warning quakes first registered in 1953, when a play by Marcelle Maurette, *Anastasia*, premiered in London. This was the year of the coronation of Elizabeth II; jets sped film overseas so that the world could see the young queen solemnly crowned in Westminster Cathedral as peers and peeresses looked on and her own handsome husband knelt in fealty before her. The play was a resounding success, and another version co-authored by Guy Bolton appeared on Broadway the following year. Twentieth Century Fox was quick to pick up the option. It was said that Marcelle Maurette had no idea the woman her heroine was based on was still alive, and "volunteered" to share the royalties once Franziska's survival was brought to her attention.

The truth of the matter was that Vermehren had forced a settlement for some thirty thousand dollars. Some of this would go to the lawyers, but enough remained to have a prefab cottage ("the dacha") erected for Franziska on a piece of donated land in Unterlengenhardt. Franziska reluctantly signed the necessary papers the day after Adele received a discouraging response from their Dornach contact.

In the 1956 movie, the enigmatic "Anna" (Ingrid Bergman) is discovered by Russian emigres who are amazed at her physical resemblance to Anastasia. They tutor Anna who learns quickly and sometimes "remembers." She also remembers a father who might have been a circus performer. But is this memory real? Her teacher, Bournine (Yul Brynner), soon has doubts. Bournine is a Harlequin Romance hero of a Russian prince; austere, remote, but finally moved by his protegee. He engineers a meeting between Anna and the dowager empress in Copenhagen, who recognizes "Anastasia" by her cough, clearing the way for a tearful embrace: "Malenkaia!"

Add court dresses, a ballroom scene, and Pat Boone warbling *An-a-sta-sia* ... the effect was complete. All so terribly romantic, especially when Anastasia forsook a royal suitor for true love with her Russian—all with Grandmamma's blessing. Was Anna really Anastasia, or was it all a dream ... and did it even matter?

Franziska, c. 1950

Chapter Seventeen

I

In 1957 *I, Anastasia*, ghosted by Roland Krug von Nidda, appeared. It seems to have been an attempt to capitalize on the interest created by the Ingrid Bergman film.

Franziska would later disavow the book, but Nidda based his narrative on documents, her dictated "memoirs" and other papers which had been preserved by Baroness von Miltitz. The tone, the voice of much of it is plainly Franziska's, full of her obsessions, peeves, and vendettas.

The civil trial was beginning, at long last. A German court had ruled that all the immediate family members of the tsar were dead and rejected Leverkuehn and Vermehren's attempt to have the Certificate of Inheritance revoked. A judge suggested that in his opinion there was sufficient evidence for the lawyers to sue directly for Franziska's recognition as Anastasia.

The legal action was a reversal of the past emphasis on finding assets; now the focus would be on establishing the mystery woman's identity. The only assets at stake were the relatively small amounts that had been dispersed by the Mendelssohn Bank. Barbara, Duchess of Mecklenburg, the granddaughter of "Aunt Irene," had received a portion of the account and was selected as a defendant. She was voluntarily joined by Prince Louis of Hesse. They were both represented by a keen young Hamburg attorney, Dr. Guenther von Berenberg-Gossler. They would ask the court to not only rule Anna Anderson an impostor, but to also declare that she was in fact Franziska Schanzkowsky.

Franziska knew that she could be arrested for perjury if she testified. Even if she won, both she and Gleb feared a successful countersuit that would involve other royals, including the British Royal Family.

Lord Louis Mountbatten was already emerging as an opponent. She also knew that the legal costs could sweep away everything she owned, including the new cottage built out of the film money.

Franziska refused to testify. "I know very well who I am and don't need a court of law to prove it," she would say. Only the indulgence of her lawyers allowed her to maintain this stance, although they were perhaps relieved, knowing that she would never make a good witness. Prince Frederick stood in as her proxy during the trial.

The trial opened before a three judge panel in the High Court in Hamburg on January 9, 1958.

II

Franziska shut herself up in the hut and turned against everyone. Never before had the dangers of being "Anastasia" been so apparent, so accompanied by publicity, by strangers waiting outside her house and clamoring to see her. When they could not come in person, they wrote. Letters came from New Zealand, Ireland, England, France, the United States, and all the German provinces; everyone sought to reassure the mysterious, tragic princess: "Dear Imperial Highness ... *Kaiserliche Hoheit* ... Forgive me for writing ... I am sorry to intrude on your time ... I cried so much in the movies when I saw how much you had suffered ... "

Adele kept all the favorable ones. There was nothing in the little brown boxes to cast doubt on Franziska's identity. The self-addressed envelopes, never returned, are here, as are the envelopes the letters came in. Requests flowed in: could "Anastasia" give them an old Russian coin, a Singer sewing machine, an autographed photograph? A high school girl in Richmond, Virginia was writing a paper and wanted to correspond. Others prayed for her, were impressed by her elegant manners, proposed marriage, or sent money for coffee and eggs, since "I know you're not a liar ... "

Imagine Adele showing her the latest letter, reading it aloud, while Franziska hid in bed. The hut had become cluttered with mementoes, papers and cats; as Adele aged, the clutter grew. Tatiana Botkin visited in the Fifties, and found Franziska burrowed beneath quilts and feather beds on a hot summer day. The window was almost obscured by plants and by cats that climbed over Franziska as she crooned endearments to them.

How silly yet somehow threatening the letters seem. They reflected the adulation and expectations of so many people, especially Germans. How could she live if she were unmasked? Where could she go? The stakes were high yet somehow she held herself together.

III

The spectre of Franziska Schanzkowsky came alive in court.

Doris Wingender testified that she had recognized Franziska at Seeon and that her family had always considered the matter closed. Now Frau Rittmann, she was 54, and still reckoned to be a good-looking woman.

The members of the press listened avidly. This was someone who had not only known Franziska Schanzkowsky, but had lived with her in a small apartment. Here were the romance novels, the pimply back, the single undershirt. She had seen Franziska during the famous "missing three days," and had swapped clothes with the claimant. There were even photos of the two of them wearing the famous blue suit at different times.

Franziska's lawyers treated Doris scurrilously, haranguing her until she fled the courtroom, crying "Do you think I made up the existence of Franziska Schanzkowsky?"

That was it, of course. Franziska's supporters had always thought of the "Polish factory worker" as a myth, an ugly phantom who should have turned up as a corpse in an unattended grave, not the real person described by Doris Wingender. Out of court they would slander Doris as a prostitute as if that could explain away Franziska Schanzkowsky as well.

Pierre Gilliard and Gerda Kleist both testified against Franziska, as did an affidavit from Anastasia's other tutor, Sydney Gibbes.

On the other hand, Felix Dassel, dying of emphysema and heard at home, testified, on oath, for Franziska. Lili Dehn's deposition, detailing her recognition of "Anastasia" and including the assertion about the "gold and in millions" was entered into evidence. An old friend of Franziska Schanzkowsky's had turned up and claimed to have talked to her in the summer of 1920, when she was supposed to be at Dalldorf. She had purportedly said she was going to sail on the *Premier* and take up residence in England. Franziska's lawyers would spend a lot of time trying to trace the ship, without success. Perhaps she had married in England and changed her name.

It was also possible, they felt, that Franziska had become a prostitute and had gone to South America to work in the trade. Prostitutes. Their minds kept going there. It was as if they assumed that any unmarried working woman not tied to a farm or working as a housemaid was probably selling herself, and cheaply too.

IV

Winter in the Black Forest. The trees in Unterlengenhardt are heavy with snow, the roads icy. The wind howls and in the courtyard of the local inn, The Adler, a cat cries plaintively while visitors shiver.

The visitors were Dominique Aucleres, a Parisian journalist writing pro-Anna Anderson articles for *Figaro* and now helping Leverkuehn and Vermehren with paperwork; Serge Kolesnikoff, a Russian ex-officer who had known the imperial family; his wife; and Tatiana Botkin. They have come to visit Franziska in her hut, but she refuses to see them and does not answer the door or the telephone. For days they have trooped over the ice, Kolesnikoff and Aucleres hanging back while Tatiana cries out, "Anastasia Nicholaevna! It is I, your old friend Tatiana!"

Nothing. The hut is dark. Not even the faithful Adele comes to the window. Inside sits Franziska in her nightdress, threatening to throw Adele out into the cold if she answers the door. The visitors have been a nuisance all week. Why should she see them?

They have put things in the mailbox, but she has forbidden Adele to empty it. Frederick and Mrs. Madsack had visited, but that was all right; they had delivered a dress from the tailor. "You will not answer the door! You will not! Do you understand, Frau von Heydebrandt?"

How small the hut is. Sometimes Franziska cannot bear the sight of the older woman, more and more ill these days. More obedient, more cowering.

"It is a shame ... they have traveled so far in the winter," Adele ventures. "Tatiana Botkin, your old friend ... "

"Get out!" Franziska screams. "I don't want to see your ugly face anymore! Out! Out!"

In The Adler, Aucleres reads and takes notes, Mrs. Kolesnikoff knits. Tatiana, having fallen on the ice, nurses a swollen ankle. Have they come all the way for this? To sit in the inn while the snow falls and their beloved Anastasia bars them from her presence?

Kolesnikoff has been reciting poetry, he is becoming more Russian by the minute, and imagines Anastasia examining, perhaps with tearful, shining eyes, the photograph from long ago which he has left in her mailbox. She is so close, merely down the road, and thus the past is close again, almost recoverable. They have dubbed Franziska's hut the "little Kremlin."

The tension is relieved by the arrival of Prince Frederick and Gertrude Madsack. Well, now, company. Frederick "of the butterfly mind" regales with stories of South America and measures their skulls to determine "ethnic descent."

Frederick is amazed when he learns of their treatment; he sighs and dispatches Mrs. Madsack to reason with Franziska. She is back in an hour. Mrs. von Heydebrandt has been ousted from the little Kremlin.

A village girl has brought Her Imperial Highness supper. "I can't ... I am dying ... " Franziska had told Mrs. Madsack, refusing to see anyone before closing her eyes and growing silent. Once alone, Franziska digs into the meal supplied by the girl.

Adele, repentant and worried, is back at the hut the next day and scurries quickly out of the road when she sees Tatiana Botkin approach. Just in case Her Imperial Highness is watching from the window. "Hide in the road where she can't see you," Adele whispers, looking over her shoulder.

They learn Mrs. von Heydebrandt has received permission to empty the mailbox and that Franziska silently stared at Kolesnikoff's photograph for hours. After seven days everyone goes home. They have not been given leave to enter the little Kremlin.

V

Adele died of a heart attack in May 1959, days after Gertud Ellerik testified in nearby Bad Liebenzell that she had recognized her sister in Hannover in 1938. Gertrud—so close, just down the road, within walking distance. Did Franziska think that in a normal life Gertrud would have visited her? What if Gertrud came to the hut or stood in the road, like a tourist, to stare? Or called out to her? There was nothing to keep her family from trying to quietly see their long lost sister.

Franziska found Adele in the garden. She was stunned and knelt beside the body for hours, repeatedly saying, "That's enough now, Frau von Heydebrandt! Get up! Get up!" They were commands Adele was finally unable to obey.

The death of the companion who had cared for her daily for over ten years was a blow, but Franziska may also have had a guilty conscience. Or did she? Was her life so internalized that she had little feeling for outward reality, or how her actions might affect others? Could she have genuine emotions for someone she fooled every day, someone who did not really know her at all, and who doubtless loathed Franziska Schanzkowsky as all the others did?

Even after Franziska's own death, her treatment of Mrs. von Heydebrandt was remembered. A local recalled an incident from the month before Adele's death. Elderly and ill, she needed to make frequent trips to the outdoor privy during the night. Franziska had the door barricaded. Adele tripped and did not reach the door in time. She "made a mess" of the hut and Franziska's big dogs had attacked the old woman while Franziska "showered abuse" on her.

At least Adele's death gave Franziska more privacy. Without Adele as a witness, Franziska could be herself in the barrack. She wrote:

I am and stay as I have been

God knows my way, I'm in his judge[ment]. *The day comes nearer, where I left this world and make another way—and without sorrowness;*

For life for me has not been short

Almighty God: Justice itself! What only have I done

Driving the worst in by the Romanovs

What crime reproaches one to me

When yet I stand as Anastasia?

No one knew just what it was she did alone in the hut. Her scars had multiplied and would come to include a star-shaped "bayonet" wound which went right through her foot. Long ago, Gleb had mentioned something about the grand duchess being stabbed in the foot with a cruciform Moissant-Nagant 98 bayonet. Franziska's foot was unmarked at the time but eventually the scar appeared, so prominent that it could be clearly seen when she wore sandals. Her supporters never seemed to note the discrepancy.

It is not clear what was causing the abscesses either. She hadn't had active tuberculosis for years. During the second trial she would have a medical examination to please the court, and her lawyer would emphasize that this was the first time in seven years that she had left her "compound." It must be that she'd had no hospitalizations or even office visits during that period—quite remarkable for a woman of her age. She would, after all, live to be nearly ninety. If it wasn't for the self-starvation and possibly self-induced abscesses, she might have been quite healthy. Her convenient illnesses ("she had decided to be sick") were widely known, but her supporters seem to have been willfully blind to the extent of the problem.

Was she so angry, yet so desperate for attention that she took to harming herself? No one was noticing. The abscesses and starvation did bring her sympathy, but it was never the kind she really needed. Alone at night, facing ruin, Franziska suffered dreadfully.

VI

Dominique Aucleres and Tatiana Botkin returned to Unterlengenhardt in the spring of 1960. The new cottage, the "dacha," was ready for Franziska, but she opposed the move.

Naturally she said she didn't want to see the guests. No one knew what to expect. Miss Mutius and Miss Mayhoff, another "lady-in-waiting" who carried Franziska's meals twice daily to her, nervously tried to talk her into at least having tea in the new house with Tatiana and Aucleres. Nothing doing. Franziska hovered in the old, ramshackle hut that was now, without Adele's presence, a complete shambles behind a high wire fence and overgrown weeds.

Would Franziska see them or not? They couldn't see her from the road, but they heard her voice through the window, directing Miss Mayhoff to offer them biscuits. Mayhoff replied that the guests would eat at The Adler, and anyway, there was no food, not a crumb, at the dacha.

"What a shame," they heard next. "The voice growled in English," is how Aucleres put it.

Franziska seemed to waiver and even offered to let the two women stay at the dacha, but Aucleres was not in the mood to accept the hospitality of the strange owner of the dacha, who "was capable of never letting herself be seen."

Franziska knew she would let herself be seen, but she could not appear too eager. She had recently received another journalist, Alain Decaux. Her friends had called out "Her Imperial Highness Grand Duchess Anastasia" as she stepped into the room, dressed in layers of cloaks and dresses. Franziska hid her mouth and promptly announced she wanted to die and be buried in Russia; she would contact Khruschev to arrange it. This announcement was followed by an hour of gossip about the royalty and film stars Franziska read about in her beloved illustrated magazines. It all seemed to have gone well, but Decaux turned around and wrote an unflattering book about her.

"She's changed her mind!" Miss Mayhoff happily told Tatiana and Aucleres the next day as they were promenading yet again through the tiny village. "Hurry up! We must make sandwiches!"

It was off to the baker and the butcher. Tatiana Botkin busied herself making sandwiches and perogies in the dacha, but by five no one had come. Would Franziska appear at all? But Franziska had invited other ladies; surely she would not disappoint everyone ...

At five-thirty the sky darkened. Thunder sounded.

"She won't come," Miss Mayhoff said sadly. "She's afraid of thunder."

But soon the three other ladies, Miss Mutius at the head, appeared, "wonderfully dignified and antique ... they wore hats, gloves, flowered dresses from Le Belle Epoque. One could say three ladies-of-honor have come to visit their sovereign."

Suddenly the door opened: "The strangest creature I have ever seen in my life entered. It was a small Madame Butterfly, disguised as a Tyrolean. She wore a Japanese kimono covered with a loden coat and over this a black cape. The hood was covered with a small Tyrolean hat which showed auburn hair with white strands. The face had great finesse, but the mouth twisted behind a napkin held in a black leather gloved hand. She wore fur-trimmed boots, and when she walked, the indecision of her steps gave her a floating movement that was quite unreal, like an apparition. Another would have appeared ridiculous but not her. This was a great lady and her dress was incapable of changing this."

The ladies sat. Aucleres ran for the teapot. When she returned, Franziska held out her hand and looked at her out of the corner of an eye. Her voice was sarcastic: "We have taken a long time to meet."

Were there no sugar tongs? Franziska grumbled to Miss Mayhoff.

Aucleres was stunned. "Then something happened which I would like to properly describe and hope to do so here. The person before me, herself, her eyes lit up, her small face shone, she wasn't any longer this fascinating old woman who had come in, but another, transformed person ... "

That wasn't all. Asked if Franziska took milk first in her cup, in the British style, she adroitly answered Aucleres in French: "Oh, oui!"

So Franziska, who had refused to speak French to Gilliard, knew the language after all! Or at least enough to answer "yes" as the cream jug lingered over her cup.

Something supernatural had happened, Aucleres concluded: "I was so enchanted that words failed me ... I had seen this face before and I couldn't stop looking at her fine profile with the lightly tipped nose. Suddenly I said to myself ... 'That's it! I've found the answer. It's the photograph of the Grand Duchess when she was a little girl bent over her work' ... No, there was really nothing in common between the portraits of Madame Anderson and the photos made of her as an old woman, sometimes monstrous, and the transparent creature I found before me, neither old nor monstrous but simply radiant."

VII

Franziska finally agreed to allow one of the judges from the panel to stare at her for exactly ten minutes. There had been the usual telephone hang-ups, voices from the window of the hut, people waiting in the road. Miss Lamerdin and Miss Mayhoff trembled as they ran in and out of the barrack. The court stenographer, from the road, heard a voice: "I have nothing to do with the court!"

In the end, Judge Backen was allowed to sit on the porch with her. He asked a few general questions and got gruff responses. When he asked her to give him the Russian names for things he was told that the interview was at an end. It was all over and she had managed not to take an oath of any kind.

Franziska's refusal to be properly examined or to testify would be cited against her, but at least she could not be charged with perjury.

VIII

In the spring of 1959 German attorneys flew to North America to interview witnesses for the court. Gleb gave a positive statement. The Leuchtenbergs, who now ran a ski resort in the Laurentians, were heard in Montreal, and presented Faith Lavington's diary, with its provocative entry about Franziska "laughing up her sleeve" at the denizens of Seeon. Princess Xenia, now Mrs. Judd, said she hadn't recognized Franziska visually, but remembered that her manner and memories had reminded her of the tsar's family.

The Grand Duchess Olga now lived in Ontario. She and her family had emigrated after the war and farmed before buying a small house in Cooksville.

She testified on March 23, 1959, at the German Consulate in Toronto. Her statement was much as it had been back in the Twenties; the claimant's features were wrong, her statements had been full of errors and she had lacked the family feeling that had been so strong in the undoubted Anastasia. Testifying was difficult and a doctor had to be called.

The worst moment was when another Anastasia waylaid her as she left. "Aunt Olga! At last!" Olga rushed from the building.

Other claimants had bothered her over the years but none caused the distress that Franziska had. "Anastasia will continue to haunt me as long as this unhappy person in Germany is alive," she told a friend, while admitting that family pressure had influenced her all those years ago in Berlin. Olga died in November 1960, at the small apartment of her good Russian friends, the Martenianoffs, in Toronto.

IX

Gleb was becoming just as eccentric as his "grand duchess." After the war, he founded the Church of Aphrodite and styled himself "The Most Reverend Gleb Botkin, Archbishop." He sewed red velvet drapes into a robe and conducted daily masses in front of a plastic replica of the Venus de Milo.

Although he was still associated with Grandanor he continued to oppose the Hamburg legal action. He hoped she might return to the United States. Franziska seems to have begun to give this possibility serious thought. Someone—Prince Frederick?—had postcards made labeled "Anastasia's House" and tour buses continued to make excursions to Unterlengenhardt so eager Germans could see "Anastasia" herself. Letters still arrived, expressing support and dispensing advice.

Franziska herself seems to have grown to distrust all of her German friends. The pristine dacha was sliding into the same chaos that had overwhelmed the hut. Her many cats slept on a bed that was said to have belonged to Queen Victoria and her four large dogs terrorized visitors. Weeds and bushes took over the garden.

She began, according to the reports of horrified friends, to fantasize about the past, recreating it in ways that contradicted the accepted version that had been refined through the years. The Grand Duke of Hesse had been merely misguided; Xenia's husband was at the bottom of her troubles at Oyster Bay; Miss Jennings was now heaped with honors. It might be that her confabulations included the fantastic stories she would enlarge upon in a few years' time about doubles who were killed in the place of the Romanovs. Whatever she said, her friends realized that Franziska's loose talk was extremely dangerous in light of the ongoing trial and moved to isolate her further from people who might spread the stories.

By the early Sixties Gleb had moved to Charlottesville, Virginia. Charlottesville would be a wonderful place for Franziska to live, he wrote. He had also met someone who was very interested in the "grand duchess." Jack Manahan was an enthusiastic genealogist, historian, and book collector whose special passion was the bloodlines of European royalty. Soon he was so enthralled that he made a trip to Germany and succeeded in meeting Franziska, whose eccentric manner apparently did nothing to dissuade him. He was prepared to finance Franziska's journey to the States and to guarantee her expenses there.

Franziska told her Unterlengenhardt friends about Jack but none of them took her seriously.

X

Prince Frederick and the lawyers were encouraged by the reports of Minna Becker, a handwriting specialist, and Otto Reche, a professor of anthropology, who had been appointed as experts by the court and who both concluded that Franziska was Anastasia.

Becker, who authenticated the diaries of Anne Frank, had "never seen this many identical traits in two scripts that did not come from the same hand." Similarly, Reche concluded that "Mrs. Anderson is not the Polish factory worker, Franziska Schanzkowska ... Mrs. Anderson is Grand Duchess Anastasia."

XI

On May 18, 1961 the High Court at Hamburg decided against Franziska. She had refused to submit to the medical and linguistic examinations ordered by the court and did not appear to know Russian, they asserted. No one had recognized her spontaneously and she had not recognized any of the witnesses from Anastasia's past without prompting.

Reche hadn't compared her to her sister Gertrud and had failed to take blood typing results, which showed a probable relation to Gertrud, into consideration. Minna Becker's report was rejected also; the orthography from Franziska's Russian samples, taken from practice sheets submitted as evidence, did not correspond to the pre-1918 script used by the genuine Anastasia.

The court did not allow for the counter claim that she was Franziska Schanzkowsky, deeming it "irrelevant," but also stating that it was "highly likely." Irrelevant; this thin tissue was all that stood between her and the oblivion she had feared for forty years. As it was, she was ordered to pay three-quarters of the massive trial costs.

"Well, the only thing left to do is die," she said, and shut herself up in the dacha.

Prince Frederick and Kurt Vermehren decided to appeal. It took Frederick weeks to convince Franziska "for the sake of the truth and the honor of the family she survived" to acquiesce. An appeal would blunt the finality of the finding, allowing life in the little Kremlin to go on as if nothing had really been decided.

It would also give her time before she lost her house, time to make other plans. In 1962 the High Court of Appeals agreed to hear the case.

Chapter Eighteen

I

Paul Leverkuehn had died early in 1960; Kurt Vermehren was killed in a car accident just as the appeal was getting under way. Prince Frederick, perhaps guilty of the ingratitude of princes himself, referred to the death of this loyal and largely unpaid attorney as merely another "miserable misfortune" for Franziska. As the holder of Franziska's power of attorney he had obtained the "rights of the poor" for her so that German taxpayers would not only have to bear the cost of the appeal, but something towards her legal counsel as well. It was nonetheless difficult to find a suitable lawyer who would work for nearly nothing. In the end Carl-August Wollmann, a Prussian monarchist of the old school, agreed to take the job without a retainer.

At about the same time Franziska met Alexis Milukoff, a friend of Gleb's who had lurked at the edge of her case for some time. After a series of letters and small gifts he was finally allowed into her presence. Milukoff arrived with a tape recorder and Franziska did not seem to mind having their conversations taped for use in the book he intended to write about her.

There were conversations from which responsible parties like Prince Frederick and Baroness von Miltitz were barred, confidences that left little to the imagination. Over the next few years, Franziska delighted Milukoff with details about her life, royal gossip, and fantastic statements about the "fifth daughter," Suzanna de Graaff-Hemmes. Transcripts reveal a playful and sly woman who, as Gleb told Milukoff, was still vain although she was now an old woman.

Her Unterlengenhardt supporters became increasingly worried that her statements would become public. Even Gleb became anxious, writing that the tapes would have to be censored.

II

The hearing of Franziska's appeal did not start until April 1964, giving Franziska a three-year hiatus from legal action. Once it convened, the court quickly moved to correct what it felt had been the deficiencies of the original court. They would not concern themselves with side issues in the form of secret bank accounts or conspiracies. The burden of proof would lie with the plaintiff. She would have to see the judges, and not at her house, either. She would also have to undergo a complete medical examination.

Seeing how things were stacking up, Gleb began to investigate ways of bringing Franziska to America immediately. Jack Manahan unsuccessfully tried to engage a Frau Jager to act as an escort for the journey.

Franziska's family—her real family—was stirring. The letters they exchanged with the opposing lawyers corroborate her niece Waltraud's statements and leave no doubt that they knew perfectly well who their sister was and what she was doing.

"There, dear uncle," Gertrud's daughter wrote to Felix. "Something new has happened. It is about your sister Franziska ... you recall what you said at first and you maintain that and nothing else. One never thought this would come up again. There, dear uncle, you know how to settle things."

Waltraud recalls a family visit in southern Germany at around this time. It was the only time she met her younger cousin, Karl Maucher—"a little lad." In the end he would be the most significant witness of all. The purpose of the visit was to discuss the Franziska affair and how it might be managed.

III

This time the court heard Otto Reche and Minna Becker, who testified that, in their professional opinions, Franziska was the Grand Duchess Anastasia. Karl Clausberg, the expert retained by Berenberg-Gossler, disagreed with Reche, particularly in the area of the ear. To settle the matter, the court sent another expert, Willy Beutler, to take pictures of Franziska in Unterlengenhardt.

Another surprise: Beutler returned with the photographs and said, "What? Are they crazy? Can't they see it's the same ear? The same face? You'd have to be blind not to see it."

It is interesting that the court did not pay more attention to these findings, in light of the later interest in them. It might be that Reche and Beutler went too far in their assertions. If the faces were identical, why didn't they look more alike? One could see why a teenaged Anastasia and an elderly Anastasia would look very different, but why were the early pictures, some taken less than two years after Ekaterinburg, so unlike the undoubted Anastasia? It was something which had always troubled her supporters. They had developed a variety of explanations for the discrepancies, but the problem remained.

The medical report was not helpful to the plaintiff. Later in Charlottesville, physicians would be astounded by the many scars covering Franziska's body, but in 1965 the doctors were surprised they didn't see more bayonet scars. X-rays showed no signs of the head injuries her supporters always claimed were responsible for her memory losses and facial changes. The suspicious foot injury was there, though. One of the doctors expressed the opinion that some of her wounds were self-inflicted.

Doris Wingender repeated her testimony, as did Gertrud and Felix. Franziska herself was heard from on September 16, 1965, at the town hall at Bad Liebenzell by Judge Bathge and a Russian language expert.

They questioned her for about an hour and a half in Russian; she answered in English, sprinkling a few words of Russian here and there. Finally they asked her to read Russian poetry. She didn't have her glasses with her. Prince Frederick handed over his, but she couldn't read the Russian words, and didn't impress either the judge or the language expert.

The Court of Appeals ruled against Franziska on February 27, 1967.

"The plaintiff is defeated in appeal," Judge Peterson stated. " ... I will say that the plaintiff who has asked for recognition as Anastasia Nicolaievna, Grand Duchess of Russia, has not been able to provide sufficient proof for that recognition, any more than she was able to do in the first place."

A little piece of theatre was enacted as the reporters ran out to file their stories. A woman in a brown coat stood in the hallway, crying "The decision is just! I am the real Anastasia!"

The reporters rushed after her.

There would be another appeal.

IV

Franziska's time in Germany was running out. She remained largely incommunicado, and her house got filthier, as if she was only waiting to escape.

After much argument she accompanied Prince Frederick and friends Ian Lilburn and Countess Elisabeth Oppersdorf to Paris that August. They were driving; it must have been a relief to to see something beyond the grimy walls of her house. Franziska was going to meet Gilbert Prouteau, a director who was filming a documentary about her case. She was also supposed to visit the Grand Duke Andrei's widow, Mathilde Kschessinska. The former ballerina was ninety-five and still believed in "Anastasia," whose eyes had reminded her so much of the tsar's.

Franziska gave a good performance. She traipsed along to see the Eiffel Tower and Notre Dame Cathedral in full "Anastasia" drag despite the sweltering summer heat: fur coat, scarves, and hat. She wept in the studio when Prouteau showed a film of people storming the Winter Palace ("You are killing me!") and expressed disappointment when she was unable to see Kschessinska after all.

After Paris, Unterlengenhardt and her filthy house palled. Franziska allowed things to deteriorate even further, causing the mayor and health department to issue clean-up orders. Franziska didn't care. Her friends thought she was depressed about the appeal, but she was more likely thinking about getting away somehow. Why should she care about the dacha? It would soon be lost to her anyway.

What about her pets? Her cats had multiplied and roamed the countryside, despoiling gardens. She probably did not realize that the farmers were beginning to shoot them. How could she know? She sat in the piles of garbage in her house. The legendary "precious goods"— the treasures given to her over the years, the tsarist relics, the bed belonging to Queen Victoria—are nowhere to be seen. She had painted all the walls red. A film of the kitchen shows heaps of refuse spilling over chairs and tables. The scene is beyond ordinary clutter and dust. It's as if Franziska tossed everything, old bottles, papers, and cartons, willy-nilly on the floor. There are cat messes too, that Prince Frederick and Ian Lilburn will scrape up after her departure. Add stench, flies, rotting food, moldering clothes: how could anyone live this way?

But there is Franziska in the middle of it.

V

Franziska's friends and neighbors decided to celebrate the May 1968 centennial of the tsar's birth. Robert Massie's joint biography, *Nicholas and Alexandra* had recently come out, rekindling interest in the Romanovs and in the love story of the last tsar and tsarina in particular. If Franziska read it, the tale of nurseries and mauve boudoirs, of the girls and the little tsarevich, may have seemed an ironic counter to her own life.

The comparison might have been ironic for her friends too. The portrait of Anastasia in the book is of a winsome little princess in a white dress. Massie's words about Franziska must have chilled: "The pathetic story of Mrs. Anderson's lifelong attempt to prove herself the Grand Duchess has become world famous. Nevertheless, she has been challenged by numerous other Anastasias living in far corners of the globe."

Is that really how their own lifelong struggle, and "Anastasia's" karmic mission would end, this dismissive footnote in a popular book?

Franziska was in no mood to celebrate the tsar's birthday, and stayed in the dacha while the villagers partied outside. A surviving film clip shows a smirking Franziska at the window, eyes dark, mouth hidden by a paper napkin, head nodding. She seems disjointed, unreal, like a figure peeking through the curtains of a puppet show.

By the end of May she refused the delivered meals, causing her friends much distress. This tactic had worked before. They fretted for three days, and then Louise Mayhoff ordered the door of the dacha broken down. They found Franziska semi-conscious on a sofa, crying for "Mama." An ambulance was summoned, a shot of morphine administered, and the protesting Franziska—"I will not go to the hospital! I will not!"—was carted off to the hospital in Neuenberg on May 29.

She would stay there for six weeks. Her friends worried about her heart, but her heart was fine and the doctor said she would live for years. What was wrong with her, then? She was seventy-one now, weak and malnourished, but she would be strong enough to fly to the States by the end of her stay.

Franziska settled into the hospital, enjoying the care of the nurses and organizing her guest list. The fainting spell and self-starvation had at last gotten her away from the dacha. Franziska, not at all depressed, was full of plans. She refused to see Prince Frederick or any of the ladies, but Milukoff was encouraged to visit with his tape recorder.

Her animals had been destroyed; Baby, the largest of her dogs, had pined and howled for her before being put to sleep. The loss of her animals remained a grievance and a sorrow, but others had at least solved the problem of what to do with them before she left.

Yes, she was going. The airline ticket and her care in the States were guaranteed by Jack Manahan and all that remained was to fill out the papers for a visa. Prince Frederick and her German friends knew nothing of this. Frederick wanted to put her property in his name, sell it, and place her in a nursing home, but Franziska was having none of it. Her own plan was incredible: she wanted to persuade Jack to give her money so that she could buy Castle Seeon and turn it into a hotel. Soon to be homeless, almost penniless, her scheme seems grandiose beyond belief, until one remembers the high opinion she still held of herself, her will to live, and her essential practicality: she knew she had no real way of supporting herself.

"We might as well make a trip and see America," Milukoff suggests on the tapes. " ... you talk to Manahan, you talk to Botkin, and say you'd like to come back and ... open a hotel with [me] ... but first we must have lots of money."

"And that we must in America get somehow together." Franziska adds.

"America will help," Milukoff agrees, "because especially if you get interested in this Mr. Manahan, he has lots of money. You say, 'Mr. Manahan, why don't you make together, like partners'."

Franziska called the project "getting a footing," the beginning of a new life. She even suggested lecturing in the United States to raise money for the hotel.

Reading the transcript of Milukoff's tapes, Franziska sounds happy, cagey, conspiratorial. Not at all an invalid, she is clearly delighted, despite her protests, about her improved health and prospects for a longer life. This is the Franziska of old, plotting with Clara, plotting with Gleb, hoping to raise $100,000 with Jill and Irvin, bragging about "contacts" in the Thirties.

"All right, then I consent. I go [to America]," she told Milukoff.

"As soon as we shall get visa then we shall simply take an airplane, a jet, and start moving at once."

"At once," Franziska says firmly.

She had always wanted to see Washington, she said. Perhaps she would even visit the president ...

Milukoff quickly obtained the visas and airline tickets. Franziska was released from the hospital and arrived at Frankfort the next day to board her flight to Dulles International Airport. Her escape from Germany was like an elopement. None of her friends knew of her plans and she never returned to Unterlengenhardt, where she had lived for nearly twenty years.

Chapter Nineteen

I

Virginia in summer. Charlottesville is noted for its writers and storytellers; William Faulkner was writer-in-residence at the university in the Fifties and wrote *The Rievers* there. John Grisham and Rita Mae Brown live nearby. In May it hosts a giant literary festival. What better place for Franziska, the consummate storyteller, the heroine of her own fiction, to live?

And yet—here: Franziska? Here on the Highway 29 which she traveled after landing at Dulles Airport in Washington, D.C. in July 1968, wearing "clothes different from ours" at a time when hemlines were rising, even among the matronly. Old-fashioned longish woolens? One of the suits, the *Kostum*, the black wool or elephant grey, a friend, Miss Freyan of Munich, had obtained for her in July 1967? The two suits, three white blouses, and a little lingerie. *Etwas Unterwaesche.* There was a summer dress, too, better for a hot Virginia July. Franziska surely tried to make a good impression and wore her dentures. She probably did not slurp at the Boxwood House where Jack's mother's friend, Mrs. Flynn, acted as chaperone, or require soft food as she had in Paris.

The refuge in Virginia would last the rest of her life. Did she sense this? Or did she still hope to get enough money together to buy Castle Seeon and run it as a hotel? In the meantime, here was nice Jack Manahan, who had visited her in the Black Forest. Jack and his money and his fascination with royalty. And Gleb, her old friend whom Jack would call her hero, was waiting in Charlottesville. He had not met the plane, but soon she would see him again. Gleb would figure out how to extricate her from the legal difficulties in Germany.

II

John Eacott Manahan is the key to Franziska's life in Virginia. Franziska called him "Hans," short for Johann, the German form for John. People still talk about Jack in Charlottesville, the eccentric book lover, genealogist and history buff who had a "heart of gold" but little common sense. He could tell you who your cousin twice removed was if you bumped into him emerging from a bookstore, his arms loaded with old books to add to his collection. Everyone has a tale about Jack: bizarre, touching, funny or plain nutty, but enjoyable in the retelling. He made Charlottesville a more interesting place, many felt.

Jack was the only son of Margaret Lucille (Becker) and John Levi Manahan, a Professor of Education Administration and later Dean of the School of Education at the University of Virginia. Jack's father by all accounts was the boss, a demanding parent. Jack was always different, the brightest in his class, devoted to his mother ("he was a slave to her"); a precocious child who turned into an impulsive young man who got into difficulties when he pursued a prominent young woman in Florida "to save the world for peace."

"He never could look after himself," said a relative.

Academically Jack did well. He attended the University of Virginia and started law school at Harvard. The war intervened and Jack became a naval officer, serving in Europe and Labrador. He returned to the University of Virginia, where it was said that "they gave Jack his Doctorate and approved his thesis with the stipulation that he never teach or publish his thesis. He did both."

For a time Jack taught in the extension program of the University of Maryland. History suffused his life. The house on University Circle had a "byzantine room ... a baroque room ... I remember the swords and the coats of armor and the armies of chess pieces," recalls a man who visited the house as a boy.

Was there a better man to have taken Franziska under his wing? She would become his link to European royalty. Jack would even come to feel he might, just might, be tsar of Russia, "even though we are low man on the totem pole." If Franziska took advantage of Jack, she surely made life more interesting for him. In their wills, his parents stated that his inheritance be kept in trust until he married, hoping a sensible wife would control his eccentric ways.

III

A story: "Another book dealer and I were coming back from Washington when I saw Jack and Anastasia parked in their car along the road. Their car was piled with junk and dogs. I said to my friend, 'Let me introduce you to some people I know. Just keep a straight face'.

"Jack jumped out and I introduced him to Bill. Jack said, 'Let me introduce you to my wife. Anastasia, this is Mr. Smith. Mr. Smith, I would like to introduce you to Anastasia, Grand Duchess of all the Russias'.

"Jack turned to me. 'Anastasia's traveled a thousand miles to Georgia in her nightgown. She just wouldn't change from her nightgown'."

Paul Collinge, the storyteller, owns Heartwood Books in Charlottesville.

"Jack got a trust check once a month, came in and bought two hundred dollars worth of books.

"Franziska always waited in the car, sometimes for hours. Once she kept the windows of the station wagon rolled up in the hundred degree heat. There was a goat in the back.

"We took a polaroid picture of Anastasia sitting in the car parked across the street."

Did she read?

"We never saw her read. Sometimes she broke sticks for kindling. She used to gather big sticks out at the farm and break them up for kindling."

A picture is emerging: Franziska, the old Pomeranian farm woman

...

IV

But that was later. At first Franziska behaved well, living out at the farm with Mrs. Flynn. The main house is more of a white mansion than a typical farmhouse, a place where you could imagine Scarlett O'Hara sweeping down the steps. It's set way back from the road, approached by a long drive fronted by iron gates. Barns, tenant houses, and outbuildings dot the 650 acre spread which had been a model farm in Jack's parents' day. It was still lovely then, with flowers blooming lavishly in the summer heat.

There is a 1968 photograph of Franziska, draped in a silk scarf, beside the ornate mantle of the farm house. Dentures in, hair combed, she's holding Gleb's book, *The Woman Who Rose Again*. In her hand is the old crumbled handkerchief, which Jack always nagged her about.

She gave a lot of interviews in those first months in Virginia. All graciousness, Franziska told the reporter that she was impressed by the courtesy of Virginians. She had been to the tourist sites, including Monticello, and wondered why anyone would want to live in Europe after seeing Virginia.

Still, she castigated the ladies in Unterlengenhardt, saying an injection of morphine was "administered by conspirators against her. Doctors gave her two weeks to live." Fortunately she "made liars out of the doctors" and successfully escaped to the United States.

But the farm palled. By August, she was living in the house on University Circle, a pleasant villa in a typical university neighborhood of senior academics; not the "opulent" area it is sometimes described as, but rather a laid back place where people have other interests than pristine lawns.

Maria Rasputin, daughter of Grigori, soon turned up with her friend Patte Barnum. They were publicizing their book about Rasputin, and Maria "instantly" recognized Franziska as Anastasia.

In a photo, Franziska, without dentures (here was someone who had seen the real Anastasia's mouth), is flanked by the young Ms. Barnum and a plump, jovial Maria Rasputin. Franziska's eyes are closed, there's a scarf around her neck, and she looks pretty pleased with herself. Franziska did well, according to Maria: "She reminded me of things I had forgotten. There was one time when I was dressed up like a Red Cross nurse, the kind who accompanied wounded troops home on the trains. I'd entirely forgotten about the incident until being reminded."

The press returned the following week to enlarge upon the story. Gleb was also interviewed in his "musty" house. The Archbishop of the Church of Aphrodite, in fancy cap and velvet cloak, was photographed beside his plastic statue of Aphrodite. "He has her on a gold-covered, homemade altar with vases of plastic flowers at her side and candlesticks in front of her," and "offers services in her honor Fridays, Saturdays and Sundays."

Franziska calls Gleb "her oldest friend in the world." He had already informed the press about the conspiracies against "Anastasia." Next he expounded his philosophy of love, based on his forty-seven-year open marriage. "The Archbishop has a patriarch's beard and a gentle, humorous manner … He is fond of recounting his triumphal arguments of joyful paganism against the 'supposedly emancipated youth of today'."

When Franziska received a *Washington Post* reporter Jack read stories about her life as she made "gestures of weeping, with her shoulders shaking, but there were no tears behind the kitchen towel she held to her eyes."

She won't discuss her past ("I can't hear you") but says she wants to see the Ingrid Bergman movie about Anastasia and to either remain in America as "a permanent guest of Dr. Manahan or someone else" or to buy the castle, despite her enemies in Germany—an old baroness had poisoned her dogs and cats. Franziska ate her ice cream "close-range, spoon-in-the-fist."

"I am ill, deranged and tired," she told the reporter, while Jack mused that "world opinion in America will help her finally win her case ... We're just putty in the hands of circumstance, drifting in the tide."

Already in Jack's mind, he and Franziska were "we."

V

Franziska refused to apply to the German consulate for an extension of her six-month visa, and Jack married her on December 23, 1968, allowing her to stay in the United States. Jack always emphasized the voluntary nature of their union, claiming that Franziska had "other suitors and preferred me." Franziska herself always mentioned her immigration problems and implied that the financial machinations of her Unterlengenhardt supporters had motivated the marriage: "People lived on me as though I was the milk cow of Europe."

Little has been written about Franziska's love life. Some said that she'd hoped to marry Prince Frederick, but the whimsical Prince with his high-pitched voice was not the stuff of dreams. He too might have hesitated, knowing the temperamental "Anastasia" as he did. Carl Vett apparently gave Franziska money for their "honeymoon in California," but nothing came of this. Then there was Prince Heinrich XLV of Reuss, a distant relative of Prince Frederick's, who was supposed to have been Franziska's true love, but died in Soviet custody after the war. She enjoyed teasing questioners by dramatically falling silent at the mention of his name.

Actually Gleb Botkin, now a widower, had been the only other candidate, but the Archbishop had managed to dodge the commitment. Jack was a better match, anyway: younger, wealthy (although not the "millionaire artifact collector" of local legend) and rooted in the community. "We accepted her because of Jack," at least one friend would say.

Franziska had to swear an oath that she was Anastasia before Jack married her. Did Jack have doubts? Later he would admit he still wasn't sure when he married Franziska that she was Anastasia. "In the beginning I did not know if my wife was who she said she was, but so many claimed to recognize her and my wife was [so] consistent, that I gave up my disbeliefs," he said years later.

Still, he came to deeply love his wife, catering to her whims and wishes. The marriage would grow beyond the "marriage of protection" Franziska said she had always wanted.

Jack and Franziska slept in one room and Jack claimed they had sex, although Franziska, being "royal," was not an enthusiastic partner, staring at the ceiling like a proper Victorian princess.

"He loved buying her hats," recalls Mildred Ewell, an old friend whose husband had gone to school with Jack. "They came for dinner, for birthday parties, for Thanksgiving and Christmas. We enjoyed her … she didn't say much but liked to read … She could be imperious with Jack though. I never doubted her identity."

Sometimes they ate at the exclusive Farmington Country Club, where Jack had inherited a membership from his parents. At other times they drove to Ken Johnson's cafeteria in the Barracks Street Mall, a spot where they were also known to all.

In the Seventies, they flew to Texas, drove to New Jersey and New England and through the south. They visited Jack's cousin in Ohio. His car didn't move unless she was in it, even later when she came to re- semble an apple doll.

"Sometimes I thought to myself she could be dead under that hat and Jack would just keep driving her around," mused artist Tim O'Kane.

She had learned long ago how indispensable she was to the people around her and it did not take her long to act as badly with Jack as she had with everyone else. Like the others, he accepted her behavior, alt- hough he did argue with her, even yelling at her in front of visitors to "Shut up! I told you we couldn't do that today!"

They were friends, Jack said later. She believed anything could be possible; this sense of hope made every day with her an adventure.

The photo following the wedding shows a casually dressed Franziska, (the bride's slacks—*Hosen*—earned a giggle in the European press), smiling smugly beneath a Russian fur hat. She clutches the old hanky and a grinning Jack, looking young enough to be her son, stands behind the wing chair. Gleb, perched on the arm of the chair, looks both enigmatic and satisfied.

Franziska, safe at last.

VI

Franziska's marriage astonished her friends in Unterlengenhardt. Franziska didn't mind informing these latest "enemies" of her new status.

"With really biggest astonishment as well as joy, we got the news I should like to say 'fairy tale'—about your marriage by Prince Frederic [*sic*] evening of the 27th— following day we received your message! So we have to believe it! We can only answer God Bless you and your husband—lifelong love—it is a beautiful place to be seen from everywhere and remembering us daily, 'There is somewhere in USA our beloved Anastasia'," wrote Miss Mutius.

How drab their world became without their tempestuous "grand duchess." They wanted to keep her clock, to remind them of her, and hoped "this clock may hang with your agreement in our room looking down so on us, at the time sitting around the Christmas tree…"

Alexis Milukoff, seemingly undaunted by the collapse of their plans for Seeon, was dispatched to try and recover some of the things she had left behind in Germany.

Unfortunately, no one could find Franziska's copy of a book on Kaspar Hauser, which she particularly wanted sent to Virginia. Steiner's influence remained. She discussed reincarnation with her new friends, and came to believe that departed human souls lived on in her cats. She strictly avoided meat and remained concerned about trees. A taciturn Franziska turned to a young man Jack was giving a lift to on a rainy day, and said with wonder at the wet, shimmering leaves, "The trees, the trees!"

Jack had other concerns. Shortly after marrying Franziska, he wrote to Ludwig Berger in Unterlengenhardt regarding her debts. Berger was happy to add it up for him: there was something like 25,000 marks owed to two banks, as well as 270,000 marks in unpaid legal fees. Prince Frederick had spent something like 30,000 marks on Franziska, but did not expect to be repaid. Baron von Gienath had spent 30,000 marks too, and did seem to expect reimbursement. In addition to this was an unpaid bill for Franziska's recent hospitalization. Altogether it came to at least 325,000 marks. There is no record of what Jack made of his bride's debts. He would never enquire about them again.

Chapter Twenty

I

The Seventies started out badly for Franziska. Gleb died just after Christmas in 1969. "Czarist Historian Dies at 69," wrote the *Charlottesville Daily Progress*. His death was troubling. Without Gleb's assistance she would have ended her life in a German nursing home. His help in adjusting to her new country had been useful as well. "Everything is changed entirely with [Botkin's] death," Franziska said.

The Supreme Court at Karlsruhe denied Franziska's appeal in February, affirming that the Hamburg judges had not been mistaken in ruling that Franziska had not presented sufficient evidence to prove she was Anastasia. Jack was disappointed, but said the "bar of history" would reveal all after "Anastasia's" death. Franziska must not have been surprised by the court's ruling. Perhaps she was relieved, as this decision would finally end the legal actions and the unpleasant surprises they produced. As it was, the endless wrangling had succeeded in nullifying the monumental court costs that had been levied against her in the early Sixties. No one would ever attempt to collect them.

II

The show went on. In the early Seventies, Franziska accompanied Jack to speaking engagements where he related the story of Anastasia. The butler, James, was still alive and the house on University Circle, while cluttered with "oil paintings, icons, heraldic shields and dime store playthings in a disarray to which Manahan alludes apologetically," was still suitable for admitting the press.

Franziska let Jack do the talking. "Drawing Mrs. Manahan into a cohesive conversation is difficult, at best." Sometimes she stayed in her room, emerging sporadically to chase her cats, a "slightly hunched wisp of a woman dressed almost entirely in red, the color of the Romanovs … Knotted hands hold a wad of pink tissue to over her mouth to cover a slight deformity her supporters say was caused by the beatings of Bolshevik guards in Ekaterinburg."

She and Jack conversed in German. James did their cooking, but "Anastasia" recalled "hundreds of recipes that were known to be served in the royal household," Jack claimed. This was new. Maria Rasputin's own recipes would form the basis of an excellent cookbook in later years; perhaps food at court had come up in their conversations.

They still entertained friends and dined at Farmington, where Franziska refused to eat meat. "Nor does she like sauces or runny gravies," Jack explained, "She saw too much blood running in that cellar in Ekaterinburg."

Mick Jagger and Keith Richards had noted that "Anastasia screamed in vain" in the sinuous Rolling Stones classic, "Sympathy for the Devil." The Massie biography, *Nicholas and Alexandra* was made into a blockbuster movie in 1971. These had been anxious years for Franziska's new country. Riots, a divisive war, the rise of strange prophets; a nervous fascination with "that cellar" gave Jack ample opportunities to talk about "Anastasia."

He addressed the Welcome Wagon Club: a chubby figure standing before a pile of books while Franziska, wearing a faux leopard skin coat and fur hat, covered her mouth and looked attentive, if skeptical.

She was less polite when a reporter from the the *Cavalier Daily*, the University of Virginia's newspaper, visited. She locked herself in her room, demanding to see a "red press card" and threatening to call the police. This went on during the two-and-a-half hour interview. Jack remained unruffled, explaining that his wife distrusted college students because the seeds of the Russian Revolution had been planted in the universities. His sense of the importance of her case now matched that of the Anthroposophists; "Anastasia's" recognition would cause a "world revolution," he said.

From behind her locked door, Franziska yelled that the real reason she didn't come out was because she had on the wrong shoes since they were planning to go out to the farm to feed the cats. Yes, Franziska was still vain in her fur hat and scarves. She did eventually emerge for a photo and wore the hat. She and Jack stand behind a table laden with mementoes. A miniature Zeppelin floats above them.

"You saw a picture of that Zeppelin?" chuckles John Eacott, a distant cousin. "We ate at that table once. They cleared it off and put the food on plastic Mickey Mouse place mats. We had rice and eggs. Did you ever eat green eggs?"

It was good for Franziska that Jack did most of the talking for her. You could never tell what she might say.

In 1974 she told a reporter that she had dropped a seventy-five pound piece of wood on her foot. The wound became infected, but she wouldn't see a doctor. Instead, she said she had "operated on herself," using a kitchen knife without antiseptic. The infection worsened, but the leg healed. Franziska wanted to impress the journalist with her toughness, but said more than she should have.

Charlottesville doctors were stunned by the healed wounds that covered her body. Franziska claimed Bolsheviks had inflicted them and Jack backed her up, somewhat, saying, "That's what Anastasia says." There were scars that had not been cataloged during the Twenties, even scars that had not been seen in 1965. Jack admitted that he could not explain the "horrendous old knife marks" that covered Franziska's body.

III

In 1976, a new book brought Franziska back into the international limelight. *The File on the Tsar*, by Anthony Summers and Tom Mangold, alleged that only the tsar and possibly the tsarevich were killed in

Ekaterinburg. Alexandra and her daughters were secretly transported to Perm, two hundred miles away, where they were held in a cellar. Later, the women were moved again. By then, Anastasia had escaped on her own. She was said to have been treated by a doctor whose testimony was allegedly backed by records at a pharmacy.

The Summers and Mangold book represented a shift in popular accounts of the last days of the Romanovs. By the time Franziska spoke to them in 1974, books by Guy Richards and Gary Null among others had already suggested that the tsar's family had survived their imprisonment in Ekaterinburg.

Jack and Franziska must have been aware of this. The idea was plausible then; the bodies had not yet been found, and it seemed possible that incontrovertible evidence of their survival could turn up in long-suppressed official documents. How would Franziska go? Should she alter her story to suit this new way of thinking, or risk becoming outdated by sticking to the old one? She recalled the wallpaper and the stars in the sky that night; she became emotional at the very thought of the massacre. It was one thing to tell wild stories to friends, but how should she deal with the journalists who were now asking a new set of questions? She had wound up stringing Summers and Mangold along for hours before intimating that "There was no massacre … but I cannot tell the rest."

She appeared on *Good Morning America* where she said the words, "I am a daughter of the Tsar of Russia." This fell a bit short of "I am Anastasia," but was magical and mysterious enough.

She hated *The File on the Tsar*: "It's a put together mess." Her main complaint, Jack claimed, was an old, unflattering picture of herself in the book.

"At first she insisted it wasn't her," Jack said. He was probably referring to a photo of Franziska at Dalldorf, but *The File on the Tsar* also contains the picture of Franziska Schanzkowsky as a maid in a garden. In the Twenties Harriet had included a cropped and heavily retouched version in her book, but few Americans had seen it. Now everyone, including her new friends in Charlottesville, could look and decide for themselves.

What to do?

Three days later, on Halloween, Franziska added an entirely new twist. The interview took place at Farmington, because 35 University Circle was a mess. James had died in April and now garbage and wood littered the yard. The front door was obscured by weeds and bushes, and the side door could be reached only by picking through the debris. No strangers were allowed inside; the cats and garbage had taken over.

The interview lasted the afternoon. Franziska saved everyone's leftovers for her cats and held a hand over her toothless mouth. She had a "gleeful twinkle in her faded blue eyes."

Franziska said that the imperial family was not even in Ekaterinburg in 1918, but "lived on trains for several years." Perhaps a double was executed in the tsar's place.

"More I cannot tell." She thought her life was in danger.

"Perhaps Anastasia is fooling us all on this point," Jack mused.

She also distanced herself from other elements of the old story. She never had a child or married a Russian soldier.

Had she seen the tsar after the war?

"I never answer one word."

"She has her reasons for maintaining the mystery," Jack said. "And I respect her reasons."

IV

Poor Jack. What was he to make of this turnabout? The train story would grow. Soon Franziska had the Romanovs operating a "blue train" themselves. In 1913, the tsar went to a wedding in Berlin and a double went back to Russia in his place. Doubles replaced the other Romanovs too.

A bizarre, multi-page xeroxed Christmas letter had gone out in 1974, the year of Summers and Mangold's fact-finding visit. It detailed some of the new theories; there is a lot about the lost fortune ("Anastasia's money") here, and the "fifth daughter" makes another appearance. Perhaps it is a key to what Jack and Franziska talked about when they were alone. Franziska spun stories, and Jack tried to make sense of them; Franziska repeated royal gossip gathered over the years, and Jack indiscriminately incorporated it into his historical framework.

Franziska seems to have first mentioned the doubles theory to Harry H. Davis, Jr., in 1969 or 1970. According to Davis, Franziska confessed that she was a double, and had been coached, in part by Anastasia herself, "to look, act and sound exactly like the young princess." Her "memories" therefore convinced people "because there were many experiences she had in common with the real Anastasia." Davis felt Franziska sometimes believed she was Anastasia, because, having taken on another identity at an early age, her "concept of reality and self-identity" became clouded. She commissioned Davis to write her biography, but stipulated that it could only be published after her and Jack's deaths.

Others ridiculed Davis' theory. Franziska knew Jack would back up her statements and enjoyed seeing how far he would go, they suggested.

The theory would grow to allow an almost infinite number of scenarios. If she had lived through the massacre, she was the double. Or perhaps she was the real Anastasia, and had been in Germany all along. And who had Gleb seen at Tobolsk—Anastasia or the double? But if she was supposed to be the real Anastasia, how could she then say her facial "deformities" and old scars were inflicted at Ekaterinburg? And what if there had been no massacre after all?

Franziska pitched the doubles-on-a-train story to James Blair Lovell, the man she called her "official biographer." She "looked almost moonily into my eyes, like a young girl playing the coquette," Lovell wrote. The proliferation of authorized biographers suggests another motivation for the increasingly complex stories she told them; she was accustomed to using this lure to attract attention, but the climate of the times meant that any new "revelations" had to become wilder and wilder to qualify as a "scoop."

V

The File on the Tsar offered other news. Dr. Morris Furtmayer, a German forensic scientist, did new comparison tests on the ears of Franziska and Anastasia and concluded they belonged to the same person. Prince Frederick only had to give the go-ahead and the case could go back to court. Franziska was having none of this. Whatever fluke had generated these results would not produce a favorable verdict. She still blamed Prince Frederick, who held her power of attorney in Europe, for all her troubles there. He "is the one behind this mess ... He is after the money and nothing else."

Franziska now seemed "annoyed by all the publicity and would like to withdraw from the public eye."

Jack didn't share Franziska's suspicions about Prince Frederick. He would soon invite Prince Frederick and Ian Lilburn to Charlottesville. "Those wretched cats," Lilburn recalls. He and the Prince stayed in the apartment building next door because the main house was such a mess. "Jack would bring breakfast over but we couldn't eat it."

VI

Did all these stories have anything to do with the reality of Franziska and Jack's day-to-day life as they cared for cats, drove out to the farm, and ate at the Barracks Road Mall?

Jack was always buoyant and happy and Franziska seemed content when no one was bothering her. She had more cats now, and dogs, including an Irish setter that was Jack's favorite. Sometimes in the summer they stopped on the way to the farm and Jack would go swimming with the dogs.

Without James, the deteriorating physical conditions, which had once embarrassed Jack, were growing beyond their control. Franziska had a tree stump in the middle of a living room cluttered with memorabilia, trinkets and toys, wrappers and papers, cats and dogs. The animals had the run of the house and defecated everywhere.

The outside of the house was another matter. In 1978, six neighbors swore out warrants against Jack and Anastasia because of the condition of their property. Jack said Franziska set traps consisting of banana peels, garbage bags, and firewood to keep out visitors. The garbage attracted rats. Jack conducted his own defense, introducing a caribou antler. The antler was unmarked; ergo, rats, known to chew horn, could not be present.

VII

Jack was finally jailed overnight because of the condition of 35 University Circle. Jail rules were that the inmate strip and take a shower. Jack screamed and yelled; there was no way he was removing his union suit. The guards telephoned the judge who said, "Well, probably the union suit could use a bath too. Let him keep it on."

Jack didn't mind his night in jail. The food was good, and he knew the family background of several cellmates. The air wasn't too great though.

Chapter Twenty-One

I

In 1979 an event occurred which would ultimately reveal to the world who Mrs. John Eacott Manahan really was. On August 20 Franziska underwent an emergency operation to correct a life-threatening blockage of the intestine. The hospital followed standard procedure and preserved a small amount of tissue which would later prove ideal for DNA testing.

The operation saved Franziska's life, but she rarely walked again and spent most of her time in a wheelchair when she wasn't in Jack's truck. He continued taking her everywhere, driving out to the farm to feed the animals or to the Barracks Road Mall.

One of the restaurants they frequented told Jack she was no longer welcome there. It might have been that she was starting to smell, although her unnerving habit of shrieking at Jack also caused problems in public. She needed a practical nurse to care for her, but she refused to have help in the house and Jack went along with this dictate, doing his best, helping her to bed, bathing her occasionally, and going for take-out food.

It was difficult. Caring for Franziska grew to be more and more like caring for an ageing parent. There were also the animals on the farm, not only the dogs that had been banished there, but cattle, pigs, and sheep. The burdens on Jack, who had always found it difficult to look after himself, were overwhelming and the results grotesque and sad.

II

The house in town was bad enough, but Fairview Farm had become a sort of nightmarish *Green Acres*. Tim O'Kane rented a house on the property while Franziska was alive. He is a perceptive, soft-spoken person whose paintings have an unsentimental empathy that transforms mundane objects and situations into a statement about how miraculous life really is. His memories of Jack and "Anastasia" are vivid and lack the patronizing quality of some of the accounts of them as Charlottesville characters.

"Jack could barely feed himself. The people who knew him in Scottsville put him in the role of village idiot. He smelled like he hadn't bathed in thirty years. But he could speak a dozen languages.

"The farm—beautiful once with terracotta silos—turned to shit. His father had a trust fund for him—he couldn't get money out ... The sheep needed shearing and I offered to help Jack, but he just wouldn't shear the sheep. One hot summer day they all ran to the creek and fell over dead ... The cows escaped and tore up a newly landscaped schoolyard and the pigs went wild. They lived in the woods and didn't look like any pigs I ever saw. They began tearing up a farmer's barley field and the farmer shot them. Jack said the farmer should have been shot instead.

"The bull, John, used to get out on the highway and buck cars. Sometimes there'd be thirty cars backed up on the road while big John tried to buck the first one ... the cattle were supposed to be shot, but a farmer down the road offered to take them. No sooner were they in their new pasture then they turned around and jumped over the fence. Jack said 'Ah-h guess the cows are going home'. The state shot the cows.

"Franziska waited in the truck while Jack gave minimal care to his livestock."

Tim O'Kane only spoke to her a few times over the years and did not believe she was Anastasia: "She was scared of anyone who came up to her. I knew her for about ten years. She spoke German to Jack and called him Hans. When I knew her she was senile and loony. I never heard one story to the contrary. I didn't know anybody pragmatic who thought she was Anastasia."

Franziska, he says, used a plastic container as a potty in the truck, and threw the contents out the window where the feces dried on the door. Once in a moment of clarity she told him that she wanted "to be buried in the woods by the farm and have a church built with certain bells in it."

O'Kane's friend Inge, an eighty-five-year-old artist from Finland, talked to Franziska and came away momentarily considering the possibility that she was Anastasia. Franziska knew so much about the Finnish coast and "remembered" the marble stalls the tsar's horses had been stabled in at the palace.

Was it Franziska who refused to have help on the farm or to restrain the animals? It is said that she regretted Jack's neglect of the livestock. She continued to let her many pets have the run of the house, which did not merely mean letting dogs jump on the sofas. O'Kane described the house on University Circle as a "carpet of shit. There were dead cats lying around—they left them. He didn't want anyone taking over. Jack would invite you in for breakfast; I always said I'd take a rain check."

Still, Jack retained his sense of humor. "Once Anastasia was screaming at him in German and Jack looked at me and laughed, 'We're always on our honeymoon'."

Others spoke of the fabled carpet of shit. Sandy MacIsaac, a local book dealer, prepared Jack's library for auction after his death. Before MacIsaac could reach the bookshelves, he had to clean out huge piles of books on the floor, all covered with layers of feces. He didn't see any of the Romanov treasures rumored to be in the house. Apart from the books it was all "garbage."

"My wife wouldn't go in there anymore after awhile," John Eacott says. "I went and came out with scabies."

III

June 18, 1981, was Anastasia's eightieth birthday and the Manahans had a party in the yard at 35 University Circle. Franziska, actually eighty-four, sat in her wheelchair. "A shawl and plaid jacket are draped over her blue nightgown, and she wears a pink straw hat with a feather and red quilted boots."

So many things had happened over the years, but here she was, at her birthday party, wearing her nightgown and spinning stories for a reporter who turned up.

"If Anastasia had the power, she says she would change her birthright. The title of grand duchess has served as nothing more than an albatross around her neck." Jack said, as Franziska nodded in agreement. "It has been a curse."

IV

Perhaps the ambiguity of the doubles stories troubled Jack. He had set such store in her actually being a grand duchess and his view, ennobling him by their marriage. In 1983 he decided to seek objective proof that his wife really was Anastasia after all.

A few years earlier, a polygraph expert had contacted Jack, offering to test Franziska. He had declined the offer then, but now he contacted L.T. McKean and asked him to test her.

As an ex-CID agent for the Marine Corps and with 27 years as a court expert, McKean was well-qualified. He jumped at the chance. "I went for it in case she was who she said she was. I thought she could be Anastasia because of her manner—she always held her head up high. But I know when people are playing with me."

McKean went with the assumption that she was Anastasia. He spent four to five hours with Franziska in her kitchen and ran five different tests. She sat facing away from the polygraph machine. Jack was present, coaching and translating. Franziska now indicated that she didn't speak English very well.

She failed miserably. She didn't answer certain questions, but McKean got a "silent response" when she tried to beat the machine by holding her breath during relevant questions such as was she who she said she was?

Finally McKean stopping testing. "I was ninety percent sure she wasn't Anastasia."

Jack suggested that Franziska's language difficulties might have caused the poor results, but McKean noted that Franziska and Jack spoke English together easily. Jack wondered next if his wife's senility might have affected the outcome. McKean said no; Franziska was coherent.

Afterward, McKean likened Franziska's responses to those of a career criminal. "She played it close to her chest ... she'd say she didn't understand me. I think under this whole age thing, I still believe the woman knew who she was."

McKean also felt that Jack didn't really believe in her. "I asked him several times if he believed his wife was Anastasia. He always hesitated and wouldn't look me in the eye. His body language told me he didn't really believe in her."

Jack never mentioned the polygraph testing to anyone.

Chapter Twenty-Two

I

Franziska celebrated Anastasia's 82nd birthday that year at 35 University Circle. People came from the Carolinas, but it was a smaller "do" than her earlier birthday party. Jack displayed an icon for the cameras and Franziska, wearing a hat, shawls, and boots, scowled in her wheelchair. A Fairview tenant, William Radford, a local character who had once set his own beard on fire to prove a point, was an invited guest. Jack would later go to court to have Radford removed from his property, but for now all was friendly.

Jack's cousin, Alice Nelson visited in 1983 and thought Franziska had a stroke that year. She had met Franziska, whom she still thinks was Anastasia, when Jack and Franziska visited Ohio, and on trips to Charlottesville. She always felt that Franziska acted like royalty; there was that reserve, that "regal" distance. Besides, Alice claims that Jacqueline Kennedy Onassis believed in "Anastasia" too. Wouldn't Jackie know?

There was nothing regal about her in 1983. Out in the messy yard, Alice suggested to Jack that his wife belonged in a nursing home.

Still, Franziska protested when Jack wanted to give Alice some statues that belonged to her. But "Jack spoke to her and said, 'she's my cousin. It's all right, Anastasia'."

Franziska smiled and talked to Alice about Paris.

II

Was Franziska still acting, even now? It seems so, even if she did know that Jack knew she wasn't Anastasia. Soon he would fixate on the idea that doctors had given Franziska a truth serum during her hospitalization and then interrogated her about her identity. What did he have to fear if he really thought she was Anastasia?

They kept up the pretense, probably even when they were alone. Perhaps on another level Jack had ceased to care who she was. They had been together for sixteen years of mutual dependence. His life revolved around her; she had provided drama and meaning. All the interviews and theories, but above all, the feeling of being involved in one of the great mysteries of history—he never would have experienced any of it if he had not married Franziska. It was a more exciting life than he would have led with a genteel Southern wife.

It is tempting to think that at night, alone, something—a look, a glance, a sigh—united them in the unspoken truth. Jack knew that she considered herself a *Wend*, a person from Pomerania. It is impossible to believe that as she grew older and more senile, a name or reference to her real being, a word in Polish or Kashubian, did not escape her during those close hours in the house. They were together all the time. Jack bathed her, cut her hair, dressed her, and lifted her into her wheelchair. They had become so intimate; no one had ever gotten so close to Franziska before. How could she not have revealed her true self now?

But without Anastasia, they were only a dishevelled, ageing couple living in a filthy house. They still needed Anastasia, just as they needed each other.

III

We have almost reached the end now.

Hans, mach ein Ende—Hans, end it, Franziska would yell when he rambled on.

It was her end that was coming now, the end of her "shell."

As her health worsened, Franziska took to sitting in the station wagon and yelling for Jack. Their house had been condemned and they had moved to the apartment building next door, where they soon duplicated the familiar dirt and clutter. Windows and doors were left open in all weather. The cats and dogs ran all over the neighborhood while Franziska yelled in the old car in the driveway. Increasingly delusional and confused, incontinent and noisy, she had become a disturbing presence on University Circle.

Jack had also become frail. Neighbors found him lying in the yard or on top of the hood of the car. Once it might have seemed cruel to harass the Manahans; now it seemed cruel to ignore their plight.

In the summer of 1983, Jack developed Rocky Mountain Spotted Fever and had to be hospitalized. Franziska went with him since no one knew what else to do with her.

Hospital staff alerted the Department of Social Welfare, who initiated action in August. A competency hearing was soon held in Circuit Court. Neighbors and friends testified that "Anastasia" spent most of her time in the car, "screaming at all hours of the day and night." The city had already served fifteen notices of housing violations against Jack. A guardian, William C. Preston, was appointed for Franziska on August 12.

IV

A new biography of Franziska, *Anastasia, The Riddle of Anna Anderson*, by Peter Kurth also appeared that August. It was a serious effort which compellingly presented his belief that she was Anastasia. The time when Kurth knew Franziska overlapped somewhat with the period when James Blair Lovell, her "official" biographer, visited her. Unlike Lovell, Kurth did not go into the doubles theory or the saga of the "fifth daughter," at any length. Lovell's book did not appear until 1991. He had died by then, still firmly believing in "Anastasia."

V

Preston had Franziska admitted to the Blue Ridge Hospital in November. It was the worst thing imaginable for Jack and Franziska. Away from Jack, who knew what Franziska might say or do? She distrusted strangers, fearing poisoning and kidnapping, and had infected Jack with these fears. He claimed that the Soviets had tried to blow up his car and at one point armed the tenants at the farm.

On November 29, Franziska was supposed to be transferred to the University of Virginia Hospital to undergo a CAT scan to rule out the possibility of a blood clot on the brain. She was adamantly against this and pleaded with Jack to save her. He was afraid too, "like an ignorant person would be, of anything on the brain."

On the morning of the 29th, Jack turned up at the hospital in his old station wagon, packed with supplies for six days. His favorite dog, a pregnant irish setter, was with him; he planned to use her as a decoy by drawing the ambulance attendant's attention to her. But the dog jumped out and ran away while Franziska waited in her wheelchair for the ambulance.

Jack simply picked her up and drove away while patients watched from the windows. No one knew the local back roads like Jack did and they were soon deep in the countryside, begging friends to take them in. Several refused and they spent a night in a motel. The following day they found refuge in a friend's unoccupied house in Amherst County.

A thirteen state search was under way and felony charges had been laid. They didn't hear the news as their radio only picked up a local station and were oblivious as they visited restaurants and a mall where they bought matching Russian fur hats.

"Our days were full," Jack said later. "The old house was full of books and she let me spend time reading to her."

Their car betrayed them. The battery needed a boost every morning, the radiator belt was bad, and a tire finally went flat. While Franziska sat in the car Jack walked back and forth to the mall for supplies. He was noticed. A restaurant owner called the Amherst County authorities on December 2.

Two deputies found Franziska, wrapped in blankets against the cold, huddled in the station wagon. She said her name was Jones. Fifteen minutes later Jack turned up. "Well, I see we've been caught."

The police took them to the Amherst County Sheriff's Office. While they waited for officials from Charlottesville, Jack told stories about Franziska and showed the pictures and books he carried with him. Franziska was silent under her fur hat. It was her first arrest, if it can even be called that. Not bad, all things considered. Did she think of that as Jack talked about her? Or was she too befuddled, too old, too tired to be afraid?

Back in Charlottesville, Franziska was returned to the hospital and Jack posted a thousand dollar bond before being allowed to return to University Circle. The charges against him were soon dropped. Jack was surprisingly reflective a few weeks later, saying his troubles with the law resulted from indulging his wife, and especially in allowing her to have so many animals. He had suspected from the beginning that the history of madness in her family and the gap in their ages could only spell trouble in the end.

The doctors did try to administer a CAT scan to Franziska, but she was so resistant that the staff gave up. What was the point? She was sent to Jane Holt's nursing home, having eluded examination one last time.

VI

Daily care was what Franziska had needed for years. At least in the nursing home she was clean and tidy and away from the disorders of her house. Unbeknownst to all, she turned eighty-eight on December 16. She was still forceful enough to refuse food unless it came out of a sealed packet opened before her eyes. She didn't want anyone touching her, even though she required bed baths and diapers. She screamed constantly for "Hans" and hardly slept.

She always wanted Jack to be there and he was. His visiting privileges had been extended so that he could come whenever he wished. It was hard. He still had the livestock to look after, but he spent as much time with Franziska as he could. He brought along photos of the Romanovs to hang on the walls and a signed photograph of Alexandra to stand on Franziska's nightstand.

Preston limited visitors to Jack, his attorney, and once, Mildred Ewell. Jack talked and talked to Franziska about the Romanovs, often asking Mrs. Holt to listen, either to give comfort to Franziska, or to remind her of who she was supposed to be. Perhaps his display of belief was the final gift he gave his dying wife. He had gone the distance with her; there was only a little left to go.

Franziska responded to Jack weakly but correctly.

"Gone, gone," she mumbled when Jack asked her about the tsar.

VII

Franziska suffered a massive stroke on the afternoon of January 28. Jack had just left, saying he would be back by 4:30. She was crying for "Hans" and kicking the sheets when her "lip went way up, her eyes drooped." Mrs. Holt ran outside, but Jack's car was gone.

An ambulance sped Franziska to the Martha Jefferson Hospital, but there was little to be done. Franziska weighed less than sixty pounds now and never recovered from the stroke. Jack was with her as much as possible.

The pneumonia that followed eased Franziska's way out of life on Sunday, February 12. Jack had stepped out of the room momentarily and she was gone when he returned.

VIII

It was sixty-two years almost to the day when Franziska left the Wingenders' apartment and sent a birthday card to Felix before jumping into the Landwehr Canal. So long ago ... it was "Hans" she remembered, "Hans" she struggled toward, as she prepared to cast off her "shell."

My life was filled with tears
With joys and sorrowness
God takes one day my soul,
I give it back into his hands.
The day comes nearer, where I let
This world and make another way
And without sorrowness;
For life for me has not been short
And is fulfilled ... not changing much.
I am and stay as I have been
God knows my way I'm in his judge[ment].

"I am and stay as I have been." The early photo of Franziska remains, the tidy girl in her clean gardening apron and polished shoes, the handkerchief in her pocket, the cap strings hanging over her collar. People are young, grow old and die: it is the same for everyone, only the paths are different. Franziska's path was one of the most unusual of her era. It was the collapse of the old order, and something in Franziska herself that allowed her fantasies to carry her so far beyond the small plot she had been allotted in life. The fame she achieved cut through class and convention and delivered her to a place few could imagine. Even after DNA testing has proved who she really was, the larger mystery of her being and of the human need to believe in myth and magic lingers.

I am fulfilled...
Was she?

Afterword

I

Sleep sweetly and see me in your dreams, and I shall dream of you, which means we'll be quits—The Grand Duchess Anastasia Nicholaevna, September 23, 1914.

Although Franziska had told Tim O'Kane that she wanted to be buried in a mausoleum in Fairview, her real wish had always been to be interred at Seeon beside the Duke of Leuchtenberg. The trouble was that members of the Leuchtenberg family did not want her buried there. The cemetery was only for the family and its retainers, they argued. The municipal authorities had to give permission as well, and feared the grave would attract too much tourist attention.

Prince Frederick stepped in. He hired a lawyer, and after lengthy meetings, the municipality overruled the Leuchtenbergs and decreed that Franziska's ashes could be placed in the family plot at Castle Seeon.

Franziska's tombstone reads:

Anastasia Manahan
1901-1984
Our heart is unsettled until it rests in You, Oh God.
God's windmills turn slowly but perfectly.

A German reporter who talked to Jack after her burial described him as "this simple American." He would live eight years beyond his "Anastasia," but they would be waning years, as he grew more frail and confused.

There would be a TV mini-series, *The Mystery of Anna* in 1986, starring Amy Irving, Rex Harrison, and Omar Sharif, among others. Very loosely based on the Kurth book, it invented a romance between Anna Anderson and a princely composite character and ended with a youthful "Anastasia" striding purposefully towards a courtroom.

In 1991, a Siberian mass grave was thrown open, and its contents inventoried and interpreted. Nine were eventually accounted for: the father, the mother, three of the sisters, the doctor, the maid, the valet, and the cook. This was an imperial family; Alexandra's body might be plundered of its jewelry, its clothing, even its face, but its platinum dental crowns proclaimed her an empress. One of the daughters—people would argue whether she was Marie or Anastasia—was missing, possibly incinerated at the site with her brother and then carried away by wind, rain, and erosion. DNA samples were obtained from living relatives, tests made, confirmed and broadcast. This, then, was the end of the story, at least as far as living people could tell it.

The skeletons in the grave hadn't been fully identified yet, but the report from Moscow hinted that all five of the imperial children were present. Jack would die the following year and unfortunately for him miss the revelation that one of the bodies of the girls was missing.

In the wake of the discovery he had fallen back on the doubles theory, insisting that the tsar's family had been in Denmark and Germany during the war. The bodies found in the woods really had nothing to do with any of it. Would Jack have dumped this theory if he had known about the missing body? He had seen Franziska's Black Forest wills by then, with their conventional versions of her escape from the murder room, and knew the results of the polygraph test. He did not speak of doubt; unlike so many others, he remained loyal to the woman he knew—whoever she was.

II

Later on, after Jack's death, the bowel sample at the Martha Jefferson Hospital would be remembered, and after arduous legal struggles, tested against the DNA profile of known Romanov relatives.

Researchers were able to locate Carl Maucher, the "little lad" of Waltraud's holiday memory. Maucher, a grandson of Gertrud Ellerik, was initially nervous. Could he be held responsible for his great aunt's debts? A family member must have alerted him to this old concern. Reassured that he was safe, Maucher agreed to give a blood sample.

On October 5, 1994, Peter Gill, Principal Research Scientist of the British Forensic Science Service, revealed the results: Anna Anderson was definitely not related to Tsar Nicholas or to Empress Alexandra, but was most definitely related to Carl Maucher. The tests were confirmed by other labs, some of them using a sample of hair discovered in an envelope tucked lovingly into one of Jack's books.

In the summer of 2007, in a clearing a short distance from the mass grave of Nicholas' family, investigators unearthed the charred, fragmentary remains of a boy and a young woman—Alexei and his missing sister had finally been found.

III

The results of the DNA tests were a relief for the members of various royal houses who had always insisted Franziska was an impostor. If the results had been otherwise, they would have seemed the selfish people Franziska had always said they were. As it was, they were vindicated. The Romanovs, the Hessians, and their allies had not been engaged in a conspiracy after all, leaving the matter of who was persecuting who open to question. Franziska's supporters had publicly questioned their morals, harassed them with lawyers, dragged them through the courts, and even forced her admittance into a private burial ground all because they had felt so certain they were right. Unfortunately they were not.

To some the results were a double blow. Not only was she not who they thought she was, she was in fact the despised Franziska Schanzkowsky, that deranged, loose-living denizen of factory floors and hayfields. There are still websites decorated with comparative studies of Anastasia and Anna Anderson, and affirmations of belief in her claims. They suggest that the samples were somehow tampered with. Intrigue ... some of Franziska's supporters longed to go back to the days of ear comparisons, depositions by elderly princesses, and the machinations of an "opposition" which could always be blamed for inconvenient events. For many it had never really been about language skills, memories, or earlobes. In the enchanting transformations of their great lady they had glimpsed old, holy Europe, where a princess of the blood could be expected to exude the subtle essence of divine kingship.

It is less clear what Anthroposophists made of the DNA revelations. Their belief in the power of "Anastasia" was, if not a closely guarded secret, then not widely known. Finding out that the one they had pinned their aspirations on was an impostor must have been puzzling, given Steiner's certainty in the matter. Most of the Anthroposophists who supported her have shed their own "shells" by now. Of those remaining, some still have faith, however. "And you believe this?" an elderly member asked when told the news.

"Could she not have been an illegitimate daughter of the tsar?" asked another. "I have heard this story ... "

IV

The imperial children have purported sons and daughters, even grandchildren now, both in Russia and in the west. "Do you know how many daughters of Anastasia have contacted me?" asks Ian Lilburn. "Sixteen! Or was it seventeen? They're mostly daughters, rarely sons, but a man rang me from New Zealand and said he was Anastasia's son. She had traveled by spaceship to New Zealand to give birth to him!"

"Yes, I know," a child of the "fifth daughter" commented, when told she resembled the last empress. "I look more like a Romanov than those people who live in Paris."

A 1997 animated feature *Anastasia* brought the mystery to a new generation of consumers via promotional devices like Burger King toy offers and Shell Oil premiums. A "sassy as hell princess," the Nineties Anastasia reused elements of Franziska's story from the 1956 film, but reached fans in a way the passive Ingrid Bergman character never could. All lonely girls want to be lost princesses, she said, but it's wrong to lie about who you are.

A recent internet search of Anastasia-themed products turned up music boxes, valentines, anime drawings, prom dresses, Franklin Heritage dolls, cosplay costumes, pillow cases, picture frames, tattoos, and a wedding cake. Enough! Make an end, as Franziska might have said.

V

Nicholas, Alexandra, three children and "all the retainers" were buried on July 17, 1998, in the Cathedral of Sts. Peter and Paul, eighty years after their murders.

Let us name the "retainers" now: Dr. Eugene Botkin, Anna Demidova, Alexei Trupp, and Ivan Kharitonov. The bells that rang, the cannons that roared, and the choirs that sang *Eternal Memory* were for them too.

VI

There was talk of Franziska's ashes being removed from the Seeon cemetery once the DNA results were in, Irina Lomasey, the Duke of Leuchtenberg's step-granddaughter said, but her half-sister is an Orthodox nun in France and thought the remains should stay where they were.

"My sister is so Orthodox, so Orthodox ... she said, 'Let her rest in peace'."

Acknowledgements

The writing of *Almost Anastasia* involved reading many, many books, conducting interviews, and accessing various archives. The project took years as we assembled various drafts, shortened, rewrote, considered options. It is hard to believe how much time has gone by and we hope we have identified all the sources. Many of the books we read are long out-of-print; it was difficult to verify the present day copyright holders, if there are any. Many of these books have been cited by other writers. Authors such as Kurth have drawn on original sources, the Edward H. Fallows archive in Harvard as we have. He has also consulted earlier books, as did James Blair Lovell and recently Greg King and Penny Wilson whose book came out after we wrote ours.

When possible, we have tried to draw on original archival sources. It was interesting to see the original documents and letters quoted in books we have read.

What started as a straightforward telling of a familiar story as seen by us, became a tour through a labyrinth of side streets, strange alleyways and busy main thoroughfares. Putting the pieces together gave us a new perspective on Franziska Schanzkowsky who emerged from the labyrinth as a person in her own right.

We have done our best to indicate the sources; however, the interpretive story-telling is our own. We apologize if we have omitted a source in error. Our intention was to cite all sources. We will gladly correct any omissions or errors.

Translations from the German and French are by Vera Green.

Images courtesy of the Romanov Collection. General Collection, Beinecke Rare Book and Manuscript Library, Yale University, pages 15, 16, 17, 93.

Images courtesy of the Houghton Library, Harvard University, pages 35, 132, 144, 245.

Notes

Chapter One

Geh und nimm Alexandrov, 148.
a rotten town Massie, 1968, 105.
When you see Maylunas and Mironenko, 318, 336.
Today it is Ibid., 307.
When God thinks Ibid., 320, 335.
I am so sorry Ibid., 364, 372, 431, 376.
Perhaps I have Ibid., 320, 354, 404.
I hope our nurse Ibid., 330.
Now you can see Massie, 1968, 239.
I am simply Radzinsky, 2000, 173.
Please forgive me Maylunas and Mironenko, 406.
we shall see you Ibid., 550.
stormy sea Ibid., 507.

Chapter Two

Information on Berlin came from Friedrich, Kollwitz, and the Berliner *Insight Guide* (1994). Franziska's attempted suicide and hospitalization have been written about by Harriet von Rathleff, Pierre Gilliard, Peter Kurth, Rene Decaux, Buxhoeveden and others. Schwier and Krockow were helpful for information about Pomerania during Franziska's era, as was Dr. Zygmunt Klimek.

Waltraud von Czenskowsky, Franziska's niece, was generous with her time in telephone interviews in 1999.

Bill Boehmer was helpful with maps of Pomerania.

Chapter Three

I could not eat Nidda, 84.

Chapter Four

higher circles ... Empress' shoulderline EHF.
spoke German quite fluently Ibid.
I thought they did not know Nidda, 93.
I arrived in Berlin Gilliard and Savitch, 49-56.
Patient is very sorry EHF.
The young woman I took in Ibid.
All these trials ... I am sure she would Ibid.
She ruined every chance Ibid.
choking feeling Ibid.
The missing three days EHF; Hans Nogly, Lovell, and Kurth write about the missing three days. See Kurth for the elements of the basic story, as well as King and Wilson.

Chapter Five

mentally shattered ... quite exactly and correctly EHF.
guilty conscience Ibid.
saw immediately that she could not be Gilliard and Savitch, 51-53 (V. Green translation).
Must implore your forgiveness King and Wilson, p. 112.
refrain from the further sending Kurth, 60-61.
Polish vagabond Gilliard and Savitch 75.
always made Grunberg nervous Nidda, 110.
virtually impossible to communicate Ibid, 113.
Dreadful weeks Ibid 111.

I have reached the firm conviction Rathlef, 25.

The activities of 10 October 1922 are further described in Friedrich, 166-170. There is much about the affair of the photograph in EHF. Franziska and her complicated relationship with the Schwabes is further discussed in Gilliard and Savitch, 75-76, and in EHF.

Chapter Six

By Anastasia the life side by side communication from the Gotheanum

Her life is a life of Karma struggle private archive.

representative of the holy on earth Ibid.

During the next three days Davy, 117.

I am personally convinced private communication to the authors.

Innocence and goodness of heart Tradowsky, 35-36.

the truth of the story is vouched Ibid., 39.

inadvertent suicide Ibid., 55.

Additional information on Anthroposophy, Kaspar Hauser, and the life of Rudolf Steiner was found in EHF, Barnes, Meyer, and Steiner's own writings.

Chapter Seven

She was small, very thin … her movements and bearing Rathlef, 26.

eyes swollen with weeping Ibid., 26-27.

Indoors or outdoors, the July heat Ibid., 43.

She was not a girl of twenty-five years Ibid., 125.

completely without any understanding Ibid., 126.

In the spring Ibid., 129.

On my first visit Klier and Mingay, 100.

I liked her fearlessness Vorres, 98-99.

What I don't understand Kurth, p. 95.

as before they said we had Ernie here Radzinsky 2000, 338.

Ah, they will all come Rathlef, 47.

Her feet are very like those Ibid., 57.

She is my father's youngest sister Gilliard and Savitch, 67.

to save her life Rathlef, 234-235.

I shall do everything possible Phenix, 151.

Heaven only knows Gilliard and Savitch, 81.

Do you know me Gilliard and Savitch, 82-83.

The visit and the excitement ... did not know her Rathlef, 98.

I knew at once Vorres, 175-178.

vulgar manners Gilliard and Savitch, 82.

May I now go to Grandmamma Rathlef, 100.

unwearying guardian ... courageous champion Ibid., 9.

radiant ... turned red Ibid, 100.

tension-ridden meal Gilliard and Savitch, 82.

not the one she believes Kurth, 119.

The letters are reproduced by G. Botkin, Nidda, Kurth, and others. In the German version "one" is used, neither *Sie* nor *Du*. Kurth's letters (113-115) are translated into English.

wept bitterly Rathlef, 77.

It was difficult to watch Gilliard and Savitch, 82.

That child was as dear Vorres, 177.

Information on Prince Frederick of Saxe-Altenburg and his involvement in Anthroposophy can be found in Samweber and Keyserlingk.

Chapter Eight

If one really states EHF

By way of a categorical denial Kurth, 114.

Dynastic difficulties Rathlef, 259.

Is there a letter EHF

I only want to get well EHF

very excitable person Rathlef, 127.

very long conversation EHF

anxious to be well-dressed Ibid.

shattering letter Nidda, 179.

of course we had to economise Ibid., 175, 178.

then there were the extras Ibid., 175.

dreadfully hard Ibid., 179.

she says that she wrote Hoover Institution.

one can sense the animosity Nidda, 180.

forbidden letters Hoover Institution.

Here at Oberstdorf Ibid.

as long as I control Ibid.

would cease to believe EHF.

nervous, very correct Ibid.

always fearing dreadfully Baroness v. Miltitz, Gothenum.

most unpleasantly surprised Rathlef, 135.

So blue ... in her face Ibid. 136.

horribly altered Hoover.

Did you know them Rathlef, 139.

dancing and funny things Kurth, 146.

excitable temperament Nidda, 192.

Additional information about the Tania Botkin's visit to Oberstdorf can be found in T. Botkin, 102-103.

Chapter Nine

It's very difficult to say Hoover Institution.

I feel that after years Ibid.

I can't have anything ... extremely detrimental Ibid.

probably the best informed G. Botkin 1927, 69.

could produce incontrovertible Ibid., 68.

I do not need to see her Rathlef, 255.

I hope you will be happy Hoover Institution.

a little more elegantly prepared Therese Kustner interview, *Stuttgartener Zeitung*, Feb. 8, 1984.

entirely lost her sense Hoover Institution.

I will not stay here Ibid.

I will prove it Ibid.

long brown caftan … people would come Irina Lamosey interview.

I came here so hoping Gilliard and Savitch, 92-97.

hostile stare … too good for work … Emperor of China Nogly, 146.

Family makes impression Ibid.

heap of misery Rathlef, 172.

you would understand EHF.

There seems to be no doubt Hoover Institution.

distinctly probable Ibid.

My dear gentlemen Berliner Nachtausgabe 9 April 1927.

She knows Hoover Institution.

A lady who knows you Berliner Nachtausgabe, 9 April 1927.

Good day … Out! Out! Ibid.

Your family asked me Ibid.

A woman without culture Hoover Institution.

I noticed her vulgar manner Gilliard and Savitch, 143.

I claim categorically Kurth, 186.

She had been wild Ibid, 174-176.

Much of our information about Franziska's life at Seeon, and on her confrontation with Doris Wingender comes from interviews with Irina Lamosey and from the reports in the *Berliner Nachtausgabe*, early April, 1927 (trans. V. Green), the Hoover Institution and Decaux.

Chapter Ten

the most dangerous moment Hoover Institution.

I wish I had known Waltraud von Czenstkowski interview.

in order to completely make away with Rathlef, 174.

Do you recognize her EHF

She told an aunt of mine Irina Lamosey interview.

There exists a strong resemblance EHF.

where the child is mentioned Ibid.

You are Harriet Rathlef ... liar and swindler Ibid.

Disgusting surroundings Ibid.

To accept this material Hoover Institution.

from a graphological point of view Ibid.

not allowed into the Governor's House Buxhoeveden 1928, Chapter 30.

strangely symbolic G. Botkin 1937, 63.

tired and nervous ... adored little Princess Ibid., 51.

It would be criminal Ibid., 51.

Her finely carved features Ibid., 61.

only two dresses Ibid., 66.

Three dresses Kurth, p. 174.

respect ... proud and sensitive Ibid., 68, 79.

I could find no words G. Botkin, 1937, 74.

exercise every effort Ibid., 44.

a very short name Ibid, 201-202.

that prostitute G. Botkin, 1937, 87.

innocent martyrdom EHF

I had at last found G. Botkin, 1937, 140.

Why must I go EHF.

Why didn't I die Ibid.

Now I look at her Ibid.

I am very glad to have an ally Ibid.

She seems to hate this name Ibid.

laughing up her sleeve Hoover Institution.

my deep conviction Ibid.

If you curse ... It was very curious Kurth, p. 199.

I have seen Nicky's daughter Hoover Institution.

general family resemblance Rathlef, 11.

I'm so afraid ... All this is the fault of Kurth, p. 204-205.

Further information on the Dassel visit was found in the *Berliner Nachtausgabe,* 1927 and 1929, as well as the *Taglicher Runschau,* October 1927.

Chapter Eleven

We are all here EHF.

What thoughts are going to haunt her Hoover Institution.

quite becoming ... Your Imperial Highness G. Botkin 1937, 159.

Are you a Grand Duchess Ibid., 165.

picturesque and juicy Ibid., 194.

typical of her kind Ibid., 167.

sobbed as she kissed her hand Ibid., 167.

nonsensical and untruthful answers ... paragon G. Botkin 1930.

I have a flair G. Botkin 1937, 176.

extremely eager Ibid., 184.

well-nigh desperate Ibid., 184.

covered herself up ... all three of us Ibid., 184.

accepted the whole incident Ibid., 184.

retire to the sanctum of her bed Ibid., 185.

Do you know what I was doing Ibid., 207-208.

don't dress her like that Klier and Mingay, 110.

scurrilous hoax Kurth, 219-225..

He did not like me Ibid, 219-225; Lovell, 146-147, 150.

I went through all that Kurth, 218.

thinking of spreading nets G. Botkin 1937, 258.

Shantkovski myth EHF.

I didn't see much of Xenia Nidda, 234.

so many lies Kurth, 220.

On 8 August Nidda, 236.

restored into her own circle G. Botkin 1937, 212.

It will be impossible to avoid Hoover Institution.

We are not trying G. Botkin 1937, 231.

I am extremely apprehensive EHF.

All servants having disappeared G. Botkin 1937, 268.

leaving penniless Ibid., 264.

Further information about the tsar's finances and their ramifications for Franziska's claim can be found in Clarke (pp.125-127) and in EHF.

Chapter Twelve

What food for her enemies G. Botkin 1937, 272.

Anastasia and I were now Ibid., 276.

free to love others Washington Post 11 September 1968.

In other words G. Botkin 1937, 306.

mysteriously threatened EHF.

dullest and most injudicious ... void G. Botkin 1937, 289.

Mischievousness ... seemingly restless Ibid., 311-312.

We are not giving up EHF.

For us, the nearest relatives Ibid.

Twenty-four hours did not pass Ibid.

any person or corporation Ibid.

All is lost Ibid.

Gleb's methods Ibid.

will destroy her chances Ibid.

miniature Ivan the Terrible G. Botkin 1937, 291.

What she does need Ibid., 319.

I cannot see you EHF.

I, Grand Duchess Anastasia Ibid.

Because of Gleb Aucleres, 157-158.

simple people Nidda, 107.

several million roubles EHF.

here you must take ... Go to the Court of Chancery Ibid.

not the first, or last, foreign visitor Clarke, 194-195.

working plan EHF.

Some lovely things Clarke, 162-164.
As the daughter Lovell, 161.
sulks and mopes Rathlef, 129.
called a daughter Nidda, 238.
fantastic and unnecessary sums G. Botkin, 1930.
make millions EHF.

Additional information about Annie Burr Jennings and Franziska in New York and Connecticut was gleaned from EHF and from the Fairfield Historical Society.

Chapter Thirteen

I am going to speak EHF.
Royal Fraud ... victimized Ibid.
thick ankles and wrists Kurth, 241.
officially and actually G. Botkin, 1930.
You know there is no doubt EHF.
Nobody sends the cook Ibid.
She usually carried a fan Information from the Fairfield Historical Society.
materials furnished Cossley-Batt, xvi.
She apparently has had EHF.
I would have liked the freedom Ibid.
you realize I spent hours Ibid.
I wish I had never seen Ibid.
exemplified to me Ibid.
I have nothing more to say Ibid.
go to hell Ibid.
when we could not do that Ibid.
It was only ... Baird did that Ibid.
We have ways Ibid.
Do think over my suggestion EHF.
I am not referring Ibid.

She believes attempts are being made Ibid.

one of her more comfortable phases Ibid.

my last souvenir Nidda, 244.

therefore delivering myself Ibid., 244.

many pieces of valuable jewelry EHF.

After the parrot incident Nidda, 245.

planned to adopt EHF.

If Grandanor dead Ibid.

has applied for an extension Ibid.

Nothing has as yet Ibid.

I have never lived through Ibid.

In the colloquial sense Ibid.

We have had the good fortune Ibid.

controversial aspects Ibid.

our Lady Ibid.

He got quite pompous Ibid.

I don't know Ibid.

Info on Four Winds: phone interview with Four Winds re rumors, *NY Sunday Times*, August 2, 1931. Also August 19, 1931, *Herald Tribune.*

Chapter Fourteen

Aber sie hat sich Waltraud von Czenskowsky interview.

the expression on the faces EHF.

It would require ... unique character Ibid.

now proved without a doubt Ibid.

I hope to soon have the honor Ibid.

chipped and cracked dishes Ibid.

I think of you always Ibid.

never works through Ibid.

I keenly appreciate Ibid.

insane lady Ibid.

I have had my own problems ... changeable, capricious Ibid.

Impostor Unmasked Ibid.

pathological mistrust of everyone Hoover Institution.

left everyone who had helped Ibid.

If the German individual manages T.H. Meyer, 12.

new bridge to the realms Ibid., 131.

the lifestrength of the Russian ether life Baroness von Miltitz, Gotheanum.

Her feet were bleeding Kurth, 271-274.

Why do the demons have to be in me Baroness von Miltitz, Gotheanum.

I am nearly broken EHF.

I always kept it Samweber, 6

Polish farm worker ... This was for me irrefutable evidence Ibid, 43.

Since Anastasia only spoke Ibid, 44.

Are you still in touch EHF.

Chapter Fifteen

Certain officials higher up ... the person she claimed to be EHF

black angels Ibid.

beneath her imperial dignity Ibid.

Please act for me Ibid.

nervous hysterical collapse Ibid.

demented Polish peasant ... black, decayed teeth G. Botkin 1937, 44, 86.

I know of nothing which would contradict EHF.

Our client is too ill Ibid.

Today is Ascension Day Ibid.

Only recently have I learned Ibid.

kind of resemblance which a horse EHF.

She is my sister Ibid.

Following your confrontation King and Wilson, 318.

worked with him EHF.

appeared willing, for a price Ibid.

angry and ugly … Schanzkowsky mess Ibid.

Could you ever forgive yourself Ibid.

Leverkuehn had seen Ibid.

he could not do otherwise EHF.

I shall persevere Ibid.

she wouldn't have anything to do Baroness von Miltitz, Gotheanum.

completely aristocratic Ibid.

She is so obviously aristocratic Ibid.

like thunder … All she wanted was to go Ibid.

very weak, undernourished Ibid.

sometimes lit by moonlight Ibid.

why do the evil spirits Ibid.

lived in a state of fantasy Schellenberg, 235.

silent adherent of Rudolf Steiner Ibid., 235.

Two tall, handsome guards Lovell, 198-199.

never recorded … All Hannover washed away Lovell, 202-206.

You have no idea what it was like Private information.

taken the daughter Lovell, 211.

Long live our secret Germany Baigent and Leigh, p. 307.

how sometimes they seemed to be Baroness von Miltitz, Gotheanum.

that my head is still on my shoulders Kurth, 285.

Additional information about the Kreisau Circle, their milieu, and other resistance movements was found in Bielenberg, Moltke, and Norton. More on Rudolf Hess, and on biodynamic farming can be found in Schellenberg and Keyserlingk, "Twelve Days with Rudolf Steiner," by Countess Johanna Keyserlingk, particularly.

Chapter Sixteen

but we don't have the money private archive (trans. V. Green).

Mrs. Anderson knows how to protect herself Ibid.

I wanted to write Ibid.

Never have I felt such evil Baroness von Miltitz, Gotheanum.

My thoughts are always with the hut private archive.

Please return the borrowed books private archive.

only the shell ... I only became a human Baroness von Miltitz, Gotheanum.

sowing and weeding ... thick abscess Ibid.

She knew how Ibid.

many, many cousins private archive.

The day comes nearer Ibid.

controlled by me and Gleb Botkin Ibid.

no statute of limitations Ibid.

Anastasia's 20,000,000 golden rubles Ibid.

sick in bed private archive.

It will be the concern of my heirs Ibid.

I should follow the Imperial Family Dehn, Part Two, Chapter IV.

At least we shan't have to beg Massie 1996, 184.

for although we were wellborn Dehn, Part One, Chapter III.

autocratic demeanor and behavior Summers and Mangold, 194-195

I do accept Mrs. Suzanna Lovell, p. 443-445

my old brown color private archive.

parcel will give you joy Ibid.

You promised me, if I approved Ibid.

worked to clear up my fate private archive.

I establish this foundation Ibid.

Further details on postwar Unterlengenhardt can be found in Aucleres, 169.

Chapter Seventeen

I know very well who I am Kurth, 318

Dear Imperial Highness private archive.

I know you're not a liar Ibid.

Do you think I made up Frankfurter Allegmeine Zeitung May 22-23, 1959.

Anastasia Nicholaevna! It is I Aucleres, 235.

You will not answer the door Ibid., 235.

It is a shame Ibid., 235.

Get out Ibid., 235.

little Kremlin Ibid.

butterfly mind ... ethnic descent Ibid., 235.

I can't Ibid., 235.

Hide in the road Ibid., 235.

That's enough now "News Review" *The Sunday Times* 9 October 1994

made a mess ... showered abuse Ibid.

I am and I stay as I have been private archive.

What a shame Aucleres, 248.

capable of never letting herself be seen Ibid., 248.

She's changed her mind Ibid., 248.

She won't come Ibid., 248.

wonderfully dignified Ibid., 248.

The strangest creature Ibid., p. 248.

We have taken a long time to meet Ibid., 248.

Then something happened Ibid., 248.

I was so enchanted Ibid., 248.

I have nothing to do with the court Kurth, 310.

Aunt Olga! At last! Information from Pat Phenix.

Anastasia will continue to haunt Ibid.

Mrs Anderson is not the Polish factory worker Kurth, 326.

irrelevant ... highly likely Ibid., 317.

Well, the only thing left Ibid., 318.

for the sake of the truth Ibid., 318.

For further detail on the court cases see Kurth, 289-317.

Chapter Eighteen

miserable misfortune Kurth, 319.
There, dear Uncle King and Wilson, 318.
a little lad Waltraud von Czenstkowski interview.
Are they crazy? Decaux 273.
defeated in appeal Ibid.
The decision is just Kurth, 357.
The pathetic story of Mrs. Anderson's Massie 1968, 531.
I will not go Lovell, 287-8.
We might as well make a trip Milukoff tapes, quoted in Lovell, 293.

Chapter Nineteen

clothes different from ours Mildred Ewell interview.
a slave to her ... never could look after himself private interview.
They gave Jack his doctorate Ibid.
byzantine room ... baroque room Ibid.
low man on the totem pole Shenandoah Valley Magazine, November 1981.
Another book dealer and I Paul Collinge interview.
administered by conspirators Ibid.
We accepted her because of Jack Mildred Ewell interview
She reminded me of things CDP 17 November 1968.
gold-covered, homemade altar Washington Post 11 September 1968.
gestures of weeping Ibid.
other suitors CDP, 12 January 1969.
milk cow of Europe Ibid.
In the beginning I did not know CDP 23 March 1990.
loved buying her hats Mildred Ewell interview.
Sometime I thought to myself Tim O'Kane interview.

With really biggest astonishment private archive
The trees, the trees Sandy MacAdams interview.

Further information about Franziska's life in Charlottesville was found in the collection of the McIntrie Public Library and in the archives of the *Charlottesville Daily Progress* [*CDP*].

Chapter Twenty

Czarist Historian Dies At 69 CDP, 30 December 1969.
Everything is changed entirely Lovell, 327.
Oil paintings, icons, heraldic shields AP story 29 April 1972.
coherent conversation is difficult Ibid.
almost entirely in red Ibid.
hundreds of recipes Ibid.
nor does she like sauces Ibid.
world revolution Cavalier Daily, 20 November 1973.
You saw a picture John Eacott interview.
operated on herself CDP 7 September 1974.
horrendous old knife marks Lovell, 347.
There was no massacre Summers and Mangold, p. 239.
I am a daughter of the Tsar GMA, 28 October 1976.
put together mess CDP 28 October 1976.
lived on trains CDP 29 June 1981.
look, act, and sound exactly alike CDP 1 October 1994.
looked almost moonily Lovell, 347.
the one behind this mess AP 1 March 1977.
Jack would bring breakfast Ian Lilburn interview.
the union suit could use a bath Tim O'Kane interview.

Chapter Twenty-One

Jack could barely feed himself Tim O'Kane interview.
sheep needed shearing Ibid.
scared of anyone who came up to her Ibid.
carpet of shit Ibid.
always on our honeymoon Ibid.
garbage Sandy MacAdams interview.
My wife wouldn't go in there John Eacott interview.
shawl and plaid jacket ... a curse CDP 18 June 1983.
I went for it in case she was L.T. McKean interview.
silent response Ibid.
I was ninety percent sure Ibid.
She played it close to her chest Ibid.
I asked him several times Ibid.

Chapter Twenty-Two

Jack spoke to her Alice Nelson interview.
Wend "A Christmas Card Like No Other," 1974.
screaming at all hours Klier and Mingay, 163.
like an ignorant person would be Kurth 453-454.
Our days were full Ibid. 454.
Well I see we have been caught CDP 3 December 1983.
Gone, gone Lovell, 369.
Her lip went way up Ibid.
My life was filled private archive.

Afterword

Sleep sweetly AN to her father 23 September 1914, Maylunas & Mironenko.

this simple American Frankfurter Alllegmeine Zeitung June 1984.

And you believe this private interview.

Could she not have been Ibid.

Do you know how many Ian Lilburn interview.

I look more like a Romanov Lovell, p. 430.

My sister is so Orthodox Irina Lamosey interview.

Selected Bibliography

Edward Huntington Fallows "Anastasia" Papers (MS Am 2648). Houghton Library, Harvard University. [EHF]

Sergei Dmitrievich Botkin Papers, 1917-1935. Hoover Institution, Stanford University.

Alexandrov, Victor, William Sutcliffe, trans. *The End of the Romanovs.* Boston: Little, Brown & Co., 1966.

Andrew, Christopher and Mitrokhin, Vasili The Mitrokhin Archive, *The KG in Europe and the West.* Harmondsworth: Penguin, 1999.

Aucleres, Dominque *Anastyasia Qui Etes Vous?* Paris: Hachette, 1962.

Baigent, Michael and Richard Leigh *Secret Germany: Claus von Stauffenberg and the Mystical Crusade Against Hitler* Harmondsworth: Penguin, 1995.

Barnes, Henry *A Life for the Spirit: Rudolf Steiner in the Crosscurrents of Our Time* (Vista Series, Vol.1.). Sterling: Steiner Books, 1997.

Bielenberg, Christabel *Christabel* Harmondsworth: Penguin, 1989.

Botkin, Gleb "This Is Anastasia," *The North American Review,* Vol. 229, No. 2, February 1930, pp. 193-199.

Botkin, Gleb *The Woman Who Rose Again.* New York: Fleming H. Revell Co., 1937.

Botkin, Gleb *Lost Tales: Stories for the Tsar's Children.* New York: Villard, 1996.

Botkin, Tatiana *Anastasia Retrouvee.* Paris: Grasset, 1985.

Bulygin, Captain Paul and Alexander Kerensky *The Murder of the Romanovs: The Authentic Account.* London: Hutchison Co., 1935.

Buxhoeveden, Bss Sophie *The Tragic Empress, the Life and Tragedy of Alexandra Feodorovna.* London: Longmans, 1928.

Buxhoeveden, Bss Sophie *Left Behind: Fourteen Months in Siberia During the Revolution.* London: Longmans, 1929.

Clarke, William *The Lost Fortunes of the Tsars.* New York: St. Martin's Press: New York, 1996.

Clay, Catrine *King, Kaiser, Tsar: Three Cousins Who Led the World to War.* London: John Murray Publishers, 2006.

Cossley-Batt, Jill L. *The Last of the California Rangers* New York: Funk & Wagnalls, 1928.

Crawford, Rosemary A. and Donald Crawford *Michael and Natasha: The Life and Love of Michael II, the Last of the Romanov Tsars.* New York: Scribner, 1997.

Davy, John, et. al. *A Man Before Others: Rudolf Steiner Remembered* Bristol: Rudolf Steiner Press, 1993.

Decaux, Alain *L'Enigme Anastasia* Paris: Edition de la Palatine 1961.

Dehn, Lili *The Real Tsaritsa.* Boston: Little, Brown & Co., 1922.

Disebach, Ghislain de *Secrets of the Gotha: Private Lives of the Royal Families of Europe.* New York: Barnes and Noble, 1993.

Doblin, Alfred, Joachim Neugroschel, trans. *Journey to Poland.* New York: Paragon House, 1991.

Dydynski, Krzysztof *Lonely Planet Poland.* London: Lonely Planet, 1993.

Eagar, Margaret *Six Years at the Russian Court.* 1906.

Everett, Susanne *Lost Berlin.* Greenwich: Bison Books, 1979.

Friedrich, Otto *Before the Deluge: A Portrait of Berlin in the 1920s.* New York: Harper Perennial, 1995.

Gilliard, Pierre and F. Appleby Holt *Thirteen Years at the Russian Court: A Personal Record of the Last Years and Death of the Czar Nicholas II and His Family.* London: Hutchinson & Co., 1921.

Gilliard, Pierre and Constantin Savitch *La fausse Anastasie: Histoire d'une pretendue Grande-Duchesse de Russie.* Paris: Payot, 1929.

Gordon, Lois G. and Alan Gordon *American Chronicle: Six Decades of American Life, 1920-1980.* New York: Atheneum, 1987.

Hassell, Agostino von and Sigrid MacRae *Alliance of Enemies: The Untold Story of the Secret American and German Collaboration to End World War II* New York: Thomas Dunne Books, 2006.

Keyserlinkg, Count Adalbert *Developing Biodynamic Agriculture— The Birth of A New Agriculture.* London: Temple Lodge, 1929.

King, Greg *The Last Empress: The Life and Times of Alexandra, Empress of Russia.* New York: Citadel, 1996.

King, Greg *The Murder of Rasputin: The Truth About Prince Felix Youssoupov and the Mad Monk Who Helped Bring Down the Romanovs.* London: Century, 1996.

King, Greg and Penny Wilson *The Resurrection of the Romanovs: Anastasia, Anna Anderson and the World's Greatest Royal Mystery* New York: John Wiley & Sons, 2010.

Klier, John and Helen Mingray *The Quest for Anastasia: Solving the Mystery of the Lost Romanovs.* New York: Citadel Press, 1999.

Kollwitz, Kathe *Ich Sah Die Welt mit Liebevollen Blicken* Wiesbaden: Fourier Verlag, 1962.

Krockow, Christian von *Die Reise nach Pommern: Bericht aus einem verschwiegen Land.* Munich: Dt. Taschenbuch Verlag, 1985.

Kurth, Peter Anastasia: *The Riddle of Anna Anderson.* Boston: Little, Brown & Co., 1983.

Lehndorff. Hans Graf von *Ostpreussisches Tagebuch dvt dokumente.* Munich: Biederstein Verlag, 1967.

Lovell, James Blair *Anastasia: The Lost Princess.* New York: Regnery Gateway, 1991.

MacDonald, George, trans. *Novalis.* London: Temple Lodge, 2001.

Maples, William R. and Michael Browning *Dead Men Do Tell Tales: The Strange and Fascinating Cases of a Forensic Anthropologist.* New York: Doubleday, 1994.

Massie, Robert K. *Nicholas and Alexandra.* New York: Atheneum, 1967.

Massie, Robert K. *The Romanovs: the Final Chapter.* New York: Random House, 1996.

Maylunas, Andrei and Sergei Mironenko *A Lifelong Passion: The Letters of Nicholas and Alexandra.* New York: Doubleday, 1996.

Meyer, T.H., ed. *Light for the New Millenium: Rudolf Steiner's Association with Helmuth and Eliza von Moltke: Letters, Documents and After-Death Communications* Sterling: Rudolf Steiner Press, 1998.

Michael of Greece, Anthony Roberts, trans. *Living with Ghosts: Eleven Extraordinary Tales.* New York: W.W. Norton & Co., 1996.

Moltke, Helmuth James von *Letters to Freya: 1939-1945* New York: Knopf, 1990.

Nidda, Roland Krug von, Oliver Coburn, trans. *I, Anastasia: The Autobiography of the Grand Duchess of Russia.* Harmondsworth: Penguin, 1961.

Nogly, Hans *Anastasia: A Novel* London: Methuen, 1956.

Norton, Robert Edward *Secret Germany: Stefan George and His Circle* New York: Cornell University Press, 2002.

O'Conor, John F., trans. and ed. *The Sokolov Investigation of the Alleged Murder of the Russian Imperial Family.* New York: Robert Speller & Sons, 1971.

Perry, John Curtis and Constantine V. Pleshakov *The Flight of the Romanovs: A Family Saga.* New York: Basic Books, 2001.

Phenix, Patricia *Olga Romanov: Russia's Last Grand Duchess.* Toronto: Viking Press, 1999.

Radzinsky, Edvard, Marian Schwartz, trans. *The Last Tsar: The Life and Death of Nicholas II.* New York: Doubleday, 1992.

Radzinsky, Edvard, Judson Rosengrant, trans. *The Rasputin Files.* New York: Doubleday, 2000.

Rathlef-Keilmann, Harriet von *Anastasia: The Survivor of Ekaterinburg.* New York: G.P. Putnam's Sons, 1928.

Samweber, Anna *Memories of Rudolf Steiner and Marie Steiner von Sivers* London: Rudolf Steiner Press, 1991.

Savitch, Marie *Marie Steiner-von Sivers, Fellow Worker with Rudolf Steiner.* London: Rudolf Steiner Press, 1967.

Schellenberg, Walter, Louis Hagen, trans. and ed. *The Schellenberg Memoirs* London: Andre Deutsch, 1956.

Schwiers, Liselotte *Das Paradies liegt in Pommern* Munich: Droemer Knaur, 1989.

Solokov, Nicholas *Enquete Judiciare sur l'assassiantde la Famille Imperiale de Russe.* Paris: Payot, 1924.

Steinberg, Mark D. and Vladimir M. Khrustalev *The Fall of the Romanovs: Political Dreams and Personal Struggles in a Time of Revolution.* New Haven: Yale University Press, 1997.

Steiner, Rudolf, et al. *Education as an Art.* Sterling: Steiner Books, 1979.

Steiner, Rudolf *How to Know Higher Worlds.* Hudson: Anthroposophic Press, 1994.

Steiner, Rudolf *Reincarnation and Karma: Their significance in modern culture; five lectures given to members of the Anthroposophical Society during January to March 1912 in Berlin and Stuttgart.* Hudson: Anthroposophic Press, 1997.

Steiner, Rudolf, Catherine Creeger, trans. *Outline of Esoteric Science.* Hudson: Anthroposophic Press, 1997.

Steiner, Rudolf Autobiography: Chapters in the Course of My Life 1861-1907. Hudson: Anthroposophic Press, 1999.

Sullivan, Michael John *A Fatal Passion: The Story of the Uncrowned Last Empress of Russia.* New York: Random House, 1997.

Summers, Anthony and Tom Mangold *The File on the Tsar.* New York: Harper & Row, 1976.

Tompkins, Peter and Christopher Bird *Secrets of the Soil.* New York: Harper and Row, 1989.

Tradowsky, Peter *Kaspar Hauser: The Struggle for the Spirit.* London: Temple Lodge, 1997.

Trewin, John Courtenay *The House of Special Purpose: An Intimate Portrait of the Last Days of the Russian Imperial Family Compiled from the Papers of Their English Tutor Charles Sydney Gibbes.* New York: Stein & Day, 1975.

Troubetzkoy, Alexis Imperial Legend: *The Mysterious Disappearance of Tsar Alkexander I.* London: Arcade Books, 2002.

Van der Kiste, John and Coryne Hall *Once a Grand Duchess: Xenia, Sister of Nicholas II.* Stroud: Sutton, 2002.

Viktoria Luise HRH Duchess of Brunswick, Robert Vachon, trans. *The Kaiser's Daughter: A Memoir.* Upper Saddle River: Prentice-Hall,1977.

Vyrubova, Anna *Memories of the Russian Court.* New York: MacMillan, 1923.

Vorres, Ian *The Last Grand Duchess: Her Imperial Highness Grand Duchess Olga Alexandrovna.* London: Hutchinson & Co., 1964.

Yuzupov, Prince Felix *En Exil.* Paris: Plon, 1954.

ABOUT THE AUTHORS

Vera Green is a Canadian author with a number of published novels and a biography. She works as a writer and editor and is also a poet. She lives in Ontario with her artist husband.

Victoria Hughes is an independent researcher who became fascinated by the Anna Anderson saga after a teenaged reading of Summers and Mangold's *The File on the Tsar*. She lives in rural Montana with her husband and cats.